Louisa E. Rhine

The Invisible Picture

A Study of
Psychic Experiences

McFarland & Company, Inc.,
Publishers
Jefferson, N.C., 1981

By the Same Author

* * *

Hidden Channels of the Mind
ESP in Life and Lab
Mind over Matter
Psi, What Is It?

Library of Congress Cataloging in Publication Data

Rhine, Louisa E
The invisible picture.

Includes bibliographical references and index.
1. Psychical research. I. Title.
BF1031.R39   133.8   80-10545
ISBN 0-89950-015-3

To our grandchildren,
yours and mine.
May their horizons be broadened
by the meaning herein glimpsed.

Contents

A Preview

The peculiar nature of the material of this book, spontaneous psychic experiences, calls for a bit of explanation. In the first place, it is not widely enough recognized that still today, as throughout history, many a person has had a "true" dream or hunch, or even a glimpse of someone who "wasn't there" just when, as he later learned, that person was undergoing an extreme crisis.

Even though the persons who have such experiences cannot explain them, neither can they convince themselves that they did not have them. Willingly or unwillingly then they have to tell themselves that the occurrence must have been psychic. But they don't know what that means either.

At this point reactions vary. A few individuals may feel that something special, almost miraculous has happened and they may read a religious meaning into it. Or, they may take it as a sign of special ability, a "gift," something they should use for the benefit of humanity.

On the other hand, an unknown number of persons today, especially the well-educated, feel embarassed by the occurrence and keep it secret. They know that if they tell it their story will almost certainly be discounted, explained away, if not actually disbelieved. "You just imagined it." "It was just a dream," and perhaps be thinking, "How can anyone be so credulous?" Better then, be silent. And so the fact of such occurrences gets played down. And, as I said, few people realize how frequent they may be, while those to whom they happen can only go on wondering, "How could it be?"

The reason for the embarassment is largely because of the close association of the psychic with superstition. Those persons abhor the latter and deny the former. And their feeling is all the stronger because of the exploitation of the psychic in fiction, which ranges all the way from simple mystery to unbridled horror stories just as wild as those on any other topic.

This book is not like that. Instead, it is a factual account of a decades-long study of a large number of personal experiences that seemed to be psychic. The objective of the study was to try to understand them and the processes that produced them. The book then will disappoint those who expect the psychic to be sensational and hair raising.

To more thoughtful readers, however, I hope that this account will bring, as the research itself did to me, a glimpse of a side of human personality that has been almost entirely hidden. And to those who find herein prototypes of their own experiences, it should give a measure of understanding and assurance.

As I explain in the text, I undertook research on this material with considerable hesitancy, doubting whether it could add much meaning to the facts of parapsychology that were slowly being established in the laboratory. But after these decades of study my attitude has changed drastically. The cases add up to more, much more, than I expected. They give a "picture" of an aspect of human personality that has been all too long scientifically "invisible." While at the very least they are bits of life, of human experience, they point to something greater, to a meaning that is not self-evident in the fragments and bits that unaided nature scatters.

It is the same meaning, of course, that is slowly, laboriously, being chipped out as if in a stone carving, by the experimental methods of the laboratory. The result shown here, however, is an airplane view and essentially, I hope, a promise for the future.

Perhaps I should add that when I undertook this research I was, as I still am, a deep-dyed devotee of the experimental method of modern science as the best and most reliable road to truth of any that has yet been devised. I was as unconvinced as my parapsychological peers by the anecdotal methods of research that had long been the main ones used in attempts to unravel the mysteries of the psychic — and yet I came to make this, the most comprehensive anecdotal study of personal psychic experiences of any so far reported.

This is an account of the reason for that research and of the main findings it yielded.

Chapter 1

Miracle — or Psi?

We did not know the man, but his employer, our host, had asked him to drive us to the airport. He did not know us, but he had been told that my husband, J.B. Rhine, was "the ESP man."

As we drove along, he ventured, "My wife believes in that ESP stuff. I don't know if I do or not." And then, "But the darnedest thing happened to me, once. I never could figure it out."

With a bit of encouragement he continued, explaining that he had lived in northern Vermont before he came down here to Florida. He said that it was good deer country and that in the fall he and a friend often went deer hunting. One such time it had been snowing and more was coming, and so even though it was only about four o'clock, it was already getting dark. They therefore started back along an old woods trail to their car.

Then he said he suddenly left that trail, "and I'll never know what made me do it!" He turned aside into the deep woods and pushed his way through a grove of hemlocks so thick he had to brush the branches aside with his hands. He went on like this a ways and then came upon a man sitting in the snow, his back against a tree. He had been shot through the side and was almost unconscious.

Our driver said he then fired his gun and his companion heard it. Eventually they got the man to a hospital.

"But what made me go in there?" he wondered.

The rest of the story was that the injured man, also a deer hunter, had had a freak accident earlier in the day. He had propped his gun against a tree and then somehow stumbled over it and shot himself. Too badly hurt to get any farther he had managed

1

to lean against the tree—and wait. But not for help. He had given up hope of that.

It came, however, because of "the darnedest thing," and after long and difficult surgery in which at one stage even the surgeon thought that the case was hopeless, "by a miracle," as our driver said, the man survived. But if the story was true, then another miracle besides the medical one took place. If, as the narrator said, he had no conscious reason for going off into the forest and finding the injured man, that action would have been a miracle, even greater perhaps, than the medical one, for the surgeon at least had training and experience to guide him.

An easy way out, of course, for anyone trying to explain the episode, would be to consider the story a fabrication, a bid for the attention of "the ESP man." Even though the narrator sounded sincere with something of the wonder of his inexplicable action still in his voice, we were in no position to prove even his truthfulness or at the best, that his action that led to his finding of the wounded man was anything more than a freak coincidence as inexplicable as the accident itself.

It is true, if I were ever to repeat his story, as I have just done here, it might seem that I could at least have written back to our host and asked about his employee's character and credibility. I did not do it however even though for years the research project in which I have been engaged has been the study of reported personal experiences which, like this one, could possibly be psychic.

I did not do it because I recognized that this man *could* have been guided, even inspired, to leave the trail as he did, by extrasensory perception (ESP) and if so his action, strictly speaking, would not have been a miracle. A miracle, says the dictionary, is "an effect which surpasses all known human or natural powers and is ascribed to a supernatural cause." But ESP is not an effect which surpasses all known human or natural powers, not any longer, as will be discussed in greater detail in Chapter 2. Because of experimental tests in the field of parapsychology it is now known to be a natural human power, or ability, the result of an obscure mental capacity to know or to get information about the world without the use of the senses. It has in addition an extra-motor aspect called psychokinesis (PK) by which objects may be affected by mind or thought alone. The two aspects together are spoken of as psi, or psi ability. Psychic experiences are the occurrence of psi in life situations.

As practically everyone knows, psychic or psi experiences have been reported since the dawn of history, but even yet, practically no one knows just what they are. The main reason is because no comprehensive study of them has been made and besides that, like fingerprints, they vary so greatly from person to person. In fact, they are even more unique than fingerprints because if the person should have several of them, each one might appear to be different from any other.

A few examples of experiences which the person involved thought might be psychic will illustrate some of the many variations. The examples given here are short and simple, selected mainly because they are easy to present. However, just as with the example cited above, they are not given as tried and proven instances of psi in daily life, but only as experiences that *could* involve psi, some less certainly than others. But in all of them, the question is left open whether or not they actually do so, or are instead a mixture of coincidence, exaggeration, bad memory, faulty reporting or mistakes of still other kinds.

A 17-year-old student at a kindergarten training school in England took the 9 a.m. bus to school each morning. One day she waited as usual as the bus approached. The conductor opened the door for her to enter but for some nameless reason she just could not get on. Disgusted, the driver told her to make up her mind before stopping him next time.

As the bus drove off without her she knew she would be late for school. It was a three-quarters of an hour walk. How silly could she be?

Five minutes later the double decker bus had brake failure going down a hill, could not make a curve at the bottom, dashed over a low stone wall and onto a road below. Many persons were killed.

Word of the accident reached the school before the girl did. She was received "like a ghost" when she arrived. Why had she *not* been on that bus?

He was only 2½ years old. His father was an aviator and

to him every airman was a "daddy." He was playing outside one day when he suddenly began to cry and rushed into the house. "Mommie, Mommie, a big airplane fall down. Daddys are hurting."

His mother tried to calm him. But then the news came over the radio of an airplane crash in the Pacific.

In 1904 on a cold and windy night in December a family had gathered to pray for the grandfather who was very ill. Three raps came on the window. "It's the death call," said the mother. Grandfather died the next day.

A young mother in a Utah town had been home so much since the baby came that one evening her husband urged her to go with a neighbor to a nearby movie. She noticed that it was a sparsely attended one, as it happened, and the rows of seats behind them were empty until her husband came in, leaned over her shoulder and whispered, "You'd better go home."

Angrily she followed him out. Had he not said she should have this one night free? He went out the theatre door before her. But when she got outside he was not in sight.

At home she walked into the bedroom. He was lying on the bed asleep. He could not have come in just moments before. "I thought I was nuts," she reported.

She went to the kitchen for a drink and noticed a glow on the sun porch. She found that her husband had heated the baby's bottle and set the hot plate on the ironing board. He had forgotten to turn the current off, and the cloth on the board was about to break into flames.

A high school girl in Ohio was writing a theme for English class. Her right arm began to hurt. The pain got worse. She had to stop writing. The pain was so bad she could not finish, nor could she find a reason why.

That evening her father was late home from work. At 6:30 word came that that afternoon his arm had been caught in the gears of the crane he was operating. The arm had to be amputated.

When, during World War II, an RAF pilot on furlough to his home in Scotland told his sister that he had been transferred to bombers a chill of fear ran through her, but trying not to show it she replied lightly, "So that is that."

A few months later his plane blew up on take off and he was killed instantly. It was found that his instruments were faulty. Sabotage was suspected.

His sister, away from home at the time, returned days later and found that a picture in her room had fallen from the wall. "That picture fell the night James was killed," her old housekeeper told her. "I think he was here looking for you."

The girl then recalled that a picture had fallen one night when she was a child. The next day the family was informed that her father's mother had died at the time the picture fell.

These experiences are obviously as different as the people who reported them; but they do have one common feature. In each instance, it was as if the person acquired information without any ordinary source. It is on that account that these could have been psychic experiences. Today with the evidence from the parapsychological laboratories that extrasensory mental processes do occur, it seems a logical necessity to look for and try to recognize spontaneous examples of its operation.

However, if any of these given above actually are instances of extrasensory perception (ESP) they pose the difficulty of recognition, because, in each one even if the facts as given are reliable, as they may or may not be, the mental process that produced the experience was a very obscure one. Every individual's mental processes go on as in a closed and secret box. He himself does not know all about what goes on there, but he does know something at least about the instances that somehow come to consciousness. The reports such persons make in instances like these, constitute spontaneous evidence of psi. Or, at least, evidence of spontaneous psi lies among such reports.

Experiences like these examples represent what is known in parapsychological literature as the non-recurrent kind of experience in which psi may be involved. They are non-recurrent in the sense that if the person should later have another which seemed to be the result of psi it would not necessarily be on a similar topic or come in a way similar to the first. However, some types of psi such as poltergeist effects and haunting cases do tend to recur in ways similar to each other. These will be omitted in this presentation, not because their basis is actually different, but because the methods of studying them are different and more complicated than those of the unrepeated or non-recurrent kinds.

Another group of presumptive psychic experiences are the automatic, like mediumship, divination, automatic writing. They will not be included here, not only because their methods of study are different, but also because their expression in consciousness represents secondary as well as primary kinds of mental processes.

As a matter of fact, the simple unrepeated experiences that bring the person information not secured directly or indirectly by the senses are the ABC's of spontaneous psychic effects. But even so, they have never been examined against the advance of knowledge achieved by parapsychological research, to see what they might suggest as to the mental processes involved in their production.

As later chapters will show, all earlier studies of personal psychic experiences made before the present one and reported in the serious literature had been concerned only with certain kinds that were suspected by the investigator of giving evidence on some problem other than that of the nature of the experience itself.

This neglect of case material in parapsychological studies was, in a way, the result of taking each account singly. Thus, just as in the deer hunter's report above, each one could be dismissed quite easily. It might have been only a coincidence, a lie or a hoax. In fact, this impression about the unreliability of case reports was so general when I myself began to make the collection of cases that turned out to be the material of this research project, that I expected to find little evidence of psychic effects in a great mass of superstition. Now, as I will explain in later chapters, I have had a rare, really an unequalled opportunity to know how right or wrong that idea was and I hope in the following chapters to make the answer clear.

Chapter 2

Parapsychology:
Experiment and Anecdote

Psychic experiences, outcasts even in the field of experimental parapsychology, have never been recognized in the established sciences. They have been beyond the fence marking the limits of propriety as to topics suitable for scholarly investigation. However, in the past, they did give the suggestion that led to the investigations of parapsychology. It then took decades of experimentation in this unpopular field to show that human beings do have psychic ability. In the meantime no guidelines were laid down by which to define its spontaneous occurrence in life situations. However, to understand fully the situation in regard to the spontaneous experiences, a short historical sketch of parapsychology up to 1948 is necessary.

Parapsychology is the Cinderella of the sciences. The stepmother, Science, has never favored her. She got a late start and the big sisters like physics, chemistry and biology almost cold-shouldered her out of recognition. It remains to be seen if any fairy prince will rescue her. Lately, however, an encouraging sign is visible.

The sign is that the reality of psi and the field of parapsychology too are gaining wider acceptance. The reason can be traced to the fact that the method of investigation is really precisely the same as that of other sciences, for it has consisted of objective experimental research with statistical evaluation of results. The general realization of this, however, has been tardy because, just as with the older sciences, the experimental stage was preceded by an earlier one that was mainly anecdotal. That stage for physics, chemistry and the others is so far back in history now that it is almost forgotten. But because of parapsychology's late start, the earlier pre-experimental stage was still visible in modern times, long after the others had passed out of it. In addition, a long-standing bias had developed against phenomena that seemed to many to be only relics of superstition. This made the field known first as psychical research, now more generally as parapsychology, seem unscientific and therefore, unimpressive to its neighbors.

This bias against psychic phenomena, part of the reason for parapsychology's late start, also contributed to its low image on the scientific firmament. The reason for both the bias and the low image was that the signs of psi, its spontaneous expression in daily life, were difficult to identify and therefore easy to overlook. They could be denied and ignored by the scholarly world, even including that of psychology, the field in whose province they most logically fell. This was at least partly because they were not reported by more than a scattered few. Besides, they conflicted with the ancient belief that nothing can get into the mind except by way of the senses. For both reasons, when they were occasionally reported, they were easily charged off to superstition, chance, illusion and mistakes of other kinds.

It was only because of a few persons, particularly in England, who came to be known as psychical researchers, that this situation ever changed. In the 19th century, long after the major sciences were fairly well organized and their method of making sure their results were reliable through the use of experimental techniques had become routine, these psychical researchers became impressed with the possible meaning of these atypical, psychic occurrences. Consequently, they began to take them seriously enough to study them. They did so, however, not so much because of interest in a possible unrecognized mental phenomenon, but for the philosophical and religious meanings such occurrences might have. This viewpoint, although logical enough as an historical development, tended to slow psychical research from growing into a field that could command the respect of the older "step-sisters."

Tracing back to the early studies of the psychical researchers, two methods of procedure can be distinguished, the anecdotal and the experimental. The anecdotal way was that of studying reports of occurrences in which the phenomenon of interest seemed to have occurred, for instance, telepathy. The experimental method, in contrast, called for the actual testing under controlled conditions of pairs of individuals to see if evidence could be obtained to show that telepathic exchange could occur, in that the thought of one could become known to the other without any overt sign being given.

In the studies reported in the late 19th century, those involving mediumistic records (discussed later) predominate. Today they would be classified an anecdotal, or at best as demonstrational or semi-experimental. Even so, many of them were careful, scholarly and in the forefront of the methodology of the time. In the 1880's an outstanding instance of the anecdotal method (based on the study of the non-recurrent kind of spontaneous cases) was undertaken and reported in 1886 as *Phantasms of the Living* (reference 2) (reviewed in Chapter 3). This study, like the mediumistic ones reported in the *Journals* and *Proceedings of the Society of Psychical Research* (SPR), exemplifies the most scholarly methods of the day, in the field of psychical research, as those methods were then recognized.

The status of an anecdotal approach, however, was affected over succeeding years by changes in the methods accepted in the scientific world in general, which in turn was greatly influenced by the development and use of statistics. The result has been that the experimental method has come more and more to replace the anecdotal in all areas of investigation where it can be applied.

Some experiments were reported, however, almost from the start of psychic investigations. But they were sporadic, scattered, almost incidental. Those that were reported in the late 19th century consisted mainly of attempts to see if a subject could identify a hidden target or match a concealed drawing. Often the results of such tests looked positive by a common sense evaluation, but that was no more convincing in regard to experimental results than was the same kind of evaluation of spontaneous cases. In parapsychology, the superiority of experimental method for permitting reliable conclusions had not yet been widely recognized; the method awaited the general use of statistics.

By the early 20th century, statistical methods were well developed in science in general. It then became possible to evaluate test results in psychical research so that the guess work could be reduced and experimenters could tell whether or not their results were significantly beyond the mean expectation of chance. Early in the 20th century this method was introduced into the field. By 1934 a continuing line of research on a strictly experimental basis was reported. It was in a university psychology department and the objective was to find evidence of telepathy, if in fact such an ability existed.

This research had begun at Duke University in 1927 because Dr. William McDougall was located there. He had recently been appointed head of the Psychology Department at the University. He was an English psychologist who had been at Harvard before coming to Duke, and he was deeply interested in the question of whether a non-mechanistic element is included in human nature. The behavioristic movement had already become dominant in American psychology, but it was in conflict with McDougall's idea of human nature. He himself had long been attempting to learn whether objective experimental evidence could be obtained to support his viewpoint of mind as including a nonphysical reality.

Meanwhile, at the University of Chicago in the early 1920's, J.B. Rhine and I, his wife, were graduate students working toward the Ph.D. degree in plant physiology. Our studies entailed considerable work in other sciences besides plant physiology, especially chemistry. In the course of these studies, we became deeply impressed with the efficiency and reliability of the experimental approach to problem solving. But at the same time we were troubled by the fact that the subjective or spiritual nature of man seemed to be entirely ignored in all the sciences with which we came in contact. We very much wanted to know whether any evidence for it existed that could stand up under the same strict conditions we were learning to use in the study of enzyme action or the development of an embryo.

Some extracurricular reading of research reports of the London Society for Psychical Research (SPR) proved especially interesting because of the bearing they seemed to have on the question of the nature of man. In contrast to the purely physicalistic picture we were getting in the laboratories, these suggested another aspect that did not appear to be of the same kind. These were accounts of mediumistic studies bearing on the question of survival after death. The mediums (certain sensitive people, working under controlled conditions) gave messages that purported to come from deceased persons. The SPR investigators were trying to find out if the messages really did come from that kind of source. The results of these inquiries made over a period of decades were buried deep in volumes of records of mediumistic utterances and writings which had been produced in "sittings" and recorded carefully as given by the medium. The evaluation of the material depended on whether the references the mediums made were correct when checked against memories or records of any kind, and if so, whether they could have been obtained by the medium from any source other than the deceased person.

The result over the years had been that in trying to evaluate the accounts as given, a continuing series of judgments was necessary. Of course, such judgments varied with each person. No final verdict acceptable to all could be expected and in fact none had been obtained. The research by a number of different investigators had gone on for years and no unequivocal solution had resulted. Even the psychical researchers themselves, careful scholars most of them, were not agreed as to whether survival had or had not been proved. They did appreciate the implications, especially of the "cross-correspondences," a body of material that certainly gave evidence of an intelligent element in the interlocking messages of different mediums, which was difficult to account for without the spirit theory. But these and all the other articles in the psychical research journals had been ignored by the world of science in general; even the most meticulous mediumistic studies had been passed over in silence, if not in scorn, by the scientific world.

However, the material, to anyone who did look at it seriously as we did, seemed very impressive in volume and possible significance. It was puzzling, inexplicable, and certainly evidence of *something* still unknown. But all of this work with mediums was still essentially anecdotal; and there always remained an alternative or two that prevented a final conclusion. To us a sharper, more decisive method seemed called for if a conclusive and reliable answer was to be obtained. It seemed that the same simple but tight experimental techniques used in the other sciences could be adapted and applied here too.

Then we came upon McDougall's book *Body and Mind* (reference 3) and realized that the author was an authority who was asking in a wider perspective the same question that was increasingly unsettling us. And so by 1927, a few years after our stint at Chicago ended, we were at Duke University to work unofficially under McDougall. The immediate subject matter of our study was that of some mediumistic records which seemed significant. We wanted to see if a reliable experimental approach could be devised to determine their origin.

The status of such a study on any of the topics of psychical research was so low in universities world-wide that few of them would tolerate it. Duke, a new university with barriers to unconventional ideas not yet in place, and McDougall, a transplanted English psychologist with an unconventional idea, were rare exceptions. And J.B. Rhine (JBR), who wanted to devote six months at least, he thought then, a life time as it developed, to the unpopular question, was also an exception among postgraduate students. This set of unique circumstances helped the field of parapsychology to develop as the more general experimental investigation of the evidence for a non-mechanistic aspect of human nature.

Eventually, JBR was given an appointment on the psychology staff at Duke University by McDougall. Soon, along with teaching duties and with the collaboration of several colleagues in the Psychology Department, he began giving tests for telepathy to his students. Telepathy seemed the topic on which to begin because if mediums could receive thoughts from other minds, as in the mediumistic reports, which meant from the minds of deceased persons, they would have to have such an ability.

The general procedure in testing for telepathy, as first used, was to have students in psychology classes attempt to guess a series of targets, numerals or letters, which the experimenter had in mind, to see if they could do so better than could be accounted for by chance coincidence between their guesses and the targets. Before long, the symbols on playing cards were used for targets, and this in turn led to the forming of a special card deck which was more convenient. (It was first called the Zener deck. Later, when extrasensory perception was being established, it was renamed the ESP deck.) It was made up of only 25 cards, five each of five different symbols. The point was that the deck was easier than playing cards to manipulate and the evaluation of results was also simpler. With this special deck five hits would be expected by chance, and so it would be easy to tell whether a series of guessing runs through it yielded a rate of correct calling greater than would be expected by chance.

To us, the almost unexpected outcome of these experiments was that they were encouraging from the beginning, for the scores of many of the college student subjects showed that they could succeed in such "guessing," to a statistically significant degree. As the tests continued, it seemed more and more likely that something unaccountable was in evidence. Otherwise, of course, the attempt would have been given up in due course.

Instead, the inquiry grew and as it did more and more excitement among those involved was generated. It was not that anything was proved by the early series of above-chance scores obtained from some of the subjects being tested, but those scores did seem like promises to JBR, indications which should be followed up to see if they might really constitute the clue to an unknown "extra-sensory" factor in man, the existence of which he had been questioning.

By 1935, the other psychology staff members had withdrawn from the research, which was not essentially their own, but JBR had continued. He was able to support a full-time colleague as well as a few students helpers by a research grant from the University, supplemented by one from an interested laywoman. Now he was partly relieved of his teaching duties to give more time to the parapsychological research, and a separate laboratory for it was formed, with JBR as director. This laboratory, the Parapsychology Laboratory of Duke University, was independent of the Psychology Department but still under

McDougall who had followed the experimental developments with great interest and continued to encourage the research until his death in 1938.*

It was soon found that the subjects could succeed not only when the target material was known to another person, a situation that was then considered to be <u>telepathic</u>, but also when no other person knew the target order. This was the clairvoyant test situation. Both findings showed that the old idea that nothing can enter the mind except by way of the senses is wrong, but that an extrasensory way of knowing exists and can operate on both "thoughts and things" (reference 12).

Later, experiments were made to test whether such perception can occur only when the targets involved are presently existing, or whether they can be identified if they are future ones, as would be the case if the mind could also know precognitively. The tests for this involved having subjects *predict* the order in which a deck of cards would be later, after the deck had been shuffled. This kind of experiment also yielded positive results, so that the concept of extrasensory perception (ESP) was expanded to include precognition, as well as telepathy and clairvoyance.

In 1934 research began at the Parapsychology Laboratory to see if matter could be affected by mind alone. In time positive results were obtained of sufficient magnitude to establish the psychokinetic effect or PK on moving objects (reference 32). Later evidence has since been obtained to show that certain life processes are also affected and increasingly reasons are found to think that a PK effect also may occur on static matter. (See Chapter 14.)

In general, research on PK shows it to be a real and demonstrable phenomenon, evidence of which is fairly widespread among the subjects so far tested and, in general, occuring under the same influences and conditions that affect ESP. It therefore seems to be but a different aspect of the same ability.

Ever since psi ability was established, research in para-

*JBR continued, full time after 1950, as director until his retirement from the University in 1965. After that, the organization moved to a nearby location but became independent of the University. It now was under the sponsorship of the Foundation for Research on the Nature of Man (FRNM), which JBR, with the help of interested persons, had formed for the purpose. (I myself joined the Parapsychology Laboratory in 1948.)

psychology has been devoted largely to an attempt to understand the influences that affect it. They are mainly psychological and involve such topics as the relationship of personality types to psi, and the influences of moods and attitudes and the effect of different mental states on its manifestation. However, the psi process gives only a "weak signal" among the much stronger ones produced by the senses. It is more fragile, obscure and difficult to work with than the familiar psychological processes.

The difficulties confronting objective research in parapsychology were great enough, in fact, that the question had sometimes been raised whether experimental procedures could ever be used for these kinds of phenomena. Perhaps it was more like astronomy, or geology in which basic data can only be studied as they occur in nature and not produced by experiment. But time, trial and ingenuity showed that experimental methods could be adapted in this field too. By their use the reality of psi ability has been established and an understanding of the processes involved is gradually being achieved.

The research carried on at the Duke Laboratory was a continuing effort to establish the full reach of the mental abilities that the experiments were disclosing.* But it was at a certain stage of the research at the Laboratory that my own project, a return to the anecdotal method, occurred; it was originally conceived as only an adjunct to the experimental research. Since it is the topic of central interest here, the setting for it must be given, especially the conditions at the Laboratory during and directly after the close of World War II.

The staff at the Laboratory had always been relatively limited in numbers, supported, still, by a small Duke research fund and such contributions from outside sources as could be obtained. But during the war years practically all the male members of the staff were drawn off to the war effort. JBR, disqualified

---

*The effort at the Parapsychology Laboratory had been the main one by which the reality of psi was being experimentally established. In England, the war, so much more devastating than in the United States, had nearly put a stop to all investigation. In America, largely I think because of psychological bias, only a few places, mainly the American Society for Psychical Research in New York City, had continued to carry on research. The Duke Laboratory, with its combination of fortunate circumstances, was about the only place where experimental projects could be carried out with a degree of continuity and where even a few fulltime workers could be supported.

for military service in this war, kept the laboratory in operation with the help of a few female colleagues.

In spite of this slowdown, by 1948 those familiar with the research results from the Laboratory and the few projects that had been carried out elsewhere felt that the reality of psi had been established even though it was not so recognized by any great part of the scholarly world.* But the assumption that psi could be considered a reality and that it included the types of ESP, clair-voyance, telepathy and precognition as well as PK, was a necessary background for my own case study, initiated in 1948.

It may be unnecessary to say that during all the preceding years at the Laboratory, the study of case material would not have been considered appropriate. The swing away from the anecdotal method was too definite and pronounced even to suggest such an effort. From the first bit of publicity about the reported "discovery" of experimental evidence for telepathy, members of the general public had begun to respond. Many of those individuals who thought they had themselves experienced it did so. However, at the Laboratory their letters had only been accumulating with little more than polite and noncommittal acknowledgment. No one had time for them, although JBR him-self had given some of them a hasty reading, and eventually he asked me to help out by seeing that the individuals at least had replies.

At the same time the atmosphere at the Laboratory was changing. The war was over and several of the men had returned, but the first euphoria of discovery that had marked the 1930's when the realization was dawning that an entirely new (mental) continent was being glimpsed, had worn off. It had been worn down partly by the mere struggle against the counterculture, the bias on every side against results like these that showed the reality of psi. Some kind of injection of new spirit and enthusiasm was needed. It was then that JBR had the idea that perhaps the

*Instead, the results from the Parapsychology Laboratory had been so widely rejected and so severely criticized in the years following the first publication of them that it sometimes seemed a good question whether it would not be necessary to "shut up shop." And that, certainly, would have happened had it not been for a tolerant University administration and if the critics had been able to show an inherent flaw in the methods that could nullify the results. But they could not do so, although it was not for lack of trying. Because the work was essentially sound, the critics need not claim further space here.

material in those letters, which purported to be spontaneous occurrences in people's lives of the ability proved in the Laboratory, might provide a valuable stimulus. He explained his idea in an editorial in the *Journal of Parapsychology* (reference 10).

Recognizing that the experimental investigations had been instigated because of spontaneous happenings that suggested forces unexplainable by customary laws of psychology and physics, he emphasized the fact that such experiences, no matter in what number, could not explain themselves. It was not possible to authenticate each one so that no possibility of mistake remained or to be certain that the desired meaning of the experience was the only possible one. The material could suggest an extrasensory method of getting information but it could not prove it. It was to miscast the case material to attempt to have it do so.

But, he felt that the suggestive value such experiences had had in leading to the experimental investigation of a possible extrasensory ability was *still inherent* in them. That value need not be entirely lost. It could be utilized to raise questions even yet, questions that could be studied experimentally, and then the answers to the experiments could be decisive. As he said in the editorial, "Ideally, the types of spontaneous experiences that initiated experimentation ought to have been kept in perspective throughout the course of the research. As it is, they have been neglected, and we must now go back to them again for a fresh outlook. And while we are no longer concerned with the original problem of psi occurrence, the very same types of experience that led to the original experiments in telepathy and clairvoyance may now be of service again in giving us clues as to the nature of these capacities."

This, therefore, in 1948 was the setting in the experimental Parapsychology Laboratory for a study of cases to begin, and as mentioned, the material for such a study was already at hand, as the many appreciative letters to the Laboratory testified. What seemed like a surprising number of people wrote not only to show their interest in the research, but usually also to tell about experiences of their own which they thought might contribute to the research and about which they would like comment or explanation.

As I said, these letters had been accumulating, and with each added publication, whether article or book, a new influx of such mail resulted. It was material which had not been used, both because it was anecdotal and also because of the preoccupation of the Laboratory staff with experimental projects which would have had first priority, even if these personal experiences had seemed important, which they didn't.

But a return to cases was called for and I was the one who eventually undertook it. At first a small group from the Laboratory staff, myself included, was appointed to do it. But the others soon found their own experimental projects more interesting, while I, with the last of our four children off to school, could not only see that the incoming letters received replies but in case any of their stories seemed of sufficient interest I could report on them at Laboratory research meetings. And so it began but with no great expectations on my part. While it seemed possible that a few persons might have experienced an actual instance of ESP, I knew that the history of psychical research had yielded very few persons who appeared to be "gifted" in this way. So I had no reason to expect that many of the authors of these letters had real instances of it to report.

I found no stopping place. Before I had read perhaps fifty of the letters, I began to realize that whether they came from Portland, Maine, or Portland, Oregon, some of the experiences reported were basically identical.*

Some such similarities — different kinds of them — were sufficiently pronounced that they could not be ignored and I began to be excited, for in spite of the diversity of the individual cases, these similarities suggested that a certain degree of lawfulness must be underlying them, a lawfulness that purely chance coincidence, which I had feared most of them might be, would not show.

JBR felt similarly. In the experimental research at the Duke Laboratory he had always been alert for signs of lawfulness in the data, because there too seemed to be a reassurance against

---

*When I began, about 300 case letters were waiting to be addressed, answered and judged. Probably only about half of them contained usable accounts, although some had more than one acceptable case. But by the time of my first study (reference 15), I had culled 1,600 acceptable cases from the continuing influx of letters.

the chance hypothesis. He was as excited as I and I was soon launched in earnest on a study of this material.

But the anecdotal method of research had a history just as did the experimental. It is outlined in the next chapter.

Chapter 3

An Early Case Study
and Its Background

Twenty-year-old Willis had been away from his Pennsylvania home for several years, but he returned for frequent visits, especially after his grandfather's stroke. The two had always been close. Two of Willis' most prized possessions, a watch and a gun, had been gifts from his grandfather. But now at each visit, the old gentleman seemed weaker.

One night soon after his return from a visit, Willis struggled awake to his grandfather's call, "Willis, Willis." The room, ordinarily very dark, was lit up brightly and, momentarily, he saw his grandfather smiling at him.

Startled, uncomprehending at first, Willis lay motionless for a bit, but then he put on the light. It was 1:10 a.m. He could sleep no more. At 6 a.m. a phone call from his brother came, but Willis spoke first: "Grand-pop died last night!"

"Yes, but how did you know?"

"He came to see me — it was about one-ten."

"Yes, that was when he died."

That experience is a modern one and it does not stand alone. From ancient times right up to the present, occasional persons have been "visited" by a distant friend or relative who they later learned was dying at the time. The message, the apparition, comes seemingly by actual personal contact. Small wonder that over the centuries experiences of this kind suggested to those to whom they occurred that they were direct evidence of a spiritual (and surviving) element in man. Such occurrences were especially convincing because the impression was so real that the experiencing person (the percipient) could not believe that the person he saw (the agent) was not actually there, even though in the flesh he could not have been. The alternative seemed to be that his spirit, somehow freed in dying from its bodily restraints, had been present.

Naturally enough, then, in mid-19th-century England, as in earlier ages, too, apparitions suggested to many that the spirit had survived the death of the body. However, although such experiences were reported again and again, educated people tended more and more to disregard them and to put them down to ignorance, credulity and superstition. However, eventually, in the 1880's, circumstances came about that led to a largescale study of them. It was the first time a comprehensive survey was undertaken and brought to completion by persons who could carry it out in a competent and thoroughly scholarly way. As a result the study, published in 1886 as *Phantasms of the Living* (reference 2), became a landmark of its kind in psychical research as much because of the method developed for the treatment of the material as for the careful and exhaustive examination of it and the insights arrived at as to its nature and genesis.

The background reason for this study was the fact that with the development of the sciences in the 19th century, the outlook was becoming ever more materialistic. The old values of religion were getting crowded out; scientifically, they had no standing. (Dr. McDougall's interest, and ours too, in the question of whether man has a non-materialistic aspect to his nature, as outlined in the preceding chapter were later-day reflections of the same conflict.)

Yet during the 1870's and 80's in England a few scholarly persons concerned about the climate of thought that was developing realized that evidence of a non-material side of man might be found in unorthodox psychic experiences such as those involving apparitions which they knew were being overlooked in the sciences. As a result, in 1882 they decided to organize a society for the study of all kinds of experiences that seemed to bear on the question of the spiritual nature of man. This became the Society for Psychical Research (SPR).

Apparitions were only one of the kinds of experience with which the London-based Society was concerned. Another was the kind that came to be called telepathic and which seemed to mean that a person had known another's unspoken thought or mental state. A modern instance of the kind is reported by a woman in Idaho.

Her husband was in the hospital. He had been burned with hot tar and the doctor was trying to grow skin on his hand by sewing it to his stomach and then cutting it loose. That morning the doctor had used a caustic on the wound and then had left. Very soon the pain became intense but the doctor had given no word for a sedative and therefore none could be administered. Soon the patient was in agony and became delirious.

His wife at home did not expect to go to the hospital until night and had allowed her son to take the car for the day. She was out raking the lawn when it seemed almost as if she could hear her husband calling out in agony. She thought she might be imagining it because there was no reason she knew of why he should be suffering, then especially. But the impression continued until finally she left her task, went in, dressed, and caught the bus to the hospital, where she at once was able to call the doctor and relieve the situation.

Then, as now, such happenings were reported. Even granting that they suggested telepathy, however, no one had proved its existence. Perhaps such cases were just the result of a chance coincidence between the thoughts of the two persons.

Accordingly, the objective of the Society as stated on page 3 of the first *Proceedings* of the SPR (1882) was to investigate "that large group of debatable subjects designated by such terms as mesmeric, psychical and spiritualistic." All of these topics were then outside the bounds of orthodox scientific investigation and all of them seemed to have antimaterialistic implications.

Research committees were set up in the Society to investigate these various topics. The first of these was assigned to examine "the nature and extent of any influence which may be exerted upon one mind by another apart from any recognized mode of perception" and the fourth was "apparitions at the moment of death or otherwise, or regarding disturbances in houses reputed to be haunted."

The method followed by the researchers assigned to these committees was anecdotal, although as mentioned previously, some experiments on telepathy had already then been made and some rather striking results had been achieved that seemed to indicate that a transference of thought had occurred (reference 2, page 31). But statistical methods were not widely used, nor was science in general yet at the stage of precision to which it later came in which anecdotal material was superseded in conviction value by the more precise results secured by statistical analyses.

Besides that, in the experiments that had already been reported by various researchers, at least one and usually both persons in telepathy situations knew that a test was being made and therefore were consciously trying to play their assigned parts of sending or receiving. But in the spontaneous cases like that with the wife at home when her husband was suffering at the hospital, neither one was consciously trying to have a telepathy experience. This kind of situation, then, it seemed, might conceivably be different from that maintained in an experiment. Therefore, the study that was undertaken under the sponsorship of the SPR was quite intentionally anecdotal. The experimental or semiexperimental efforts that had earlier been made were therefore accorded only a minor place in the book *Phantasms of the Living*.

Perhaps another reason too influenced the approach that was used in this study. Apparitional experiences were spontaneous and it was an explanation of them that these psychical researchers were seeking, even more than, or rather beyond, proof of telepathy. At least indirectly then, this inquiry of the 1880's was made as an attempt to get *proof* of a spiritual element in man, and not in order to understand such spontaneous psychic experiences as had impressed them, which were mainly apparitions and cases that suggested telepathy. The concept of psi had not then been born and telepathy, its historical forerunner, was still far from being generally recognized as a reality.

Two special requirements faced the committee that set out to see if the case for telepathy was reliable. One was to find instances in which one person seemed to know another person's thought without the ordinary avenues of sense. The other requirement was to be certain that the experiences so found were reliable, that they really occurred as reported. This second requirement proved to be even more difficult to fulfill than the first. With a number of persons collecting cases, many reports accumulated over the years between 1882 and 1886. But the problem was that of authenticating the facts of each one. Human testimony at best is far from reliable. Memory is imperfect, observations may be faulty, descriptions may be incomplete, judgments biased. The task of winnowing out incorrect details in material like this and arriving at the absolute truth was formidable. In the report, the authors of the book took over fifty pages (Chapter IV) just to indicate the ways in which human testimony may be unreliable—even if the person giving it is sincerely trying to report the unadorned facts.

One of the obvious first needs to impose on a person reporting experiences then was to require that he produce one or more witnesses to the main elements of the occurrence and especially that he report it before he learned of the outcome. Another was that the experience and event coincide in time, as with Willis, at the time of his grandfather's death. Also, if the occurrence involved any event that could be documented, as for instance a death notice, that too should be verified. In the final report, the committee was able to publish some 700 cases, most of which had passed these and other corroborative tests. Securing the corroboration of all of these points had involved no inconsiderable labor, including numberless visits, trips and personal interviews. But the gravity of the objective had made the labor necessary, for proof that telepathy occurs must not be based on flimsy evidence.

The analysis of the cases in the collection led first of all to a breakdown into two main classifications: those in which the impression was sensory and externalized (Willis' impression of his grandfather) and those in which it was not, but more internal and impressionistic (the woman raking the lawn when the idea that her husband was suffering came to her). In addition, four secondary divisions were recognized: (a) the feeling of pain or illness alone, which later was found to be ascribable to a distant person who was at the time undergoing similar sensations; (b) a division of dreams; (c) experiences occurring on the borderline between sleep and waking; and (d) reciprocal and collective cases (reference 2, pages 186-187).

The use of dreams, however, called for special explanation because their status in 1882 was much lower than today when the Freudian influence has had a magnifying effect on their significance. But, at that time even an attempt to use dreams as evidence in a serious way needed justification because of the common assumption that since everyone has innumerable dreams, the chances are great that an occasional one, by simple coincidence alone, should resemble a real situation (reference 2, Chapter 8).

However, a number of especially impressive dream cases were found which the authors could not dismiss for they seemed like evidence of telepathy because the event dreamed about was *distinct, unexpected* and *unusual*. But the rules that isolated such instances were stringent. For instance, one dream was rejected when one of its elements was shown not to have been entirely unusual in the dreamer's experience. That situation was that the dreamer told her family one morning that she dreamed that a certain cousin of theirs would come to see them that day although he had been in bed with "a quinsey," a malady he had never had before. The report of the dream was corroborated but, nevertheless, the case was rejected when the SPR collectors learned that a governess in the dreamer's family had had "a quinsey," so that the item was not entirely unusual to that person.

One finding among the "true dreams" seemed significant. It was that one of the most frequent topics was death. Out of 149 of the accepted dream cases, 79 concerned an unexpected death. It seemed that this was many more on this theme than should be expected on the chance basis alone (reference 2, page 303).

Even though this was not yet the age of experimental procedures in psychical research, these authors recognized the value of statistics for they made an attempt to strengthen their dream material by resorting to numerical evaluation. By a fairly involved calculation (covering several pages of explanation) they made out a case for the rate at which, by pure coincidence, dreams of death should be expected to coincide with the reality.

By their calculation, they were able to show that the death dreams in their collection occurred about 24 times too often to be only coincidences. But even with this numerical basis for taking this dream material seriously, they stated that they would not have ventured to offer it as evidence of telepathy if it had stood alone. However, it was not alone, for they held all of their material labelled A, the hallucinations, to be stronger evidence.

The next chapter of the report was on the material which was "sensory and externalized." This, as evidence of telepathy, was stated to be "the most important of all." It was characterized as instances in which "the impression is sensory and externalized" and which seem to have a distant cause or reason, one that could be considered to be available by telepathy.

The authors classed such experiences (slightly paraphrased) as "those in which something is presented to the percipient (the experiencing person) as really there but is not, and which is instead a phantasm, belonging to the general class, hallucination."* It is, however, a species which is a veridical hallucination of the sane, one which psychology has so far not recognized (reference 2, page 457).

The later chapters of Volume 1 of *Phantasms* are devoted to experiences that occur on the borderline between sleep and waking (Willis' experience would classify here) and those that occur when the person is up and presumably wide awake. Each case is presented along with numerous quotations from corroborative testimony, often more lengthy than the report of the case itself.

Following all this, the authors discuss in detail the considerable evidence found for the genesis or development of an hallucination. It was not simply a case of telepathy, but more complicated. Their primary conclusion was that the evidence pointed to an idea's being received by the experiencing person from the agent, which would of course essentially be a telepathic transfer. But that transferred idea was only the central theme and did not account for the entirety of the experience. For instance, the clothing of the figure seen might be that which the percipient remembered rather than that which the agent was actually wearing, or which the agent himself would have had in mind. But in other cases the clothing might be factual, but unfamiliar to the experiencing person.

*The terms percipient and agent were chosen to represent the two persons involved in a telepathic transfer on the assumption that a thought in the mind of one person is sent to the other. The person who receives the thought, the experiencing person, was called the percipient; the one who was assumed to have sent the thought, the agent. It may be less confusing here, however, to speak of the percipient as the experiencing person, or to use the terms interchangeably.

All this was confusing of course. It is interesting to have the authors refer to what today can be recognized as an actuality but which was not so recognized then, when they say, "another conception no doubt there is — that of some *independent* exercise of the percipient's own faculties" (reference 2, page 555). Today, that reality is ESP.

Then the authors continue: "But in the absence of more distinct contemporary evidence for such exercise, I think we should avoid even provisionally resorting to a theory which introduces problems as formidable as any that it can be employed to explain. And in the present cases, since nothing is perceived that is definitely outside the agent's range of knowledge, the extension of the percipient's faculties — his *clairvoyance* — may still be perfectly well regarded as a *telepathic* extension, an abnormally increased power of receiving impressions from another mind ... under conditions of crisis or excitement" (page 555-556). And then the author argues (page 556) that in the majority of cases no special features troublesome to explain are introduced and it therefore "seems to me reasonable to refer the details of the appearance (of the agent) to the percipient's mind," rather than to think that the whole thing was projected from the agent.

In this statement one sees a bias toward telepathy and against clairvoyance as a type of perception in its own right. It was the direct result of the reason for the inquiry, the quest for proof of telepathy. It took many years of research and many later experiments to establish the fact that telepathy (i.e., the extrasensory awareness of another person's thought) is only one of the types of ESP ability, clairvoyance and precognition being others. The old bias in favor of telepathy, however, imbued with the possibility that it could provide an explanation for postmortem survival and thus for a spiritual element in man, has clung tenaciously. In fact, one can find remnants of it today.

The result of the inquiry covered in *Phantasms* was meant to establish the occurrence of telepathy as a process in which the initial impression originated in the mind of the agent. The authors felt that no reasonable person, fully cognizant of the burden of the report, could fail to accept the weight of proof of it based on the hundreds of cases that had been individually authenticated about as far as they possibly could have been.

However, no general acceptance of telepathy as a reality did follow. In fact, it has taken forty years of strictly experimental research since then on extrasensory perception in general even to begin to crack the hard shell of bias against the idea of a non-mechanistic element in human nature that the concept of telepathy introduced; research that in the doing has even brought into question the concept of telepathy as a mind-to-mind transfer itself.* Perhaps in the 19th century, the weight of bias and indifference was too strong for any kind of proof of an extrasensory way of knowing to have been sufficient. Also, because the two-volume *Phantasms*, with its over 1,300 closely packed pages, makes what today would be formidable reading, it may be that few people in the general stream of science read it. Another reason too was that the scientific attitude against anecdotal material as proof of a revolutionary thesis was becoming more adamant. In such experiences as these, even if all the facts were proved to have been as reported, still it could be argued that they were just a series of chance coincidences. In Willis' case, for example, it might have been only a nightmare which by chance occurred at the time his grandfather died; in the other instance, perhaps the wife's anxiety just happened to coincide with the time of her husband's ordeal. And so, since even the most stringent authentication of an individual's experience could not exclude all other explanations for it besides telepathy, the accumulation of evidence of this kind should not be expected to be wholly convincing to the skeptical. This inadequacy of the anecdotal method was not generally recognized by those in the field, however, and succeeding workers often came to expend their main energies on the authentication of cases rather than the study of them and their interpretation.

A few years later another study, called the *Census of Hallucinations*, was undertaken by members of the SPR (reference 4). This one dealt with apparitional experiences directly. Its object was to show that more than just coincidence is involved when an individual "sees" the figure of a distant person at the time that person is dying.

This question is based on the present day uncertainty as to the proper definition of a mind. Is it an independent "entity," as assumed in the usage here, or is it dependent in the final analysis on the physical structure of the brain? If the latter should prove to be the case, then telepathy would be only a sub-category of clairvoyance.

In this study, first, a questionnaire was circulated asking members of the general public whether they had ever had an apparitional experience. The feature of special interest among the respondents who reported having had such an experience was whether it occurred at the time the person was dying. The result was that about one apparitional experience in 43 did correspond with the time the person seen was dying. However, the average annual death rate in England was then 19.15 per thousand. The researchers could therefore arrive at an estimate of the rate such coincidences could be expected on a purely chance basis. It was 1 in 19,000.

The numerical estimate of one apparitional experience at the time of death out of 43 seemed to indicate that among apparitional experiences, those coinciding with the death of the agent were so frequent that a connection other than chance must exist between the apparitions and the deaths to which they seemed to relate.

At the time and for many years afterward the results of this "census" were considered as evidence that apparitions at the time of death had a bearing on the question of survival.

Later, however, when the reality of psi in living persons was established, this data could be construed only as probable evidence of ESP. This will be clear after the discussion of the forms of psi experience in Chapter 7 and the further discussions of hallucinatory and apparitional experiences in Chapters 12 and 13.

In the following years numerous studies of case material on various different specific points were made by various investigators, all of them using the approach of *Phantasms* in that the material used consisted mainly of reports of spontaneous experiences with emphasis on authentication (reference 14). Exceptional among them was one by Mr. H.F. Saltmarsh (reference 34), who, using already authenticated cases, put his emphasis on their study and analysis. He selected experiences that seemed to be precognitive, a type, it should be noted, which had been excluded in the SPR study because one of the authenticating criteria was that the experience and the event should coincide in time or within a 12-hour period (reference 2, pages 138-139). Saltmarsh, by an analysis of the state of mind and content of the

349 cases he was able to find, convinced himself that precognition is an actuality and developed a theory to account for it. This, of course predated by some years the eventual establishment of the phenomenon by experimental research, and although it was an anecdotal study, it involved some very insightful internal analyses, the results of which stood the test of later experimental confirmation.

Another notable study of case material, this time that of apparitions, was reported by Tyrrell in 1953 (reference 38). This author, using the old accumulated and authenticated published reports of the phenomenon, again showed that they could be the result of telepathy between the agent and the experiencing person and not necessarily evidence of a spiritual element. Both Saltmarsh and Tyrrell went beyond the bounds of strict anecdotal method by analyzing the case material in such ways that something of its essential nature was revealed. Also Tyrrell at least had some of the advances made by experimental method to guide him, except in the area of hallucinatory experience, in which even today no suitable experimental method of study has been devised.

It should be noted that most of the above studies and others not mentioned but made in this period were concerned with special kinds of experiences and were not carried out in order to arrive at an understanding of the processes that might be involved. Instead, nearly all of them except Saltmarsh's were concerned directly or indirectly with the question of survival. In the main one, the *Phantasms* study of the SPR, as already stated, the attempt was to use the cases themselves as proof of the thesis under study. It was this method of approach that set the stage for numerous later ones and was still the predominating model for case studies when my own project for studying cases began in 1948.

Chapter 4

A Different Kind
Of Case Study

The situation at the Duke Parapsychology Laboratory in 1948 was different in many respects from that at the Society for Psychical Research in 1882 when the case study already referred to was started there. More than sixty years of research had intervened. Even though the rate of progress of research in the field did not compare with that in the other sciences (the number of pioneering individuals in parapsychology had always been small and almost all were self-supporting), still some very significant advances in understanding had been made.

The changes of those intervening years however had not affected the basic methods of studying cases. Those methods still followed the model of the 1880's. But the status of anecdotal studies in general science was now the reverse of what it had been then. The use of experimental techniques was now in the ascendancy and very few case studies were being reported in parapsychology. To undertake one in 1948 almost called for an apology and certainly did for an explanation.

The most significant change the years had brought was that concerning the basis of knowledge on which a study of cases could be predicated. That basis in 1882 had been entirely conjectural. The psychical researchers then had only reports of two pertinent kinds of human experiences on which to go. The first was that of apparitions. They *looked like* communications from the dying or the dead and therefore suggested a spiritual element in humans that was separable from the physical body. The second

31

was the telepathic kind, which *looked like* a means of communication between minds that was not dependent on the physical channels of sense. The suggestion, then, as already mentioned, was that telepathy could be the means by which communication between the living and the deceased could occur.

In contrast, in 1948, telepathy as the ability of an experiencing person to become aware of another person's unspoken thought had been established experimentally.* In addition, there were clairvoyance, precognition and even psychokinesis, so that all of them together, psi, could be considered a unitary mental ability. It was now recognized at the Parapsychology Laboratory to be a widespread capacity by which the mind can get information about (and even affect) the external world without using the senses or the muscles.

This change, of course, meant that the objectives of the two case studies were very different. In 1882 it had been to find proof of telepathy, if such an ability existed. In 1948, as outlined in an editorial by JBR (reference 10), the aim was to look for signs of the way psi may occur in life situations, in order to help experimenters in their effort to understand the psi process.

In 1882 the idea had been that cases could be used as proof; in 1948 only that they might offer indications of the way psi operates, suggestions which then could be tested experimentally to show whether or not they were valid. The argument now was that, at the worst, a few unproductive experiments would be made. At the best, a new finding would be added to the slowly emerging understanding of psi.

More important still, these differences in aim called for a change in the methods of approach. The old study required cases that were free of errors of reporting and they could only be obtained, if at all, by the stringent authentication of testimony and the elimination from consideration of any that lacked it. This meant that criteria for acceptability had to be set up in advance; one, for instance, was that the experience had been reported to a second person before its relevance was learned. Naturally some

*The researchers, however, had come to question the adequacy of any known method by which to separate telepathy from other psi processes. That is, there was no way to rule out the possibility that the awareness of the thought of the agent was only a special instance of clairvoyance; i.e., the clairvoyant perception of brain operation.

kinds of cases are more apt to be so reported than others. Presumably an apparitional experience, being very striking and unusual, would have a much greater likelihood of being mentioned to another person before its meaning was learned (*i.e.,* the death or crisis of the person seen) than a dream, which very well might not be thought of as meaningful, and not mentioned, even half-forgotten, until the fulfillment. Only then the person might recall it, and then realize, "Why, I dreamed that." Even though sometimes tricks of memory might exaggerate or change the similarity then, an entire category of possible psi experiences might be eliminated by this requirement of authentication. (Quite possibly this requirement, along with the low status of dreams in general in the 1880's, goes far toward explaining the relatively large number of apparitional experiences on record then. The method of selecting cases in itself would have tended to make them stand out.)

Another requirement was that the event and experience be simultaneous or at the most within 12 hours of each other. This was based on the then held concept of apparitions of the dying and it eliminated at the start most precognitive experiences. This may have had no serious effect on the project in 1882, but a restriction imposed prematurely in my 1948 effort would be deadly and might defeat the very purpose for which the project was undertaken.

The new need was for a broader standard of collecting, one that would avoid any preselection of data. Every kind of case in which psi could have been involved must be included in order that the collection be as representative as possible of all the ways in which psi is expressed spontaneously. That meant that any kind of experience in which a person obtained information without the use of the senses could possibly be a psi experience.

Obviously, I could therefore not use the old criteria on cases to be collected in 1948 and later. But human testimony was still just as open to error as ever. Even though most people most of the time are probably trying to be truthful, even the best of witnesses can make mistakes, and the percentage of actual liars probably has not decreased over the years. In the present situation of course the possibility of including incorrect testimony thus was as great as ever. The seriousness of such

error, however, was less because case material was not to constitute proof of anything. As JBR said in his 1948 editorial, it had
been miscast as proof, a role for which it was too weak, nor
could it be sufficiently strengthened for that purpose even by the
most rigorous attempt at authentication.

For the new project it was therefore necessary to make a
compromise between the desire for a collection of cases authenticated in the time-honored way and the need to have one in
which the kinds of experiences were not selected. The compromise that I decided on was based on *numbers* of similar cases,
rather than on individual ones. To be acceptable, a case report
still had to fulfill the requirement that it seem to be an instance
in which the experiencing person received information that appeared not to have come from sensory sources and which seemed
to be reasonably beyond conjecture and coincidence.

The requirement of this definition, simple as it sounds
however, called for an element of judgment in its application to
specific experiences. When did the information not come from
any of these sources? The need for such decisions, inexact as they
must be, is one of the considerations that make case material
inherently and irremediably unfit to be the basis for final conclusions.

Cases collected because they seemed to fulfill the
definition, however, were not to be considered on their special
individual characteristics, but only on those that were common
among a large number of instances. At the start, my plan was
that there must be at least 50 cases showing any given feature, for
instance a precognitive or an apparitional effect, before any
study of the feature would be made. The supposition was that
any actual psi effect occurring to one person would occur to
others too — not that all conceivable ones would be reported with
the same frequency but that none would stand alone, either.

By thus placing the emphasis on 50 or more experiences
exemplifying a given point, the likelihood that that point was
representative of an actual aspect of psi was augmented. At the
same time, the importance of individual errors was minimized
because the ways of unreliable reporting would vary with the individuals.

When the general criterion for acceptable cases was
decided, the next question was how best to file them individually

so that those pertinent to a given topic would be readily available. Of course, it would not be possible to foresee every future topic that might be needed. But those already in mind because of past or current laboratory projects could be isolated. Accordingly, the tentative outline I drew up and reported in my first published study (reference 15) reflected the situation in the field then fairly clearly. The degree to which it is out of date today is something of a measure of the progress I can claim in understanding the nature of these psychic experiences in daily life.

According to this early outline, the cases would be filed under the following headings: *1* Precognition, *2* Survival, *3* Manner or form of emergence into consciousness, *4* The percipient's idea of the origin of his experience, *5* Telepathy, *6* Apparitions, *7* Psychokinesis, and *8* Special subjects.

Study and comparison of ever increasing numbers of cases, in time showed that these topics were only relevant in varying degrees. No. 1, precognition, in 1948, was a recent laboratory discovery and its expression in daily life was naturally of special interest, even overshadowing in immediacy that of No. 2, survival, which claimed second place. But No. 3, the way or manner by which psi information comes into consciousness, was largely an unknown. Any ideas anyone may have had about it were little more than guesses, in which no distinctions were made between effects that might be basic and others that might be secondary.

No. 4, the percipient's idea of the origin of his experience, I soon had to drop entirely. The percipients usually had no idea about it or if they did, it was purely a personal opinion and not amenable to generalization.

No. 5, telepathy, a workable topic, was not quite what might have been expected from the familiarity of the word, as will be shown in later chapters. No. 6, apparitions, was a topic that later faded into one of the forms isolated under No. 3, while No. 7, psychokinesis, and No. 8, special subjects, were viable topics, although items placed under them were relatively few.

It was necessary now to decide on a method of procedure by which to handle the material. First, of course, acceptable cases had to be distinguished and so marked in the margin of the letter. Then they had to be copied off, each on separate sheets so they could be handled as independent units. The contributors' name had to be given on each, so that when necessary later, the letter could be consulted. For reference the letters were then filed alphabetically.*

Of course, a coding system for each individual case had then to be worked out so that the characteristics of each one on any of the points that seemed important then or might later be so considered could be located when needed. Although the one I used at first still makes sense to me because I know what in my ignorance it meant to me then, if I were recoding all the thousands of cases now in the files I could make many improvements. As a matter of fact, I'm surprised at the extent to which the system started then still makes any sense today.

One decision made at the start that was especially fortunate, was that although many cases might fit under several different headings, each one should be filed only once and into the category where it seemed it would make the greatest contribution. The total numbers given later in various studies, therefore, are independent.

Since the types of psi — telepathy, clairvoyance and precognition — had already been isolated in the laboratory, the type of each case was then first to be marked on the margin and all of them were filed into these three groups accordingly. In making these classifications, I had to remember, however, not to try to decide at this stage any less obvious point that might come up in an individual case, but to leave all such for later special study when sufficient numbers and specific objectives might dictate it. This initial classification thus was only a general one but it was sufficient to allow a sorting into major groups so that numbers in individual files could be counted and those that were ready for detailed study easily estimated.

At this early stage, as mentioned above, I did not consider that the study I was undertaking would actually come to be a

*Letters in which no acceptable cases were found were also filed alphabetically, but in separate cabinets. Today their bulk is about one and half times that of the "case letters." This is perhaps something of a very rough estimate of the relative rate at which these letters from the general public proved to contain acceptable cases — very rough, however, because many letters reported more than a single case.

research project of my own. The idea then was only to have numerous cases on hand for experimenters and to have each one classified and filed according to topic so that experimenters could quickly find those appropriate to their special needs and interest. Presumably, then, the experimenters could consult the files and see what suggestions they could get from the experiences to help them in the planning of their research.

Practice, however, soon showed that this idea was not going to work, even though very soon case files on most of the topics under investigation were available. To study them sufficiently to cull out pertinent suggestions took time and few experimenters could give it. Even when they did so, more than a hurried and cursory reading of a few cases was necessary to suggest viable leads. It took more time, patience and experience with case reports than individual researchers had to give. It was then, as I came to realize, that this was becoming a research effort of my own and any tips that experimenters might get from it would have to come from the reports I would make. These followed in due course, the first in 1951. By 1967, in all 18 had appeared. The topics of the earlier ones particularly were mainly those that were then of active interest in the laboratory, but more and more as my studies progressed, they came to be on topics in which the cases themselves suggested new meanings to me so that I thought I was beginning to see underlying processes which I hoped might in time come to be subjected to clarifying research. This I was later able to do; see chapters 8 to 13 of the present work especially.

Some of the cases, too, seemed to bear on topics not yet within the experimental focus, particularly those of apparitions and survival. Even though still beyond the range of available experimental techniques, I knew it would be of general interest to sum up what the case material on these topics seemed to say.

As the various studies were made the numbers of cases in the collection were steadily increasing. Eventually, the total number became so large that even files of less frequently reported experiences contained well over the requirement of 50 items, and new cases seldom represented a different aspect from many of those already on hand. It seemed no longer important to try to add to the number of items in such categories. On that account, by 1970, active collection practically ceased and few new cases, unless offering some exceptional hint or insight, were added to the collection.

The general approach I have taken in making this case collection is of course outlined above and also suggested in Chapter 1, where, as I said, I did not try to decide if the deer hunter was truthful or even correct in all the details of his experience, as he gave them. By the time I heard the man tell his story, its basic characteristic was so true to a great many other cases contributed by other persons that I could accept the essential outline of the case. Granting that the details, just when and where, etc., were irrelevant, an attempt to verify them would have been an empty gesture. And so it is with all the cases that are used herein as examples. Each one is given as representative in its main bearing of many others with other and different details. The point, then, in reading this book is not whether every detail in any case is absolutely correct. No effort could so verify material such as this. But the accumulated evidence, even based on the relatively small number of instances of any single kind that are given here as examples, I think, can scarcely help but suggest even to a thoroughgoing but fair-minded, skeptic, that "such things do occur." Therefore, I hope that, among other ideas, this account will lead many people to say, "Why, these experiences are happening all around and all the time much more frequently than I knew." It's not that "the Emperor has no clothes," but that the Emperor has a lot of clothes, only the citizenry has not been looking at them.

More than that, however, I hope that the story of this research and the new insights it gives into the processes that go on in these elementary kinds of psychic experiences will help to illuminate some aspects of them that too long have remained in shadow and thereby have tended either to be exaggerated in fiction or ignored in science.

Chapter 5

The Reach
and Types of Psi

No. 1

It was December 7, 1941, a sleepy Sunday afternoon in an Alabama city. In one home a man was dozing in his comfortable chair near the radio, his wife nearby reading a book. Suddenly jumping up,

"My, God!" he exclaimed to his wife. "Did you hear that?" The President announced that the Japanese are bombing Pearl Harbor!"

She laughed aloud. "Why, you are crazy. You were dreaming. You were asleep!"

"I was not asleep. I never heard anything clearer in my life!"

She continued to laugh. If there had been such an announcement she would have heard it. And he *was* asleep. While they were still arguing about it:

"Flash! The President announced that the Japanese are bombing Pearl Harbor."

With hundred of reports of personal experiences each of which, like that one, seemed to have brought the experiencing person an item of information he did not get by sensory channels, the question in my study was, where to begin? But, as I said above, since in the laboratory three types of psi, clairvoyance, telepathy and precognition, had already been established, it seemed logical to begin by deciding the type of psi each case seemed to represent. In clairvoyance tests in the laboratory, the subjects had identified inanimate targets like symbols on hidden cards when no one had the symbol in mind. In telepathy, they identified symbols without objective representation but which existed *only* in the mind of another person. Whether the target was actually the other person's thought pure and simple, or if something of his brain state was also involved, it was at least a different situation than that of pure clairvoyance and could continue to be called telepathy regardless and to mean simply the awareness by an experiencing person of another individual's thought. In precognition, the subjects had identified, even though imperfectly, the order of a pack of cards that would not be determined until they were shuffled at a later time. Precognition, therefore, meant the awareness of a target still in the future. The three types then were simple ESP of the three different kinds or *orders* of targets.

My task of deciding the type of each of these cases, however, was not as simple a matter as it might seem. Take, for instance, a case like No. 1 above. Was it a telepathy case? At face value the man seemed to have been aware of a thought from some outside source and without any sensory means. But what was that source? Was it someone's thought at the distant scene, or radio station, or was it a precognitive impression of the report so soon to come right in his own living room?

Almost from the start, in trying to classify the cases in the collection, even on this relatively simple point of their type, quite frequently I met uncertainties like the above. Provisionally accepting the testimony as given, I knew that an experience like No. 1 would probably once have been judged to be telepathic. But now with the alternatives of clairvoyance and precognition to be considered too, it could not be so classified with any certainty. Leaving it undecided for the moment, the next case to come to hand might have been like this one.

No. 2

A man, his wife and a friend of hers were driving to a restaurant for lunch one day. On the way the friend asked if they could stop a moment at a drug store. The man just double parked and both women ran into the store.

The minutes dragged by. He began to be concerned lest a policeman gave him a ticket. More and more minutes passed. He was "fit to be tied," by the time they finally appeared.

"Guess what I bought," his wife called to him as she approached the car.

"Three dozen wooden clothes pins," he answered sarcastically.

"Right!" She had them to show for it, three dozen of them.

Telepathy again? In the past no doubt this experience too would have been so classified because the wife certainly had the three dozen clothes pins in mind. Before ESP had been shown to be a real mental ability, a case like this perhaps would have suggested something like leakage or contagion from one mind to another. Telepathy was the rather catch-all word coined to cover occurrences such as this, as well as those like No. 1, even though the thought and even the minds from which it might have come were indefinite.

No one at that earlier time suspected the full reach of mind as now known, a reach that means it can get information not only of another person's thought but also of objects or events that no one knows or even those still in the future. The fact that the wife in a case like No. 2 not only had the clothes pins in mind but also *in hand* would have gone unnoticed. But those clothes pins could have been the target for clairvoyance. The case then could not be definitely claimed to be either telepathic or clairvoyant. It could not safely be considered as a clear example of either one.

In the laboratory, the distinction between telepathy and clairvoyance could be tightly drawn because the type of target material could be controlled. In that research, the objective was to be certain that "pure" instances of each type do occur. In real life it seldom matters whether such a distinction is correctly made or not. But in this collection of cases, made primarily in order to study the psi process, it seemed safest to file cases like Nos. 1 and 2 as general ESP (GESP), and not to attempt any finer level of distinction. I felt certain that if I filed cases like these simply as general ESP (GESP) they would still be of value, for they might

fit into this survey from some other aspect. I was already quite
sure that this classification of the experiences according to type
was only one of many I would eventually make. Certainly in
others the type might not be at all important. I therefore gave the
GESP cases a file of their own in which to await a future need.

Continuing then, the next case would probably be quite
different. Suppose, for instance, it was this one.

No. 3

A 16-year-old girl in Oregon was on her first job, that of
dental assistant. One morning when the dentist was not coming
to the office he instructed her to pick up a package at the post office which contained gold foil, and lock it in the upper drawer of
his cabinet.

She got the package and was unwrapping it when a knock
came and she left it lying open in the shallow drawer and answered the knock. It was "Frenchie," a town character, come to
pick up his bridge work. She went to the inner office to get it.

After a little chat, he left and she returned to the drawer,
which was no longer open as she thought she had left it, and inside the gold foil was gone. Frantically she searched but did not
find it. She remembered that Frenchie was an odd-ball, a salmon
fisherman frequently locked up for disorderly conduct. But he
had never been charged with anything serious. He was better
educated than most of the other rough fishermen and the police
chief said he sometimes picked the man up on a Saturday night to
keep them from killing him in their brawls.

She remembered that she had thought she had heard the
drawer closing softly—yet to accuse Frenchie would destroy him.
Worried nearly sick, she went to bed praying for guidance. Early,
before dawn, she woke from a vivid dream. She thought a voice
had told her how to open the bottom drawer of the cabinet, pull
it out and release a certain catch, push forward the drawer above
and find the gold foil wedged against the back wall of the cabinet.

At daylight she rushed to the office, followed directions—and found the envelope with the gold foil intact.

The next time she saw Frenchie he told her she must learn
to be more careful with valuables as he had seen that she left the
drawer open with gold in it and he had closed it (and in doing so
apparently caused it to slip back against the back wall of the
cabinet).

"You just can't tell who might come wandering in," he admonished her.

That case was very different for no one knew where the gold foil was. Only clairvoyance, of all the types of psi, could have been involved. The girl, in reporting the experience, wondered if the dream was some sort of miracle or a message from her subconscious. I knew it was a message from her subconscious, even the "voice." But without clairvoyance, she would have been as ignorant of the answer, subconsciously, as she was consciously.

As it developed, the clairvoyant type of case was the most difficult to file with certainty, because in the majority of human situations human beings as well as inanimate events are involved, and so, as in No. 2, possible clairvoyant and telepathic elements cannot be separated. However, most of the cases that could be considered clairvoyant, were "finding cases," like No. 3. The situation in them seems to be the most common kind of experience that is not "contaminated" by human thought.

In No. 3, the object found was in the immediate vicinity of the percipient. However, such instances were also reported at greater distances as in the following case.

No. 4

During the 1934-35 depression, a man in Texas needed a tow chain and had been unable to get one. One Saturday he and his brother went fishing, driving some 70 miles from home. On the way back he got the certain feeling that he would find a tow chain strung out down the center of the road. Some 50 miles farther on they found it.

When many finding cases had accumulated, however, I found that nearly all involved short ranges. Did this mean that clairvoyance is "easier" when the target is nearby?

One of the interesting questions that came up in the laboratory research that had established clairvoyance was that of what the effect would be of distance between the subject and his target material (reference 13, Chapter 4). When different distances were interposed, however, the experimenters found no noticeable differences between the short and the longer distances. If other conditions were the same it seemed not to matter whether the target material was near or far from the subjects.

Considering the experimental finding I realized, however, that the relative difference in numbers of long range and short range finding cases did not necessarily mean a conflict between the experimental result and the testimony of the cases because this kind of experience would almost necessarily be recognized only if the lost object were near enough to the person that he would come upon it easily and so verify his impression. Accordingly, it would mean that in reported instances the object would usually be in the person's near or immediate vicinity. Situations involving a fairly long distance like No. 4 then are likely to be rare, and so the *reach* of the mind over distance would probably scarcely have been appreciated from spontaneous cases alone. Controlled experiments were necessary to bring out the point strongly that longer distances do not inhibit clairvoyance nor appreciably affect it.

Now, suppose the next experience is a sort of shared dream.

No. 5

A woman in California awoke one night and recalled a dream that had been so vivid and beautiful that she told her husband about it. When she finished he said, "You can't have dreamed that! *I* did!" In her dream she thought she was standing outside a building admiring the beautiful shimmering blue sky with the moon bright, round and silver. Then, as she watched, six other smaller moons of varying sizes rose, one by one, in different arcs and at different speeds. Some were more golden than the actual moon, some paler; their light turned the sky almost to daylight.

In the dream, she watched as if entranced and not wanting her husband to miss such a wonderful sight she called him out of the building and they stood there happily watching the moons and commenting on their beauty.

Her husband's dream seemed to have been identical except that he called her out to see the moons. The dreams occurred in 1954 before publicity on space exploration made the moon or general firmament more likely subject matter for dreams. The most logical explanation of the similarity, they thought, was that she and her husband were in telepathic rapport.

Telepathic rapport? Yes, in this kind of instance, telepathy would seem the only explanation, for no clairvoyant target was involved to confuse the interpretation. I realized then that in trying to recognize a telepathic experience, the situations would be the reverse of that with clairvoyance. With telepathy, inanimate things, not people, must be ruled out, for they would be the contaminants.

Oddly, perhaps, telepathy had been more difficult to work with in the laboratory than clairvoyance, for telepathy requires two persons and a kind of target more difficult to manage than that for clairvoyance tests. Consequently, much more experimental evidence is on the books for clairvoyance than for telepathy. Clairvoyance needed only a physical object so hidden from the subject that he could have no sensory cue as to its identity. But a telepathic target had to be a thought in one person's mind with no objective sign of it that the subject could pick up by clairvoyance.

I noticed, when telepathy cases accumulated, that the majority of them, like No. 5, were between persons who were emotionally close. But here again, I realized that this may have been at least partially what could be called situational, for experiences involving two persons who were emotionally close would be the more likely to be recognized. A sufficient number of episodes between casual acquaintances, as No. 6 below, and even strangers was reported to show that telepathy does not actually depend on emotional bonds, whether or not they may facilitate it.

No. 6

A man in New Jersey dreamed he was out with a gun and with a woman companion, a person whom he knew only slightly. He thought they were shooting at different objects but the targets that impressed him most were some cows in a field. He remembered the dream in the morning, partly because the woman was no one he was interested in, but one of the people in his home town whom he only knew casually.

The next day he happened to meet her in a store. When she saw him she said she wanted to tell him about a "crazy" dream she had about him the night before. "I was stunned for a moment when she said she had dreamed that she and I were out shooting cows."

The slim chance that those two persons would ever know that they had had similar dreams and that they probably were telepathic depended on the casual meeting of the two persons soon after. So it is that telepathic exchanges, especially between persons not likely to be in contact could very well occur and never be recognized.

The effect of distance in telepathy experiments as in those for clairvoyance, was negligible. In the cases, however, it was seemingly almost the opposite of that in clairvoyance, for telepathic episodes so often involved people who, though emotionally close, were far apart actually, as to raise the question whether or not the sense of separation may not help to induce them. Many of the cases covered thousands of miles, as the next one.

No. 7

A girl in Los Angeles one night heard her mother call her as if from the next room. She turned and before she thought answered, "Yes, Mother." But then she chided herself for such a lapse, when "Mother is 3,000 miles away."

A few days later she had a letter from her mother saying that that night "I was so lonesome for you that I stood in the doorway of your room and called to you."

"Call cases" like this (more about them in Chapter 8) are one of several forms of experiences that tend to stand out especially. They tend to make an impression on people that they are unlikely to forget. And such cases are indeed fairly frequently reported. It may be that this kind of experience had much to do with making telepathy seem real to those who experienced it long before it was established by experimental research.

The reality of telepathy relative to distances and degree of emotion thus seemed to be as great as the experimental results suggested that it can be. If the GESP cases too are considered for their probable telepathic element, it would seem that telepathy and clairvoyance and both together in inextricable combination have no *objective limits* in real life, just as none have been found in the laboratory.

One of the oddities that sometimes occurs in the world of research on new ideas occurred in the history of para-psychological investigations. It was that telepathy was expected, or even needed for a long time, before it was actually adequately tested in a way that did not involve clairvoyance. The very reverse occurred with experiences like the kind that comes up next.

No. 8

A woman in Illinois dreamed that her 2-year-old daughter was hurt somehow and that she was rushing the child, wearing only panties, to the hospital. The dream awoke her trembling, and she was most relieved to find it was just a dream.

The next day the child pulled a pot full of boiling coffee over herself. The mother did indeed rush her to a hospital wearing only panties. She had had to cut off the rest of her clothing.

The dream occurred the night before the accident happened. It therefore was of the precognitive type. And this type, unlike telepathy, was not expected before it was demonstrated in the laboratory, even though it was not a new idea but a very old one, if only from the Bible. But until the tests for it were made at the Duke Parapsychology Laboratory beginning in 1933, precognition was not thought to occur among ordinary persons but only to specially gifted prophets.

The research at the Laboratory soon showed that test subjects who gave evidence of clairvoyance could also give evidence of precognition. Only after this fact was established did the point begin to be recognized that precognition too must be a general human ability just as clairvoyance and telepathy seemed to be, for the subjects who had given evidence of it, mostly university students, were not prophets in the old sense, but ordinary unselected individuals who had not even suspected that they had precognitive ability.

However, as the cases of precognition accumulated, a great variation in the importance of their subject matter was noticeable. Sometimes, as in No. 8, the target was one of great concern to the individual. But many quite unimportant events were the subject matter in other cases. The following is a typical unimportant one.

No. 9

A man from California reported his experience because he was impressed with its unimportance almost as much as by the fact that it came true.

It happened in a small town in Idaho where he was a refrigerator contractor. He dreamed one night that he was working late in a dry goods store. He thought it was just breaking day as he walked toward the front of the store with his tool box in his hand and saw the first rays of sunlight come over the mountains and shine through the big plate glass door.

He opened the door and turned around and looked back across the store. There he saw two big air conditioners hanging from the ceiling about 30 feet apart, and he wondered whether they would work for he had never seen air conditioners hanging from the ceiling. That ended the dream.

About three weeks later he submitted a bid for two 3-ton air conditioners to cool a dry goods store. They had to be refrigerated air conditioners and they could not sit on the floor for lack of available space. So they had to be hung from the ceiling.

It turned out the job had to be done at night because he and his helpers would have to tear up the ceiling to hang the units and they did not want to disrupt the owner's business. They worked all night and finished about 5 a.m. He gathered up his tools and walked to the front of the store. When he came to the big plate glass door and the first sunlight was streaming through, he got the feeling that he had experienced this once before. He looked back — and, with "cold chills down my back," he said, he could not be sure for a moment whether he was dreaming about something he had done before or doing something he had dreamed before.

The fact that, in the precognitive experiences, the importance of the subject matter ranged so widely meant that the range of emotional to nonemotional topics was similarly broad. The distances between the person and the precognized scene also varied, from fairly near together, as in the preceding cases, to long distances apart, as below:

No. 10

A woman in Hawaii dreamed she was standing alone on the prow of a rather large boat which was traveling down a small but beautiful and rapid river through dense forests of conifers. She was entranced by the beauty of the scenery. The dream was repeated several times over a period of about a year. While the fact did not mean necessarily that the dream would come true, it did serve to impress the scene very clearly on her mind.

A year later she decided to go on a trip from White Horse down the Yukon River to Damison. But she was unable to book passage on a regular boat. She did, however, obtain a berth on a freighter. She was the only passenger and stood alone on the prow of the boat as it cast off and started down the swift and lovely river, and then suddenly there she was in the middle of the dream "down to the last detail." Incidentally, she never dreamed of the scene again.

Experiences like that one not only illustrate the long distances that sometimes intervened between the place of the experience and its fulfillment, but also possible clairvoyance as well as precognition. The actual river scene presumably could have been clairvoyant since it was no doubt in existence when the dreams occurred. But it was only later when the girl actually stood alone on the prow of the ship that the dreams were fulfilled.

Of course, in precognitive experiences, the distance between the place of the experience and the event is not a factor of main significance. In these it is time, instead, that is the element of special interest. In the examples already given, relatively short time intervals elapsed, but sometimes much longer ones were reported, regardless of the importance of the topic of the experience. The following involves both a long time period and an incidental glimpse of landscape, one of no special importance.

No. 11

A railroad telegraph operator and train dispatcher, long an employee of the Southern Railroad, recalled a dream he had had twenty years earlier. He had learned telegraphy while a boy in school and by the age of 14 was so proficient that the operator at the station would sometimes let him take messages for him or even sometimes, when the operator had a date, allow him to finish out the night. However, the youngster really wanted to be a locomotive engineer instead of a telegraph operator, which his father wanted him to be.

One night he dreamed that he was an engineer on a long passenger train drawn by a powerful sleek locomotive. In the dream he was passing through a long curve. He looked back and could see the coaches and Pullman cars stretched out behind, coming around the curve. On one side of the curve was a piney woodland and on the other a beautiful meadow with a creek meandering through it. In the lush grass he could see cows, some grazing, some drinking from the creek, some lying down. It was a strikingly beautiful scene and made a strong impression.

During following years as he advanced to train dispatcher his interest in driving a locomotive continued and he used every opportunity to ride or run one. Then, twenty years later, he accepted a job of dispatcher that gave him one day off each week. He spent most of these days off riding locomotives until the engineers sometimes allowed him to run their engines.

One summer day an engineer allowed him to run the engine alone while he, the engineer, took it easy in the baggage car. On this trip in going around a long curve he looked back to see if everything was in order. There was the dream; pineland on the right, the meadow with the brook, even the cows, exactly as in the dream.

The impact was so strong that in reporting it he added, "There is surely something supernatural about dreams. Even the Bible relates many strange ones. I believe there is something to it; but what?"

Naturally, when long time periods are covered, the faults and weaknesses of memory must be recognized, especially in the recalling of details. Occasionally, however, cases were reported in which memory was reinforced by a written record. For example, a woman in Iowa was able to recognize a dream scene of twenty years before, for she had recorded it in her diary, as follows:

No. 12

In the dream she thought she was standing upstairs in the hall of a house, with her hand on the banister, when the realtor said, "This house would make an ideal home for you and it can be yours."

When the event occurred exactly, so long afterwards, it was a few minutes before she remembered the dream. When she looked up the diary later, she found that details of the entry to the house and of several of the rooms also were the same.

Such long-term experiences showed a general form seemingly no different from that of the dreams that came true fairly soon. It also seemed that the "forward memory," precognition, was little different from that of ordinary memory of past events in the way the details of the situation were reproduced.

In the collection as a whole, however, short-term precognitive cases were much more frequent than long-term ones. But I realized that that would be expected, even if their actual rate of occurrence were the same, for fewer of those covering long terms would be remembered or even recognized. The point to be made here, however, is that I found no real cut-off in the actual length of time spanned in these spontaneous experiences. While experimental tests have as yet covered a period of only about a year, the experiences seem to be the same whether the time involved is days or years. And so far as any discernible indications show, long time periods appear to be spanned just as easily as short ones.

All of the ESP experiences mentioned so far fell into the three types just outlined, the clairvoyant, telepathic and precognitive. Also, the experiences, like the experimental results, tentatively covered the entire array of the possible kinds of objective information a person might acquire, with one exception. One other dimension must be mentioned. Does ESP cover the past too, as precognition covers the future? In a comparatively few cases, it appeared as if the past had been so glimpsed. And if it had, the experience would be classed as retrocognitive.

No. 13

A high-school boy from California who was a senior, editor of the school paper, and regarded as quite normal by his associates, had a series of puzzling dreams.

They were of a large white house, with a white berry bush planted at one corner of the yard, the planting centered around a tree stump. The house was on a hill, and a curious feature of it was that the second floor consisted of seven rooms, all completely empty.

Those empty rooms had a special fascination for him. He felt that he had to climb up and wander through them.

After he had this dream several times it began to worry him. He had been used to dreaming, more understandably, about girls and school affairs, etc., and so finally he told his mother about these dreams of the large white house, with the empty rooms.

His mother was astounded. The description fitted a house in Kentucky where the family had lived 17 years ago when he was an infant. He had never been in the upstairs. The family had lived there only four or five months. What kind of a "trick of the subconscious" was this, he wanted to know.

Just why such a dream scene should have been fastened upon by the unconscious dream maker would of course, be impossible to tell. Equally impossible is it to say in such an experience whether its basis was direct ESP of a past scene (if the identification of it was correct, and ESP was involved) or if the dreams were based on the boy's mother's memory. The fact, of course, was that she did remember the house and it was her confirmation that made it possible to recognize the dream as probably based on ESP. If it could not have been so checked it would not have been even suspected of being a dream based on reality.

All of the cases that involve episodes in the past pose the same kind of dilemma. If the impression of the past event cannot be checked against a memory or record of some kind, it cannot be counted as an instance of ESP, and if it can be so checked, it cannot be certainly identified as an instance of retrocognition because it could equally well be one of telepathy or clairvoyance. Theoretically, then, direct ESP of a past event cannot be proved to occur. However, the fact of precognition does show that ESP is not confined to the present. This means that time is not a limitation on the extrasensory as it is on sensory experience. Theoretically then, it would be logical to expect ESP of the past, just as of the future. Experiences like this one suggest that glimpses of both may be equally natural.

At the same time, cases that could possibly be retrocognitive were very rare in the collection compared to the large number of precognitive ones. And so, without deciding whether or not such cases are actually retrocognitive, it looks as if the human mind has a greater tendency to stray out of the concerns of the present into those still to come than to look backward into the past. However, on the basis of the person's interest in the topic only, it would seem reasonable that the future might intrigue the experiencing person more than the past.

When all of the cases that could be assigned to one of the three types as above had been so classified, and all those that could not be so definitely defined had been labelled GESP, a few more remained that fitted none of the ESP categories. These were accounts of physical effects that did not appear to have a satisfactory natural explanation. Instead, the person who reported them seemed to feel that they had a relationship to a human situation. Usually the crisis of another person was involved, one that had emotional overtones for both himself and the other. But sometimes too, the physical effect seemed to mark a significant time or event, as in the next case.

No. 14

A young married man died and the settling of his estate was held up by lack of information that he alone had had. A friend of his, an older woman, dreamed that she had a talk with him in which he told her the needed information.

Later when the friend told the family of her dream and the information it included, a noise startled the group and they found a picture had fallen from the wall.

These were the cases that had been filed as possible instances of PK, although with reservations, because generally the only connection between the effect (the falling picture, for instance), and the human situation to which it was suspected of being relevant, was that they happened at the same time. Had it not been for my rule not to throw out any kind of occurrence that could be construed to be an instance of information received without the use of the senses, these certainly would have been discarded one by one. It was only much later (as will be discussed in Chapter 7) when a reasonable, though still small, number of them had accumulated that another similarity too could be recognized. It was that the situation was an emotion-stirring one for the percipients, though often one of which they were not consciously aware until later. And then in one of the first novel ideas that my study produced I recognized that these experiences involving a physical effect might also indicate that the person was showing psi information but evidencing it by a psychokinetic (PK) effect instead of by ESP.

With this insight, all the cases collected under the definition of experiences in which information was secured without the use of the senses, had found a classification and now special studies of them could begin.

The first of these, reported in the next chapter, added another characteristic to the list of the types and states of consciousness, which I recorded on each case report. This one, "conviction," concerned the relative degree to which each person seemed to believe that his experience was true, his "conviction" or lack of conviction that his impression was meaningful.

Chapter 6

Conviction

No. 1

She had to make a hurried trip to town that morning and decided not to take six-year-old Ruthie along but to leave her with the maid. She started out, drove down town, but just as she got to the business section, she suddenly knew that she must go back. Ruthie was in danger! She must drive fast!

"Where is Ruthie?" she shouted to the maid as she drove in.

"Oh, she's playing with Anne," Ruthie's little six-year-old friend and neighbor.

She rushed to Anne's house, five doors down. Again, "Where is Ruthie?"

"I thought they were playing at your house."

With hardly time for thought, she drove on, down a lane, over a railroad crossing, parked, ran through a pedestrian's gate, up a little hill and down to an old brick pit, now filled with water. And there at the edge of it sat both children, taking off their shoes to go wading. The water was much too deep, the sides of the pit too steep for them to crawl out of once they were in. She was just in time. Another few minutes and...

As far as either mother knew, the children had never been to the pond before. As she said, as she reported the episode to the Parapsychology Laboratory, "It was not so much a thought as an impelling message that drove me home before I had gotten out of my car to go shopping. And it drove me at once to the dangerous old brick pit pond."

"Not so much a thought as an impelling message." But she

55

never questioned it or asked herself how she could know. She
believed it, and acted on it.

No. 2

Another mother was home one day at the stove fixing
something for dinner when she had a vivid "mental picture" of her
little girl, Marjorie, who was playing outside in the yard, but now
crying, her face all red and distorted from falling off a crate. But
it was not that she had heard the crying, the radio was blaring too
loudly for that.

This mother did not rush out to see what had happened.
She did not even turn away from the stove. "What a peculiar
thing to be imagining," she thought, and went on with her task.

Minutes later, Majorie came in crying, her face all grazed
and red. She had been playing on the crate, she said and fell off
and skinned her face.

One mother believed her impression, the other did not.
Conviction in one instance, a lack of it in the other. But, I asked,
why the difference? Could the presence or absence of the element
of conviction have a meaning beyond the personalities of the
people involved? Could it tell something about what happens
when ESP occurs?

What does happen when ESP occurs? As explained in
Chapter 2, in the experiments that established ESP, the guesses
of some of the student subjects as to the symbols on shuffled and
concealed card decks averaged more hits per run than chance
alone should give, so that an explanation was called for. These
subjects could be said to have shown knowledge of some of the
symbols, even though they were unaware they had such
knowledge, and certainly they did not get it by sense perception.
Thus, it had to be *extra*-sensory perception. However, the subjects in the tests thought they were only guessing. And more than
half of their calls were wrong; usually only a few — say, six to nine
of the 25 — were correct. And of these hits, five on the average
had to be counted as chance hits. But calls that would have been
based on knowledge supplied by ESP were mixed in with them.
The subjects did not know the difference, however, and neither
did anyone else. But still there was a difference because the
origins were different.

If a way to tell the difference between hits that only oc-curred by chance and those with an ESP origin could be found, then a "key" to understanding ESP would be obtained and possibly subjects could learn to use it. They could learn to omit the wrong calls and this would mean that they could control their ESP. To gain control of the occurrence of ESP had always been one of the great objectives of the research, for neither in experiments nor in real life could any reliable use be made of it if it was not subject to conscious control.

Experimenters had early been impressed by occasional calls subjects made which they said they were certain were correct. It might happen several times in a 25-call run of guesses. The subjects were asked to make a check mark by their record of those particular calls. Then, when those calls were counted separately later, usually a higher percentage of them actually were correct than of the other calls in the same run. These special "confidence" calls, as they came to be known, seemed to be different, and to mean that in them the subjects showed a measure of information and conviction that the run-of-the-mill calls lacked. It looked as if in these calls the subjects were not just blindly guessing, but like Ruthie's mother, were "using infor-mation," however unaware of it they may have been. These "con-fidence" calls seemed to indicate certainty just as did individuals in conviction experiences, and a number of cases that showed strong conviction like this one of Ruthie's mother, soon ac-cumulated. Since "confidence calls" in experiments were crying for explanation, it seemed at the time that perhaps the cases, if carefully examined, could tell something on the topic that would be helpful in the laboratory. And so the topic of conviction was the first one I undertook to study (reference 16) and I started out on it with all the confidence of ignorance. If I could have foreseen then how far from simple it would be to untangle the confidence theme from all the connections that affect it, I cer-tainly would not have begun my studies with this topic.

At the time, however, it seemed possible that a flash of certainty such as was shown in the conviction cases might mean that an element of consciousness had crept into an otherwise un-conscious experience. If so, it seemed as if a study of such in-cidents might yield some hints as to how the unconscious process could be made conscious. This was the reasoning behind the first analysis I made.

A total of 1600 cases were then in the files, personal reports from apparently serious persons who were puzzled and concerned by episodes in which it seemed they had received information their senses did not bring them. The first step was to find out what I could about what the people themselves thought about this matter. Why did they feel so sure their impressions were correct? I wondered if their own accounts would offer any suggestions to explain their unquestioning belief. And so, I picked out, to study in detail, 100 cases that showed strong conviction. Some excerpts from these accounts will show their general tenor:

> My mother dreamed that something had happened to my brother. She was sure he was hurt. She went 90 miles to San Francisco and found him in a hospital, his arms and hands bandaged.

> I was a janitor at the high school. One night I awakened from the most realistic dream that the school was on fire. I at once dressed and hurried to the school and found a fire started that in a few more minutes would have destroyed the building.

> I was visiting my sister in another city when I suddenly felt that my little girl at home had burned herself very severely. (She had, as the mother found when she hurriedly returned home.)

> While attending church my mother became faint and my father had to help her to leave during the sermon. She said, "Oh Alex, it's John." (That was her brother. Later, they received the announcement that he had died at that time.)

The criteria I used for deciding if the experience had carried conviction was that the person either took action because of his impression, as in the first three instances, or else he "just knew" it without a question, as in the fourth. But as I re-read the

100 cases carefully one by one, in no instance did the person seem to know *how* he knew. Just as in these excerpts above, none of them even offered a hint or suggestion about it. In fact, the lack of a reason usually seemed to the person part of the inexplicableness of the experience. The survey of all 100 cases showed only that to these persons the reason for their conviction was as much a mystery as it was to me and to the test subjects in the laboratory when they made "confidence" calls in an experiment.

Since this initial survey did not yield anything, it seemed that possibly some hint might come from comparing the experiences that showed conviction with those that did not. Accordingly, I separated them into conviction and non-conviction groups by the same criteria used above. This division yielded 840 conviction cases and 760 that were either non-conviction or lacked the fullness of reporting necessary to count them as conviction cases. The conviction group, then, was reliably that but the non-conviction cases were not so certainly non-conviction.

The numbers, showing more than half of all cases as carrying conviction, seemed too high. At least in the laboratory, confidence calls practically never occurred in so large a proportion of test calls. But the fallibility of these numbers as indicating anything about the actual rates of the two kinds was obvious, for even if those listed as without conviction had been as reliably without it as the others were with it, it would not necessarily mean that the actual proportion of conviction cases in life situations is that high, for conviction experiences certainly are likely to be much more impressive to the person, more likely to be remembered and more likely to be considered worth reporting than those without. The numbers only showed what I had to work with and nothing really about frequencies of occurrence in actual life.

In an attempt to learn something about so uncharted* an effect as conviction, I had to turn to any vague impressions or suggestions that might arise, usually without any very clear indication that they would be revealing, as the one involving the

---

As it turned out most of the other effects I was to study in succeeding projects over the years were similarly little known.

100 conviction cases was not. But even, so when separating those cases I had noticed that a great many of them occurred when the person was awake and that the cases lacking conviction were often dreams. And so, now, even though I could see no reason for such a grouping it was at least a lead that could be followed, so I counted the dreams and waking experiences in both groups. I had to omit 150 that occurred on the borderline between sleep and wakefulness, but of those remaining, 1444 in all, 70 per cent of the waking cases carried conviction, but only 30 per cent of the dreams did so. The impression thus was strongly confirmed. Somehow the feeling of conviction was associated predominately with the waking state. This might mean that on a rational basis persons were more likely to discount a dream than an experience that occurred when they were awake; still with as many as 30 per cent of the dreams showing conviction, it hardly seemed that this could be the whole explanation, although of course in case studies one has no firm basis on which to decide how large a percentage must be in order to be considered significant. This analysis therefore might mean that conviction was somehow associated more with waking experiences than with dreams, but it had to be a rather tentative interpretation.

However, in the course of separating the dream and waking experiences, again I had had an impression that again needed verification. This one involved the types of ESP, clairvoyance, telepathy and precognition. When I made the sleep vs. waking separation, the cases were already filed according to types, so that I could notice the rates of conviction among them in general, and I thought that it differed among them. The next analysis was to see whether this impression was correct. A count of the conviction cases in each of the three types then showed that only 40 per cent of the precognitive cases showed it, 53 per cent of the telepathic, and 62 per cent of the GESP cases.

The question now was why conviction should be less frequent in the precognitive experiences than in the other types for the difference between 40 and 62 per cent seemed too large to be meaningless. Was it caused by a rationalization on a more or less conscious level that an ESP impression of a present event was more reliable than of a future one? That hardly seemed the explanation for it was noticeable that the persons seldom knew until the later check-up that their precognitive impressions referred to a future rather than to a present situation. Nearly all of the precognitive cases had given the impression that they were in the present. It usually was only their eventual fulfillment that led the person to the realization that he had had the dream *before* the reality. Therefore, it did not seem likely that the lower conviction rate in precognitive cases was the result of such reasoning, at least not on a conscious level. So far, then, it looked as if conviction was associated with the waking state rather than with dreams, and unequally with the types of ESP, being especially infrequent in precognitive experiences. I then recalled another observation, this one made in the original classification, when separating the cases as to type (Chapter 5). It was in connection with the manner in which the person experienced ESP in consciousness, and that the occurrence of conviction had been much more frequent in some than in others.

In explanation of this a digression is necessary to make clear that, by hindsight, a study of the manner in which ESP is expressed in consciousness should have preceded this one about conviction. These differences in manner, which later I came more descriptively to call "form" (Chapter 7) had been so obvious in my earlier classification according to type, that I had recognized three different divisions. I had named them descriptively, and on the margin of the report marked which one was involved in each case. They were: (a) photographic, if the impression was like a true picture of the reality; (b) dramatic, if it was fanciful, dramatized or a fantasy, but not realistic; and (c) symbolic, if the impression was a fantasy entirely divorced from the reality.

In making these divisions, the impression had developed that conviction occurred the least frequently in the cases that were photographic, although they showed the most information about the event of any of the forms. It now seemed necessary to follow this lead, and find out whether conviction was or was not correlated with the amount of information the person received in his experience.

The different forms were sufficiently distinct in 570 of the 1444 cases that they could be definitely separated. The numbers were 302 for the photographic, 211 for the dramatic, and 57 for the symbolic. But the respective percentages of conviction cases in each, 39, 48, and 28 per cent, seemed entirely erratic or at least the 39 per cent for photographic and 48 per cent for dramatic seemed so.

However, I recognized that if any meaning was hidden in these percentages it was obscured by the fact that the photographic groups included a large number of precognitive dreams and I already knew from the analysis above that the frequency of conviction cases in both precognitive experiences and dreams was relatively low. This no doubt depressed the percentage of conviction in the photographic cases. But even so it seemed unlikely that this would have wiped out the effect of the relatively large amount of information contributed by the photographic manner of presentation, if that were a factor in leading to conviction. Since the result of this line of inquiry thus was ambiguous, a more specific comparison was called for.

For this next comparison, again, I had another observation to draw on from my original classification of cases as to type. In making that classification, the fact was inescapable that some experiences did and some did not give the person a complete unit of information, *i.e.*, including the identity of the person and the nature of the event. Even aside from the manner or form the experience took, the relative completeness of information varied noticeably. I had found four rather natural groups to cover these variations which I had then called *complete, meaningful, fragmented,* and *blocked.* These had been marked appropriately on each case report, so that now this division, too, could easily be made.

The cases suitable for this breakdown were the 570 used above and 66 others that were appropriate here but had not been there. These 636 cases, then, fell into the four levels of incompleteness which, arranged in descending order, and with their respective percentages of conviction cases, were as follows.

> *Complete:* 201 cases with both a coherent message and relevant details; 37 per cent conviction, as in No. 3.

No. 3

A young man in Washington, "about half asleep," reported that he "saw" his mother, father, and brother traveling down a highway. He saw a car trying to pass another car in front of his father, who was forced to swerve off the road, with two right wheels hanging over the ditch. The cars passed. His father was fighting the wheel trying to get back on the road. Then the front wheel caught. The car made 180-degree turn into the ditch on the other side, and rolled over onto the roof. He saw that his father got a bloody nose and a cracked ankle, "and then I came out of it." Fifteen minutes later they came home and he knew just what had happened. When he went to the crash site it was exactly as he had seen it.

> *Meaningful*: 141 cases, giving a correct and meaningful idea but with few or no details; 72 per cent conviction; as in the next case.

No. 4

A 19-year-old girl from the East had gone to California to find work. As it happened, a boy whom she had known in high school was in the same city and one night he invited her out on a date. On their return, about three blocks from her furnished room suddenly a cold chill came over her. She said in her report to the laboratory, "I must have looked strange because my friend pulled over to the curb and asked 'What's wrong, are you ill?' "

"My grandmother is dead," she told him. She was very close to her grandmother, who had practically raised her when her mother worked to support the family. The girl knew her grandmother had recently had a fall and was in the hospital with a broken hip, but no reports had suggested that her condition was critical.

As they entered the house where she stayed, the landlady came hurrying in, and said, "Call the operator. There's a telegram for you." It said, "Grandma is dead. Please come."

> *Fragmented*: 151 cases giving some items of information but not enough to yield a coherent idea and sometimes with mistakes mixed in; 29 per cent conviction.

No. 5

A California woman whose husband had died 16 months

earlier, wrote that about two weeks before his death she had a dream that woke her out of a sound sleep. In the dream she thought she was in a pool of black water. She called to her husband to help her out. He reached toward her, but fell over onto the ground and said, "I can't make it, dear."

Two weeks later her husband and a hired boy were filling a truck in the yard with black soil and he asked his wife to get up on the truck and pull the dirt over a little. She started to rake it over to the other side of the truck bed, when her husband fell to the ground. As soon as it happened, she looked at that black soil and thought of the pool of black water. It was the same shape and size as the truck load of soil. She knew at once that he was dead.

> *Blocked*: 143 cases yielding no factual information but only an emotion or a compulsion to action which proved to have been relevant to an event of which the person later learned; 83 per cent conviction. The following is an example of emotion only.

No. 6

A man in Montana reported a remarkable experience of being very happy all day but knowing of no particular reason for it. It was sufficiently marked and unexplainable to him that he still remembered his mood that day as quite exceptional, two days later when he received a registered letter with a $1000 check in it. The letter was dated the day he had been so happy.

The sender was an elderly cousin whose wife and mother had died and who now was giving his money away before he died. He wrote that he had just heard from another cousin, "of the work you are doing for young people in teaching them music and swimming free of charge. I am enclosing a check for you to take a trip."

The next case is an instance of compulsive action.

No. 7

A young family lived on a lonely farm in Ontario. One day the husband forgot to leave the firewood cut that his wife would need to cook supper. She was a city girl and not used to using an ax but she went to the wood pile and began the job of chopping, leaving her year-old son sitting on the veranda step five steps above the lawn.

She was struggling with her task when all at once, "I felt a voice — or something — say to me, 'Never mind that. Go back to the house!' " She dropped the ax and *ran*. And there a big snake was lying the full length of the five steps with its head above the veranda floor staring at the baby. The baby was innocently staring back.

She ran up the steps beside the snake, grabbed up the baby and a broom, shouted and tried to hit the snake, and it "went slithering away."

(Then the writer continues, "But if that voice had not told me ... what would have happened? I wondered whose voice it was — and I can only think it was mine. But how could that be?")

It could have been a compulsion based on an ESP impression.

And so here was a puzzling mixture; cases with very different amounts of information but with apparently no corresponding frequency of conviction; only 37 per cent when information was practically complete, and 83 per cent when it was blocked and only emotion or a compulsive act remained to show that ESP information might have been received. These numbers showed quite definitely that the amount of information and the feeling of conviction were not directly related. They also showed that conviction was not the result of conscious reasoning. It therefore must be an element arising below the level of consciousness. The fact that the psi process is an unconscious one had already been recognized in the experimental work, and here one aspect of ESP, that of the conviction factor, was shown also to have its origin below the conscious level. This would explain why percipients in the cases and the subjects in tests also had no idea why they believed or had confidence in some of their impressions but not others.

But the study also suggested that the likelihood that an experience would carry conviction was affected by the state of consciousness, the type of experience, its form in consciousness, and the relative amount of information it contributed. In other words, it was more likely to occur in the waking state than in dreams, less likely in precognitive than other types of experience, less likely in the form that contributed the most information and more likely in those that consisted only of emotion or compulsion. And with these seemingly unintelligible findings I had to leave the topic, no other feasible leads presenting themselves at the time. My report did not show how subjects could produce confidence calls in their tests or why some people believed their experiences and others did not. It did show that conviction somehow was related to the unconscious processes in the genesis of psi experience, but not how it was related. That relationship did not come clear until after a number of other inquiries over succeeding years had been completed (chapters 14 and 15). Only then, with the increasing degree of insight they slowly permitted, w⌐s it clear that these original observations were not, after all, just meaningless vagaries, but the lawful byproducts of hidden principles, which sufficient study and observation could reveal.

This first study of conviction, even though it ended inconclusively, opened other questions for further study. The first one of these that called for a special study, because of the effect it seemed to have on conviction, was that of the manner or forms the experiences took in consciousness. What were they? What did they mean? And why did the different ones contribute such varying amounts of information as, for instance, the "blocked" and the "photographic"? These topics needed to be explored next.

They were, as the next chapter shows.

Chapter 7

The Forms of ESP — and PK

Perhaps the most insistent unanswered question raised by the survey of conviction cases of Chapter 6 concerned the manner in which ESP messages appear in consciousness. Why does it vary so much? At one extreme are instances when it comes almost like a photograph of the event, then sometimes like a dramatization instead, while at the other extreme are messages so completely unreal as to have to be called symbolic, if indeed they really do represent the event as the person thinks.

The suggestion, to me, was that the process and conditions that produced such variations must be responsible, which would mean that they vary likewise. If so, then it was logical to think that those variations in the manner, or better, the *form* of the experience offered a clear invitation for further examination to see if it would be possible to trace their origin. But the first question was, how many and what basically different forms actually occur? If I could know that, what would their identification reveal about their origin and nature?

In order to try to answer these questions, it was clearly very important to have examples of all of the forms or variations of spontaneous psi experiences. It certainly would have defeated the purpose here if any form had been excluded from consideration because the person who had experienced it had been unable, let us say, to get the necessary corroboration. It might have biased the results even if the numbers of instances of a given form were reduced because corroboration was more difficult to get for it than for others. This was just what had happened many years ago in the collection made in England and discussed in Chapter 3, when the criteria that were used resulted in a reduced number of dreams in proportion to apparitions.

My own method of accepting those cases that fulfilled the definition, without requiring special corroboration of them but studying them only when numbers of similar ones accumulated, insured me against having omitted or having artificially reduced the number of reports of any form of ESP experience. However, it did not insure me against making a different kind of mistake which I did make — for in studying the various forms that psi may take in consciousness, I at first limited the study to ESP experiences, instead of including those involving psychokinesis (PK) as well. Because the end result of a PK experience is not an idea but a physical effect and because only a few such cases were yet on file, it did not occur to me at this early stage of my studies that a PK effect too might be one of the real and observable forms of psi; that it can bear a message in its own way. Fortunately, I was able to rectify this error some years later and the results of that later study will be mentioned at the end of this chapter, and presented in full in Chapter 15.

The 1600 ESP cases that had been used in Chapter 6 were available for this study of the forms too (reference 17). Some of them, however, had been filed in the separate categories of PK experiences, children's experiences, and those that seemed to bear on survival. These special kinds, I thought, might introduce uncertainties that could be complicating in this initial study and so I omitted them here, but reserved them for later use to see if they represented any forms not included in the main bulk of cases. (It was in the later study of these that I recognized the PK form.) Also, in 77 cases the form was insufficiently distinct for use here, so that the number of those I could use in the present survey were reduced to 1073 items. Of these, 552 were dreams and 521, waking experiences.

I hoped that these 1073 cases included an adequate sample of all the forms in which ESP is expressed in real life. The hope has apparently been fulfilled so far, for in all the years since, during which the collection has increased in numbers many times over, no forms of ESP expression not represented in this initial group have been reported.

My objective now was to recognize those features of the individual cases that represented significant differences of form and to do so in a much more thoroughgoing and analytical way than had been done in Chapter 6. To do this, it was necessary to disregard the almost endless superficial and personal variations of individual cases. Neither would it matter here whether a case was clairvoyant, telepathic, GESP or precognitive. Only its form was important. The task then was to distinguish from the superficial, incidental, and purely personal aspects of each case the form in which the basic psi information was expressed in consciousness.

Since it seemed almost inevitable that a distinctive difference in mental process must divide dreams and waking experiences, I decided to begin the survey with the dreams, and then continue with the waking cases.

The Dream Forms

Each dream seemed different from the others in so many ways that it was not at once clear which feature of the many presented in each case was important and which only superficial. Something of this problem can be illustrated by a few examples such as the first three below.

No. 1

A Mr. D. in California often played tennis with a friend in a nearby park. One night he had a vivid dream that as he was playing in a strange court that was at the foot of a stairs, his wife appeared at the head of it. She looked down at him and screamed, "Ray, Ray, Angela has been hurt!"

He looked up and saw her standing there with their little girl in her arms. The child was limp, her head hung down, her eyes were closed, her mouth open, face white.

The dream frightened him awake and he could hardly get back to sleep. He told it to his wife the next morning and then tried to forget about it.

The following Sunday, some friends came by and invited the D. family to go along on a picnic to a distant park where the men could get in some tennis and the women could watch the children in a nearby play area. The invitation was accepted.

After both families had scattered to their various areas and the tennis game was in progress. Mr. D., in actuality this

time, heard his wife scream, "Ray, Ray, Angela has been hurt!"
He looked up to the top of the stairs to see the exact scene of the
dream — the child was unconscious in her mother's arms.

Angela had fallen head first from the top of a large slide.
She was still unconscious when a quarter of an hour later they got
her to the hospital emergency room. She recovered, however, but
her father could not forget that dream, so true, of an unfamiliar
park, and one in which the tennis court was *down* a stairs.

No. 2

One summer some years ago a New York family, father,
mother, and nine-year-old daughter, were on a long motor trip
through unfamiliar territory in a remote part of Maine. One
warm sunny day it was time for lunch, but restaurants in this area
were scarce and mainly quite unattractive.

At last they came to an eating place that had been adver-
tised. They stopped to look it over. It too was unappealing.
However, the adults agreed that they had better eat when they
had the chance, not knowing when they would find another
place, to say nothing of a better one. But, unexpectedly, the nine-
year-old, who had been drowsing in the back seat, spoke up.

"No, let us go on," and she told her parents that on ahead,
around a curve, was a pretty house with a blue door where they
could get a better lunch than here. Naturally, her parents thought
she was just having a fantasy and partly to prove it to her they
drove on. In about a mile the road curved sharply — and on ahead
was a most attractive inn with a blue door, and they were able to
get an excellent lunch.

Reporting the episode later, when it had become a family
joke, the girl described her experience as like "a glimpse inside
my mind, a flash of memory."

No. 3

One morning a man in New York told his wife of an odd
dream he had had, which, although he was not superstitious,
bothered him a bit. He said he thought a man had stood by his
bed and said, "James is dead." James was his wife's uncle. His
wife too did not think it meant anything, but said, "Why not
drive up to Mother's and see that everything is all right." Her uncle James lived there with her mother, his sister.

As they entered her mother's house her mother was coming down the stairs, and upon seeing them exclaimed, "Oh, I'm so glad you have come. I am unable to arouse Jim." A doctor was called and it was found that her uncle had suffered a stroke from which he died shortly after.

In experiences as different as just these three, not to mention the 1070 remaining cases, what were the basic forms? In analyzing them I realized that in those like No. 1, the dream imagery was a fairly exact copy of the actual event. It was the kind that I had called "photographic" in Chapter 6. As a copy it was exact enough to suggest that the mind that produced it must be something like a (hidden) camera. Somehow it could make a faithful copy. It seemed as if this kind of true and realistic presentation could represent a basic form.

But what about No. 2? Even though the child in this case did not specify just what her impression had been, still the details she did give were true and realistic just as were those in No. 1. This one, too, then, could be labelled realistic.

But No. 3 was different. Here the setting was not true. Although it correctly indicated the person who was involved and the event that had concerned him, it was no photographic copy. It was a dramatization, a little fantasy in which the message was imbedded. It was true, but unrealistic.

In some other instances, the degree of unrealism was still greater, as in the next case.

No. 4

A man in Illinois reported that during World War II, Jim, the son of his next-door neighbor, enlisted in the Marines. He had been overseas about 10 months when the man in Illinois dreamed that he saw the son in Marine uniform followed by another boy also in Marine uniform come through his parents' back yard, up onto the rear porch and into his father's house. In the morning the man told his wife of the dream and they decided not to mention it to the parents for fear that it might mean a tragedy.

About three days later a message came to the man to be relayed to the parents that Jim had been killed, apparently at the very time of the dream. Upon being shown a photo of Jim's closest pal, who was also killed at the same time, he recognized him as the person he had seen in his dream.

The message that dream brought could easily be taken as based on the death of the two Marines, but if so, it was only hinted at. The only correct item was the identity of those involved. The scene itself was a fantasy, entirely unrealistic and imaginative.

The next case might be like No. 5. How would it classify, if indeed it was, as the experiencing person thought, a "significant" dream?

No. 5

A man in Albany, Georgia, dreamed that a white horse from heaven, with saddle, bridle and all, complete except for a rider, rubbed his head lovingly against the man's cheek. He dreamed he asked the horse what he wanted and the horse replied, "You know what I have come for."

A few days later, the man's son was killed in an accident.

If that dream actually foretold the coming death, it was by a dramatization even farther removed from reality than that of No. 4. But, the identity of the person involved was not revealed. The next death in the immediate family would certainly be taken as the one referred to. If the reference was correct, if ESP was really involved, then a fantasy must have been quite unconsciously constructed in the mind of the dreamer. It, of course, was well below the possibility of recall. It must have been by way of symbolic imagery.

A few cases tested the reach of symbolism even further, as with the next one.

No. 6

A woman from New Jersey told about a dream she had had, aged 11. In it she thought she was chewing up her own teeth and spitting them out as tiny, hard, brittle pieces. The dream somehow terrified her awake. Just then her father came in and took her in his arms and said, "Honey, your grandma died a little while ago." Although her grandmother, to whom she had been very close, had been at the point of death for days, the news so overcame the child that she quite forgot her dream.

Two months later, she reported, "I found myself in the misery of the same dream." When she awoke from it, her mother told her that her grandfather, her mother's father, was dying of a heart attack. She still felt the horror of her dream, but did not then connect it with the death.

When she was 13, the dream recurred. That time a popular girl at school committed suicide.

These were the first three occasions of a long list, one at age 15, another at 18. At 19 she married and her husband laughed at the idea of taking such dreams seriously. The dreams continued, however, some of them preceding deaths in the family, until even he, she says, "began to wonder."

In this account, typical of its kind, the message of the repeated dream included no true fact whatever. No actual reference to death was made and there was nothing to suggest the identity of the person who would be involved. The dream only became meaningful to the person because each time it seemed to be followed by a death. Therefore, it came to be taken as symbolic, which, of course, it must have been if indeed it did involve ESP, again a question not easily decided.

However, Nos. 3, 4, 5, and 6 were alike in using imagery that was not a copy of a real event. In all of them, the imagery departed from the fact to which it appeared to be related. The element that varied was only the degree to which it did so.

It seemed then that the basic differences in form in all of these dreams were really only two, that between copying and dramatizing. It was a difference of imagery, perhaps the result of personality factors, one matter-of-fact, the other more imaginative.

It was a difference that continued to stand out among the rest of the dreams. About three times as many of them were "copies," which I called realistic, as compared to dramatizations, which I called unrealistic and which covered a great variety of degrees of fantasy as the examples given above illustrate.

In general, the distinction between the two forms was

fairly clear. In a few instances, however, both forms of imagery occurred in a single dream, as in the following case.

No. 7

A woman in California was half-dozing after lunch one day and thought she was walking along a path when she came to a large iron gate. It was open and as she looked inside she saw what seemed to be a beautiful park. She saw a long straight path that stretched ahead until in the distance between large trees on either side a light mist or fog obscured the end.

She walked through the gate and down the path. But then she became a little frightened as she came to the misty area, with great trees overhanging the path on which she walked. She began then to hear faint music and she got the feeling that she was watched. She thought she heard voices whispering, "Who is she?" and "She does not know we are here." She decided to turn back, and left the place through the open gate.

The dream somehow disturbed her and she awakened. She repeated it to a friend who merely thought it odd but of no significance.

A few years later, after her mother's funeral which was held in a mortuary, the woman was given a small white book her friends had signed. The cover of the book was quite familiar. It was the exact picture she had dreamed, the gates, the path, and trees and the mist, just as her dream had shown.

In such cases both kinds of dream imagery were recognizable. In this instance the copy of the book's cover came first and then apparently it was "embroidered" by dream fantasy. Perhaps if the meaning of that book, its relation to her mother's funeral, had been in any way indicated it might have awakened the woman before the dream fantasy was initiated. The dream then would have been only realistic, except for the fact that the woman projected herself into the picture.

Dreams, of course, are fragile creations and subject to various hazards. The person may awaken too soon or he may remember only parts of the dream, so that dream experiences are particularly unreliable as evidence of anything. The wonder is that even so they can carry some degree of rationale in an area so obscure as that of psi phenomena.

Later in studying the experiences that occur when the person is awake, I found some instances which have a bearing on this relation between these forms and the dream state. Some of them included realistic imagery, some unrealistic, even though the person was not sleeping, as in examples Nos. 8 and 9 below.

No. 8

A young woman, divorced and remarried, had not heard anything from her ex-husband except that he had enlisted in the Air Force. Her mother, who lived nearby, one day called on her daughter and found her crying. "Why the tears?" she asked.

"Mother, I was just sitting here sort of daydreaming, not sleeping, when just as in a TV picture I saw an airplane fall from the sky. I'm sure Hal has been killed or very badly injured."

Her mother tried to make light of it, but the girl was very positive. Sometime later they learned that he had led a squadron of planes in a sortie of some sort and his plane had failed. He was hospitalized at the time of her experience, and when later she met him in the medical building when she visited her doctor, he was still getting treatments from an injury so serious that he was released from air service.

Not sleeping, "sort of daydreaming." But the picture presumably was realistic. It seemed that such cases could be realistic "waking dreams." Apparently the realistic copying kind of imagery is not entirely dependent on the fact that the person is asleep. Unrealistic imagery too was sometimes found when the person was not sleeping.

No. 9

Her children were excited because an elderly magician was coming to their school. He had been doing it occasionally for a number of years and seemed to enjoy the school children as much as they enjoyed him.

She awoke the night before the magician's appearance and could not go back to sleep, so she went to the kitchen to work for a while. She began to mop the floor, still in a half-sleepy state of mind, and kept having a fantasy about the magician. She thought he was not well, had gone to a doctor who found he had an advanced case of cancer. He begged the doctor to let him go on working, for making children happy had been a vital part of his life. The doctor agreed and, as she fantasized on, she thought he worked right up to the time of his death.

At noon the next day the children came home excited. The magician had had a heart attack on the stage and died immediately. The paper ran a story telling how the man, with no children of his own, had followed his practice in the schools as a substitute, and that morning had had a heart attack in his hotel, but came to the school anyway because he did not want to disappoint the children. Her fantasy had been based only on the fact that she knew he was unusually popular with the children.

Only a relatively few cases with imagery like the two above were found among the waking experiences. And these perhaps could be called daydreams. At any rate, they show that the sleeping state is not strictly necessary for the realistic or unrealistic kinds of imagery to be used.

The Forms of Waking Experiences

Among the experiences that occurred in the waking state, a quite distinctive dichotomy of forms was evident. Cases 10 and 11 suggest it, even though it will take many more examples to indicate the modifications of these two forms that may occur.

No. 10

It was a doctor's office in Virginia and several patients had been waiting in turn. Then suddenly the one who was to go next (to get treatment for a sinus infection) knew that she must go home at once because her mother had stumbled on a rug, fallen and broken her hip. She went to the desk and said, "I must go home at once. I am needed there."

"But you are next," urged the receptionist. "It will only be a few minutes now."

"No. I must go. I'm needed at once."

"Why not phone and tell them you'll be there shortly?"

"No. I can't. The phone is out of order." And she rushed out wondering why she had said that. The phone was all right when she had left an hour or so ago. But she knew her father was there alone with her mother and he needed help. All this rushed through her mind with no time to question it.

"The feeling, the urgency, was so strong," she reported later, "that I drove beyond the speed limit." A policeman stopped her and she explained so earnestly that he went on ahead and cleared the way so that they arrived at her house in minutes.

She opened the door. Her mother was lying on the floor, her father bending over her.

"How did she break her hip?"

"How do you know she broke it? I've been frantic since she fell. I didn't want to leave and I couldn't phone the doctor. As Mother fell she hit the phone cord and pulled out the phone."

The policeman went next door and called the doctor and the ambulance.

Now compare that sudden hunch with this experience:

No. 11

A couple in Pennsylvania had retired about 11:30 p.m. and the woman had not yet fallen asleep when, as she reported to the Parapsychology Laboratory, "Suddenly I saw my mother — no surroundings — just her. She was slightly bent over and holding her left hand and screaming, 'Help me! Help me! Somebody help me!' "

Then the scene faded but it had been as clear as a projection on a screen in front of her and it terrified her. She told her husband she feared that perhaps her mother might have burned herself. She would have called home at once (her mother lived in California and it would have been earlier there) but no phone had yet been installed. She had to console herself with the thought that if her mother was hurt her father would help her and that some of her relatives would let her know, and so she tried to forget the experience.

However, the time for a letter to have come from California went by and no word came and so, still worried, she finally went to a phone and called her mother. Her mother, in surprise, asked if she had not received a clipping from the local paper that had been sent her. She had not. Evidently it had gone astray.

Then the woman learned that on the night in question her mother had left the store where she worked and was unlocking the door to her car when she was attacked from behind by a man who held a knife to her throat. He moved and her mother attempted to grab the knife, getting a bad slash along her left hand. She screamed, "Help me! Help me! Somebody help me!" The man hesitated — and ran. He was later apprehended.

In No. 10, the person "just knew" what had happened to her mother. In No. 11 she "just knew" and "just heard" it. In the first, no imagery appeared at all but in the second, visual and auditory modalities were represented. But they were pseudosensory, because while the person felt she was seeing her mother and hearing her scream, the sensation did not have the ordinary physical stimuli of actual light or sound waves. With differences as distinctive as these, the waking experiences were easier to separate into basically different forms than the dreams had been. And the difference was only in these two aspects, absence of imagery vs. pseudosensory imagery. In the "no imagery" group, like No. 10, the mental process seemed to be like that commonly called intuitive, while in No. 11, the experience fitted the familiar name, hallucinatory. In this case, however, the hallucinatory figure was a replica of a real one, not an imagined snake or goblin as in cases of drugged hallucinatory fantasy.

Sorting further among the waking experiences, however, some like No. 12 appeared.

No. 12

"A young man very close to me," a young woman wrote, "left early one morning to hunt for deer in an isolated area (in California) where the chance of getting shot by another hunter was slight." She went about her tasks without a worry. But at 9 a.m. a sudden fear gripped her, "pierced my heart." She continued, "I dislike using this ancient expression, but it does express what happened. I thought of the possible danger then of other hunters and a stray shot, but this fear had nothing to do with bullets, for when I questioned myself it was as if the question glanced off a shining shield into space, proving that it had not been part of the fear."

She concentrated on other things; nothing to do but work and wait. But the fear nagged at her until 4:30 p.m. Then sud-

denly it was gone, and, until the hunter returned at 7:30, she was
again as carefree as she had been at 9 that morning. He returned
in good spirits and she felt foolish questioning him, but finally
she asked about his day without "giving herself away."

He had started out as intended but at 9 a.m. not finding
any sign of deer, he turned toward a different more dangerous
area. At 4:30, tired, he stepped up on a fallen log and was about
to sit down and rest a bit when he saw an extremely large rattlesnake coiled up beside the log. He killed it, since he saw it just
in time and before it saw him and could reverse the situation.

In that, the only sign was the feeling of fear. The person
had no fact on which to base it. No imagery was involved,
although the woman did know her fear was for the hunter. Her
experience then was emotional. However, it came upon her
without an apparent reason, suddenly, intuitively, can one say?
If so, then its form was similar to No. 10 above, intuitive, and
only the *amount* of information which she, the experiencing person, got was different. It was much less than that in No. 10.

Occasionally, too, situations were reported when not even
an emotion seemed to mark an experience that could have involved ESP, as in the following.

No. 13

A young couple visiting at the home of an aunt were
playing bridge one evening, their 3-year-old son asleep in an adjoining bedroom. Or so they thought, when the wife, "quite
rudely," she reported, left the card table. "I didn't even know I
was doing it," and went into the bedroom where she found the
child sitting up in bed playing with a loaded revolver which her
aunt had forgotten to remove from under her pillow.

In this instance it seemed as if the action was taken quite
automatically. It was as if because of some hidden message, some
"information" of which she herself was not consciously aware.
But still, if it was a case of ESP its form was intuitive, just like
Nos. 10 and 12.

In all the other waking experiences without imagery, the
form could be called intuitive, it seemed, whether the person

knew what happened (*i.e.*, had a complete impression) or was aware only of an emotion or only took compulsive action. These variations then could be recognized not as differences in form, but in the relative amount of information the person received.

The rest of the cases, after isolating all those that had no imagery and in which the information could be considered to have come intuitively, were hallucinatory like No. 11, in that they were marked by pseudosensory imagery. Sometimes persons in the imagery, the "target" persons, were living, sometimes dying, sometimes already dead, but they always appeared just as if they were actually seen. This, of course, makes such experiences very difficult for the experiencer to understand. It is only by interpreting one's own sensations either by inference or later information that one can realize the hallucinatory character of such an occurrence. A full discussion of this form of experience will be deferred to Chapter 12.

As I continued to sort the cases and found that all of them fell into one or another of these four groups—two kinds of dreams, two, of waking experiences—it was something of a surprise to realize that the total number of different forms was so small. The general impression that the number would be much larger had been given because so many characteristics of specific cases were personal or secondary. Further, it was now emphasized as never before so clearly that these four forms were not new, or spectacular, or special, for ESP. Instead, they were old and already familiar in daily life and not at all unique. Dreams with either form of imagery are commonplace, as are hunches and intuitions. Hallucinations are not so common, at least among normal people in good health, but neither are they unheard of. Also, the evidence of these experiences that represent ESP information seems to indicate that normal people can hallucinate. However, since this form is less often reported than the others it may mean that only a relatively few persons do hallucinate. I recognized that the job of trying to understand the psi process should be much facilitated by knowing these basic forms, for their psychology is known. Dreams, with their imagery formation, are unconscious mental productions. No one knows his dreams directly, but only to the extent that he can remember them upon waking and thus bring their contents into consciousness. Intuitions too are recognizable instances of unconscious mental action in which material below the conscious level breaks through into consciousness.

All this, of course, was in line with the idea long held in experimental parapsychology that the psi process begins in unconscious mental levels.

Once I recognized these forms of ESP, I could ask some questions and make some observations that did not come up before. For instance, knowing that the forms of ESP cover extremes of mental state from dreaming to full consciousness leads to the question whether different degrees of ease or difficulty of transmission of the information are involved. The answer probably is that when the information is received in some unconscious level, and "processed" according to some plan or reason impossible to specify in each individual case, it will take the form which, for whatever reason, is most appropriate or easiest.

If so, one might suppose that dreaming would be easier than a waking form. The numbers of cases of each, however, probably do not reflect actual frequencies with any reliability since so many other considerations could obscure them. And so I had to conclude that the question of which form is the "easiest" could not be answered very clearly from this evidence.

However, one characteristic of many of the waking experiences did suggest that the ESP information in them may cause difficulties. That is the rather violent-appearing breakthrough which suggested that information was "blocked," as described in Chapter 6. This occurred especially in those cases when only emotion was shown. Such experiences suggested that an emotional build-up beneath the conscious level occurs and that it is necessary for it to be fairly strong in order to erupt into consciousness. Also, the fact that intuitive experiences, at best, have no details but just the bare meaning of the message, could be interpreted as reflecting this same difficulty of thrusting through the preoccupying stream of conscious thought.

Another peculiarity of ESP experiences, I realized now, was explained by the fact that the forms of ESP are the ones already common in everyday life. It was the reason why ESP is so difficult to recognize with certainty. Since it has no distinctive form of its own, only the information that the experience brings is unique. On that account it becomes a matter of judgment in each instance whether or not the given item of information came by ESP, or by memory, inference or accident. This can seldom be decided with finality and is thus one reason why cases — anecdotes — can never have the reliability of properly performed and confirmed experimental results.

Spontaneous Psychokinesis

But now what about PK? When it had been established in the laboratory that the human mind can affect matter (as it obviously had been in thousands of controlled dice throws), again, it could safely be assumed, as with ESP, that the same effect would appear spontaneously too. If so it would be in situations in which a physical effect in the environment occurs that cannot be ascribed to any physical cause but that seems to be relevant in some way to a human situation. As already stated, on that basis I had accepted reports for the collection, as I did all the others, without trying then to form any hypothesis as to how this could be. However, as also already mentioned, the total number of cases involving a physical effect was always small compared to the number of ESP experiences. This was part of the reason that I had not considered them in the original study of the forms of psi in consciousness. But ten years later the collection of PK cases seemed large enough to study. At that time, with over 10,000 instances of presumptive ESP on file, only 178 had been classified as possible instances of PK.

The fact that the number of possible PK experiences was so small, I recognize now, may not represent very truly their actual rate of occurrence. If it is difficult to recognize ESP with certainty, it is much more difficult to identify a PK occurrence. In the first place, the possibility of PK is even more incredible to almost everyone. If this is so only because very few persons have seen any evidence of it in daily life, those that have experienced something that suggested telepathy or other ESP effects are by comparison much more numerous. As one side result, even in fiction, ESP-like occurrences have been used much more frequently than those suggesting PK.

Another reason PK has remained incredible is because it is always difficult to be certain that no ordinary but undetected physical cause produced it. For all these reasons, the list of PK-like effects reported or accepted for this or any other collection may well be inordinately low in comparison to their actual frequency of occurrence.

However, when the possible PK cases in the collection were analyzed, I found that they were all practically alike in several features (reference 28). In nearly all instances two persons were involved, one of whom observed the effect — the experiencing person (for convenience, simply the E person). The other, usually at a distance, was undergoing a crisis. He could be considered the target or T person (roughly equivalent to the agent in ESP situations). Besides that, the two persons were nearly always relatives or friends, so that the crisis of one would naturally produce an emotional response in the other.

The kind of physical effect varied but it usually involved a household appliance, like a clock or picture. For instance, the following case.

No. 14

A man in Detroit told how he was awakened one night by a dream that his aged grandmother was standing by his bed calling his name. His dog, sleeping at the foot of his bed, awoke and was apparently frightened, making enough commotion that the man turned on the bed light and saw that it was 4 a.m. He went back to sleep, however, without thinking further of his grandmother.

In the morning his mother found the grandmother dead in bed, although she had not been ill. The doctor thought she had been dead about two hours and *her clock had stopped at 4 o'clock.*

One of the most frequent kinds of physical effect was the falling of an object from a wall, shelf or table as in No. 13, Chapter 5, and as in the next case of a woman in Illinois.

No. 15

This person was very close to her father and one night in a discussion with him on the subject of life after death, she asked him if he believed in it. He replied that he did, and she asked him if he would try to come back and give her a signal when he died. He promised to do so.

On the day of his funeral, as she was going out the door, a large mirror fell to the floor.

In a number of instances, a light switched on or off inexplicably, as in the following case.

No. 16

One night in the bedroom of a girl away from home, the light went on when no one was near the switch. She reported that she "knew" then that something was wrong at home. The next morning her sister called to tell her that her father, a miner, was in the hospital. At the same time her light had come on the night before, a motor down in the mine had fallen on her father and crushed his pelvis.

Various other kinds of effects too were reported. Sometimes an object broke unaccountably, exploded or rocked or shook, or a door opened, shut, was locked, or was unlocked unaccountably. But in each case the effect noticed by the percipient seemed to occur at the time the target or T person was undergoing a crisis. The suggestion therefore was obvious, that the two—the effect and the crisis—were connected, that somehow the E person's experiences were ones by which they were receiving information about the crisis, even though they may not have recognized it at the time or been able to interpret correctly the meaning of it until they later learned what had happened.

With the realization that these physical effects could be the bearers of messages concerning events beyond the range of the senses, it seemed that, like the dreams and intuitions of ESP, they were another form of psi. In addition to the four ESP forms, then, one PK form could be recognized, making five forms of psi in all.

But PK, unlike the forms of ESP, is not a recognized form of everyday mental life. It apparently is a specific psi form. The suggestion also is that it too originates in deeply unconscious levels where the method of processing is decided.

Now, for the first time, I could ask the question of how the form or vehicle used in psi experiences is selected. In fact, now it had to be considered. I realized that the most obvious factor that probably is involved in determining the form of psi ex-

periences is the personality of the E person. Almost from the start
of laboratory studies of ESP, efforts were made to find a special
type of personality in which the ability was expressed more
readily than in others. The attempt was not successful in general,
but one finding had been that personality characteristics governed to some extent the *direction* in which subjects in tests would
score (Chapter 16). Some subjects tended to score positively or
above chance in certain conditions while other personalities
scored in the opposite direction. A change of conditions could
reverse the process. Now a new question could be raised. Do personality factors also determine the form of experiences in consciousness? But this rounding up of the forms only allowed
questions like these to be raised. It did not answer them. For answers, many more studies, both of cases and of experiments,
would be necessary. A specific one involving the general nature
of the psi process comes up in Chapter 8.

Chapter 8

The ESP Process and the S-R Model

ESP appears in consciousness in four different forms, as my analyses showed. But what did these differences really mean? Were they just surface variations depending on each individual's personal situation at the moment or was some hidden factor involved that decided that Mrs. A. would express her ESP information as a dream and Mrs. B. hers as an intuition? How could I analyze their experiences to show the nature of the basic processes, the processes that resulted in the specific form?

At the time I was all but lying awake at night trying to find an approach to this puzzle when another case came in of a kind that had become familiar because it had been repeated so often in spite of the widely different personal situations of the people who reported it. It was another of the kind I had come to think of simply as a "call'" case. It was uncomplicated, definite, just like a hundred others I had received.

No. 1

A man who during World War II was a Merchant Marine trainee reported that after a period of relatively uneventful routine in Pacific waters he was stationed on a Liberty ship escorting a convoy from Cuba to New York City. It was August 15, a night so hot and humid that he decided to leave his room and try to sleep outside on No. 1 hatch. Of course, all the ships were blacked out and the moon was not shining. He had hardly composed his head on a pillow he had brought along when a jolt that nearly lifted him off the deck brought him back to full alertness and he saw flames against the sky, a sight that told him that the convoy had been torpedoed. He ran wildly to higher ground on the flying bridge and eventually came through the crisis safely.

When he next saw his mother in California, in spite of the fact that all mail was censored and news of the ship's sinking never mentioned, she wanted to know what happened the night of August 15th.

"You could have knocked me over with a feather," he wrote in his letter to the Parapsychology Laboratory, "but I said 'nothing' and let it go at that." But his mother persisted. She said she was awakened from a sound sleep by hearing him call "Mother!" several times. She answered so loudly she thought she could have been heard a block away, and found herself out of bed and covered with perspiration. She had awakened his grandmother, who slept in the same room, and both of them testified to that.

"How do you characterize this, Dr. Rhine?" he asked. "For myself, I have always felt that my mother was maybe 'psychic.'"

Well, I would feel that, too! And even more. It suggested to me, at face value, that in some way his mother was responding to her son — even though he did not actually call to her. But then, I questioned, if he did not call, to what was she actually responding?

Suddenly I thought I saw a way to analyze the relation between such an experience and the situation to which it seemed to be a response. In the sensory model of perception (stimulus and response, or S-R) a physical stimulus physically communicated to a physical sense organ by a physical nervous system produces a sensory response, an experience of seeing, hearing, etc.

ESP experiences, of course, have no physical chain of causation. For them the stimulus, the target, may be a physical object, as in clairvoyance, but so hidden that no physical causal chain can operate, or it may be entirely nonphysical, the thought of another person, or even a still non-existant future event. The situation in ESP is obviously so different from that in sense perception that it seems to be in contrast at every point. Still, could it be possible, I wondered, that somehow hidden below the surface a specific stimulus of some extrasensory kind does exist, some regular feature that even though hidden elicits the call response? Or is it a situation still more inexplicable, one of a response without a specific stimulus?

As I said, "call cases" had been reported again and again and now as a group they could be analyzed to see if any such regularity could be uncovered. I therefore undertook a study of them. I found over 200 of them in my files and in order to increase the number and so to make as representative a collection as possible, I found 77 more cases in old SPR publications and other sources until I had a total of 279. In all of these, the experience, the response according to the model, was a call expressed very similarly in all. The question was, could any kind of circumstance be common in them that could have been a specific stimulus to cause the specific response?

The first question to ask, it seemed, was whether the person who was in the crisis, the agent, and was heard to call, actually uttered a call to the one who heard it? If so, that call itself presumably could have been the stimulus.

In case No. 1 above, although it seemed unlikely that the man had actually called his mother, one could not be certain. The information about it was unclear. In sorting through the collection of 279, I found 73 other cases in which it was not clear whether an actual call had been uttered. In only 64 instances was an actual call specified, as in No. 2.

No. 2

A girl in Ohio was babysitting one night in an upper duplex apartment and had dozed off on the davenport, when she awakened suddenly to hear a drunk stumbling and cursing up the stairway toward the door. Sitting upright and putting both hands to her mouth, "Mother, oh Mother," she breathed.

Then she realized the drunk was on the other side of the wall going not to her apartment but to the one next door. Soon after, she heard her mother, who lived three blocks away, at the lower door calling her. She went down and let her in. Her mother asked her what was wrong. When the girl explained, her mother said she had been sitting in her rocker before the fire dozing but was awakened to "see" her daughter before her, sitting upright, both hands to her mouth, and saying, "Mother, oh Mother."

But even if the agent's actual call were the stimulus to

which the response was made in cases like No. 2, in 40 other instances the agent almost certainly did not call aloud. It is true that in all of these, however, he was most probably thinking strongly of the percipient, as in No. 3.

No. 3

A Pennsylvania man was away from home on a business trip. His wife did not expect him back for several days when one night she heard him call her. She arose and went to the door. But no one was there. It had snowed and she could see no tracks. Puzzled, she went back to bed and in the morning told the family she had been so sure that her husband had called her in the night that she had even opened the door for him.

About noon her husband did come home, but he was very ill. He said he thought she called him in the night, and awoke to realize he was very sick. He called the hotel office and they sent for a doctor who stayed with him until morning and then advised him to try to get home, which he had managed to do. He was in bed for the next six months with heart trouble.

"I could never understand," wrote his wife, "why we should have heard each other call." And, she might have added, when neither of us did so. But, I might add, when each was thinking intently of the other.

Of course, if when each call was heard the agent had been thinking strongly of the percipient, then the question would only be whether such a thought could have been a stimulus that produced the call response, however such a stimulus could operate. But such apparently was not the case in ten other instances, as for example the next one.

No. 4

One evening in Ohio a family of five dispersed after supper according to their various interests. A son, Stan, had gone to a picnic about five miles away at the home of one of the members of his church youth group. The mother was alone in the kitchen and had just finished the dishes when she heard Stan's voice calling, she thought, from the side door. She knew it was Stan because his voice was changing. He called three times.

"Mom, Mom, Mom," not excitedly, but the way he always did when he wanted to tell her something, like "Mom, I'm going over to Jim's house, OK?"

She thought, why was he home so early, and why, if he was home did he stand at the door? She went to the door. No one was there. Puzzled, she sat down with her book, again. But then a strange sensation "as of an invisible veil being drawn over me," she said, and with it the knowledge that Stan was hurt. She didn't know how seriously.

The phone rang. It was the woman at the home where the picnic was being held. She said that the gang had started to play baseball and that Stan had been hit on the head and knocked unconscious. He recovered later with no ill effects but his mother could not forget her unusual experience.

The point of interest here, of course, was the call she heard at that time when Stan, the agent, was unconscious. The knowledge that Stan was hurt, of course, came to her as an intuition (Chapter 7). The sense of being enveloped in a veil certainly was a personal item, not one of general significance. The mother in this case had the call experience just as definitely as did the mother in No. 2. Yet here her son, the agent, was unconscious and presumably could not even have directed a conscious thought to his mother. Neither an actual call nor even a strong thought, then, could have been a stimulus for her call experience.

However, one generalization could be made about the 188 cases of the three groups (in which a call had been uttered, or a thought directed toward the percipient, or neither): in all of them a living agent was involved. But even this feature was not common in the rest of the call cases. The remaining 91 included 25 in which the agent was someone deceased at the time of the experience, and 66 in which the voice was either unrecognized but heard as masculine, or without even that distinction, being "just a voice." The contrast between the two is illustrated by No. 5, the recognized voice of someone deceased, and No. 6, an impersonal voice.

No. 5

A woman from North Carolina wrote, "Because I was partly deaf and an ugly child, my mother and I were very close.

When I was 12 years old she died and my father left the city as soon as he found a home for me."

Some years later on a shopping trip this person saw a woman hurrying along ahead of her who was dressed exactly as her mother used to dress. Then she lost sight of her in the crowd. But minutes later, halfway across Main Street she heard her mother call, "Harriet, Harriet, look out." She looked up to see where the voice came from and no one seemed near enough — but bearing down on her was a street car. She had barely time to jump back out of the middle of the tracks and let it pass. She was certain that it was her mother's voice that warned her.

No. 6

A young woman with a rather uncommon given name was walking down a city street with her husband one day when they both heard her name, "Mina," shouted loudly. They stopped, turned abruptly. Just then came a crash ahead in the direction they had been going. A huge cement block had fallen from the top of a building in their path. But no one who knew that name was in sight.

Had it not been for such instances as No. 6, with an impersonal voice, those with the voice of someone deceased might have meant that, yes, an agent (although not necessarily a living one) is required for the percipient to hear a call. But if calls could be heard with *no* agent, then that conclusion was ruled out.

However, when the cases with living agents and those with deceased agents were compared as separate groups I found a difference, although it was mainly a difference of viewpoint such as logically might be expected if one party in an exchange of information were living and the other deceased. The difference was that when the agent was living (nos. 1,2,3,4) the crisis was usually his own and his voice was heard by the percipient as if to inform him of it. From the viewpoint of the percipient, the episode therefore was an information-bringing experience. And furthermore, the message usually consisted of the percipient's name only, with no added phrase. Besides, the crisis was always one of which the percipient could have become aware by clairvoyance of GESP. Also, it was never a situation in the future, but always a contemporaneous one.

On the other hand, when the message came in the voice of someone deceased, it was always either a warning to the percipient or advice about some situation threatening him or her and was usually a few words with or without the percipient's name. And while the majority of the situations were contemporaneous, occasionally the danger warned against was a coming one so that precognition might have been involved.

The fact that the voice of a person who was dead warned against dangers or crises of the living percipient rather than of the agent, of course, could be expected since a deceased agent could not be in a mortal crisis. But no *a priori* reason would prevent a living agent from seeming to warn a percipient of an impending danger. Yet out of the 188 cases with a living agent, there was only one instance, the following, in which the message was a warning to the percipient.

No. 7

A man was driving a truckload of timber down a highway from upstate New York to Long Island one morning about 3. He had fallen asleep at the wheel when very clearly and shrilly he heard his mother's voice calling him just as she used to do when he was a child at home. He awakened with a start to find that he was only about two feet from the wall of an overpass. No doubt it would have meant instant death if he had not awakened just in time to swerve the truck away from the wall. However, his mother, who reported the incident to the Parapsychology Laboratory, apparently knew nothing about her son's danger until he later told her how her voice had warned him.

The case would have been typical of others if the mother had been deceased or if, the other way around, she had been awakened by her son's voice telling her what a narrow escape from an impending danger he had had. But as it was, it was a rare exception.

As compared to the distinctiveness of the cases involving the voice of the living vs. that of the dead, the situation in the 66 cases with an impersonal voice (like No. 6) was especially significant. That example, like the cases with the voice of a deceased person, seemed usually to give a warning. But it was unlike those in the voice of a living person in which only the percipient's name was heard. Instead, many of the impersonal voices gave a more specific message, often without the person's name; they simply gave information rather than a warning of danger. For instance, the following.

No. 8

After fifteen years of childless marriage a Texas woman explained that having a baby had become an obsession with her. She even walked into a baby shop one day and put her name on a waiting list for a layette. (It was after World War II and items of baby apparel were scarce so stores kept waiting lists.) The clerk asked when she was expecting. She said without thinking, "In about two months."

The clerk looked skeptical, so she explained that she was adopting a baby. She hadn't planned to say any such thing. "In fact," she wrote when reporting the experience to the Laboratory, "I hadn't planned any part of it, but I did it and I felt good about it."

But by the next morning she was discouraged again. She was ironing and a wave of dispair swept over her, and she said, "God, I must have a baby."

Then, "just as clearly as a bell" came a masculine voice saying, "Well, go to the telephone." She looked around, no one was there. The clock just then struck 11:00. She went to the phone and automatically dialed the number of a doctor whom she knew but hadn't seen for about three years. When he answered, she asked spontaneously. "When are you going to get me a baby?"

"I was just thinking of you," he said. "I have your baby here in the hospital right now."

Then he explained that from that minute the baby was hers but she and her husband had to be approved by the woman who was responsible for the baby's placement.

The interview with this person was brief and simple. The woman asked her, "What were you doing at 11 o'clock?" After relating the experience at the ironing board the woman told her that she had been praying about the matter and at 11 o'clock she suddenly "felt complete peace" and knew that it was settled.

When the case was reported to the Laboratory, the writer added, "Our son is fourteen now and he is everything we ever hoped for. I call it answer to prayer. But whatever you call it, the source is the same, isn't it?"

I had no argument with that, and replied, "You are so right. Whatever you call it — the source is the same." But my objective here was to try to trace out a little further the route taken by such messages as they travel from their sources into the percipient's consciousness.

Summing up the characteristics of the cases with an impersonal voice, I found that, one, the event always concerned the percipient just as in those with the voice of a deceased person; two, it was often a warning, although it did not always concern a crisis as in the other call cases; three, instead of the name of the percipient, these cases usually involved a statement like "your mother is dead," or a command, as in a traffic situation, like "slow down"; and, four, as in a few of the cases with a living voice, they sometimes were precognitive — as in No. 9 following.

No. 9

A texas woman wrote, "I was pregnant with our first child. He was placenta previa, which had caused hemorrhaging and a trip to the hospital." She then described a visit she and her husband had made to her husband's parents, during which his father said she should "go ahead and lose the baby as it could never be normal."

This sent her to her room in tears and she was alone there and crying hard when a male voice, deep and resonant, told her she had nothing to fear, that she would have a lovely healthy child. As she says about it, "This was a voice I heard with my ears, not imagined, but I was alone and no one had come close to the room."

From then on she was relieved and had a feeling of inner peace. The baby was born prematurely, weighing only 3½ pounds, but was perfectly normal. At that time she wrote the Laboratory she could report that he was nine years old, normal and healthy.

In a general way, then, it seemed that as a group, the experiences involving an impersonal voice were rather less specific and more varied in kind of subject matter than those of the other two call groups. It was as if the voices of the living, and those of deceased persons too, had generally been in character, but when the voice was impersonal, no such limitation was involved and consequently information so transmitted was wider in scope than in the other situations.

My conclusion on this study had to be that since I could find no common feature among these varying groups of "call cases," the S-R model does not fit the process that goes on in psi experiences. Instead, the situation seems to be the one I earlier had considered to be still more inexplicable: one of a specific response without a specific stimulus. The response, the ESP experience, then, can be different in each instance.

Still, I did find differences in the group characteristics that apparently were connected with the state of the agent, living, deceased, or no agent. Summing them up, what explanation could I find for them?

Beginning with the cases with the impersonal voice, the wider variation in types of response contrasted quite strongly with the almost uniform kind of call associated with the voice of a living person. Also, in contrast, was the rather free range of kinds of events covered by the impersonal voice, compared to the restriction to crises of the agents of those involving a living voice. At the same time, comparison of the cases with the voice of the deceased to the other two groups showed the former to be intermediate between them in the range of topics they covered. Also the wording of the calls from the deceased was more varied than those in the voice of a living person. Precognitive cases did occur, but somewhat less frequently than when the voice was impersonal.*

The fact that cases with an impersonal voice showed the widest range of all, both as to the wording of the message and the

---

In all instances with either the living or the deceased voice the percipient recognized the voice and he already knew whether the person was living or dead. If some had involved agents who had died without the percipient's knowledge, they might have been revealing, but no such cases appeared in this collection.

kinds of events they covered, suggested to me that they could be a kind of disguised situation in which the percipients, in a way, were "talking to themselves." When ESP information was involved, then, the voice would simply be a projected vehicle, an hallucinatory one, by which the information was transferred to consciousness. Even the futuristic elements would be explicable in this way. They would be evidence of the percipient's own precognitive ability.

However, I realized that if the impersonal voice is interpreted as a projection from the unconscious by the percipient himself, then of course, the same interpretation could be applied to the other two kinds of voices. Then their differences could be accounted for as the result of the difference in the way the percipients conceived of the powers of their living vs. deceased relatives and acquaintances.

When an agent is in a crisis and a percipient becomes "aware" of it by means of a call experience, then that percipient dramatizes the situation as if, for instance, it were the mother-child relationship (which in many cases is the actual one – see Nos. 1 to 4 – in which the mother hears the child call to her). Then, if she is a person for whom the hallucinatory form is possible, she "hears" the call, but she will, of course, be entirely unaware of her own part in creating it.

With this same concept, what then happens when the voice is that of someone deceased? If the percipient is the architect of his or her own experience in these cases too, which are practically always warnings of danger to the percipient, it could mean that knowledge of the threat has become accessible by ESP and is dramatized into a warning voice. This idea was all the more plausible because in most of the instances in which the person heard the voice of someone deceased, the deceased had been a protector of the living person and so now would be the logical one to be projected to call a warning. At the same time, the percipient would be unlikely to project a warning call as coming from a living agent for, according to well entrenched and commonly accepted dicta, he would not assume that a living person had the ability to know of a threat before it materialized.

By reasoning such as this, it seemed that not only did the call cases make sense, but they also showed a basic aspect of the

ESP process. They showed that the percipients are those who "construct" the experiences by their own unconscious procedure, based on their own interests, desires, memories, etc. In the call cases they do it by an auditory hallucination, but of course not all percipients use that form. Instead they employ the other forms too, depending, one must suppose, on local or personal proclivities. But, at any rate, the form is not determined by the agent. From this viewpoint the agent, in a way, is only part of the subject matter the percipient uses to create the specifics of his or her experience.

This explanation was an answer to my question about the deeper meaning of the forms of ESP—*i.e.*, that they were apparently surface variations depending on the percipient. It also seemed a much simpler explanation than the old one which was based on the assumption that agents were responsible for telepathic experiences because they "sent" their thoughts to the percipients. That assumption also meant that the process in telepathy acted differently from the one involved in clairvoyant and precognitive experiences. This finding about the call cases, I knew, was revolutionary, but such changes are inevitable if progress in the understanding of psi in daily life is to keep abreast of the experimental research in the field. This change in understanding of the basic dynamic of the psi process will come up repeatedly, especially in the chapter on telepathy and those on hallucinatory experiences.

But first, what about precognition in daily life and the questions raised when the idea of foreseeing the future is faced? Those questions too are new ones and have never been addressed either in the parapsychological or any other nonfictional literature.

Chapter 9

Time, Imagery
and People

No. 1

"About the second or third day of May, 1812, I dreamed that I was in the lobby of the House of Commons (a place well known to me). A small man dressed in a blue coat and a white waistcoat entered, and immediately I saw a person whom I had observed on my first entrance, dressed in a snuff-colored coat with metal buttons, take a pistol from under his coat, and present it at [aim it at] the little man above mentioned. The pistol was discharged, the ball entering under the left breast of the person at whom it was directed. I saw the blood issue from the place where the ball had struck him, his countenance instantly altered and he fell to the ground.

"Upon inquiry who the sufferer might be I was informed that he was Mr. Perceval, the Chancellor of the Exchequer. I further saw the murderer laid hold of by several of the gentlemen in the room."

The narrator of this long-ago dream, John Williams, Esq., of Cornwall, England, went on to say that he told his wife about the vivid and disturbing dream. He also told some of his business associates and said he felt that he should go up to London and warn the person concerned. However, his friends discouraged him from doing so, saying he would only be taken for a fanatic.

Mr. Williams learned on May 13th that Mr. Perceval had been assassinated on May 11, a week or so after the dream. Later he had occasion to see a print picturing the assassination scene in the House of Commons and he found it a quite exact replica of the scene of his dream.

This experience was sufficiently impressive that some seventy-five years later the account of it was included by Mrs. Henry Sidgwick in a collection of cases she made for her study, "On the Evidence for Premonitions" (reference 36, pages 324-325). Even though the idea that the future could be known beforehand was practically as unthinkable then, in 1888, as it had been in 1812 when John Williams, Esq., foresaw the assassination of the Chancellor, Mrs. Sidgwick applied to this case, and to the list of others like it that had accumulated, the careful analysis of corroborative conditions that had been exemplified in *Phantasms*. Some of the cases she included, like this one, were among those that had been excluded in that study because of the time discrepancy. She found it impossible to dismiss these experiences as meaningless, but neither could she be certain that some as yet unrecognized explanation other than human precognitive ability might explain them.

Through the succeeding years as experiences suggesting precognition were occasionally reported, a number of thoughtful psychical researchers puzzled over them. However, as mentioned in Chapter 5, it was not until the later 1930's that experimental work finally provided statistically significant evidence showing that the human mind is sometimes able to know extrasensorially about an event still in the future.

Even though to the experimenters themselves in the 1930's the idea of precognition still seemed impossible, and quite inexplicable, still the data repeatedly showed it. The experimental results meant that the idea would have to be entertained of a human ability to know about a future event no matter how incredible it seemed and however much ahead of an adequate explanation it might be. As JBR said in 1938, in his first report of the experimental work on the topic at the Parapsychology Laboratory, the idea of precognition seemed to go "against all common sense and science" (reference 8, page 43).

Even by the time of this 1938 report, and before any widespread knowledge of the experimental evidence for precognition could have been disseminated, apparently the earlier bias against cases seeming to involve it was lifting somewhat, for more of them were being reported than earlier. At least by 1948, when I started my project of case collecting, it seemed to me almost from the start that the folder for precognitive dreams was filling up faster than any others.

The impression was in line with an observation made in 1944 by an English psychical researcher, Dr. D.J. West, that "the precognitive dream is by far the commonest reported psychic incident at the present time." He continued, "This has not always been so. The records of fifty years back were predominantly of apparitions of the dying, but since then the emphasis has transferred from apparitions to dreams" (reference 40, page 265).

West thought it likely that part of the reason for this change was the higher status of dreams since Freud. In the earlier days, as noted in Chapter 3, dreams were held to be comparatively unmeaningful. This fact, although it might account for a relative increase in more recent times of reports of dreams in general, would not however mean that precognitive dreams would be more frequent than those of the contemporary types, the clairvoyant and the telepathic.

I knew that the impression was deepening in the laboratory that all three types were but different aspects of a single mental ability to get information without the senses. The target materials represented different *orders* of reality, but otherwise the processes they involved seemed to be the same. But if precognitive dreams occurred more frequently than those of the other types, it presented an anomaly that needed explanation. And so, with this to explain and also because no study of precognitive experiences had been made since the experimental establishment of precognition, I decided to make one, using the cases in the collection.

The general objective would be to see if any difference could be shown between the precognitive and the contemporaneous types of cases except that of timing. For this, I could compare similar aspects of the two time groups as to their relative frequencies for any possible suggestions that might arise.

In approaching this comparison between cases in the two time groups, the unusual number of precognitive dreams seemed contrary to common-sense expectations, namely, that the percipients, recognizing the unreliability of dreams, would tend to discount them in comparison to waking experiences and even more so if they were precognitive. They should do so if they knew at the time which ones were precognitive and which were contemporary.

But then I remembered that, as mentioned in Chapter 5, when I was classifying the cases into their types, it was seldom indicated in the precognitive dreams, as reported, that the event was still in the future. For example, in John Williams' experience above, the event was given as if it were happening right then. "I dreamed I was in the House of Common," but the event, the shooting, did not actually come to pass until a week or more later. In fact, in many instances, the imagery of two experiences, one precognitive, one contemporaneous would give no clue as to which was which. For instance:

No. 2

A New York woman reported, "I dreamed soldiers were all over the refinery [where she worked] and that they were all carrying rifles. They did not seem to be at war, but a great feeling of tenseness and excitement prevailed. Two soldiers would get on the running board of the taxi, one on each side of the car, and would ride to the office with us."

No. 3

A woman from Oklahoma wrote, "My first vivid experience came to me during the war. In a dream one night I could see a bomber from a nearby airfield flying alone quite normally, when suddenly it crashed nose first into the ground, killing all men aboard."

Both sets of imagery portrayed a present scene. Yet as the sequels show, No. 2 was precognitive and No. 3, contemporary.

Sequel to No. 2

The writer continued, "That was all there was to the dream but it seemed so incongruous that I kept remembering it and wondering why I should have had such a dream."

Nearly a year after, there was a strike at the refinery and the entire place was put under martial law. The soldiers were there and two of them always rode in and out of the plant grounds with the office employees.

Sequel to No. 3

"The papers the following day revealed a picture of the

crashed plane with details just as I described them. It crashed just about the time I was having the dream."

Although in Chapter 5 I had noticed this tendency for precognitive dreams to be presented as contemporaneous, and again here, neither time did I actually stop and ask why this should be so. It was only after many later studies that the reason became clear. Here, the fact itself was the point of significance for it meant that the person, not knowing that the dream was a true one, could not make an immediate conscious decision based on the timing, between precognitive and contemporaneous experiences.

Another observation, too, was that although precognitive dreams were generally experienced as if in the present, in precognitive intuitions the timing was clear, if only by the nature of the situation. For instance, in cases like No. 4 and No. 5 below, the person knew that the event was a future one.

No. 4

A man and his wife were in the middle of a block-long, three-lane wide, bumper-to-bumper line of cars waiting for the San Diego ferry to Coronado Isle, when his wife suddenly began to panic. She "saw" their car slip between the ramp and the ferry. She began to urge her husband to leave the car, but he was skeptical of such impressions, and so she rolled the window down and, as she reported, "resigned myself to whatever might happen."

When their turn came following about twenty others already aboard the ferry, their front wheels passed over but the back ones stuck in a foot-wide and still widening gap right at the spot where she'd "seen" it would happen. After some vain attempts the car lurched forward onto the ferry, while later cars were halted until the gap was closed.

No. 5

Her husband, who worked for a bank in the city in Utah, told her one evening that in about a week he would have to go by bus to Los Angeles to pick up a repossessed car for the bank. At once, she felt a premonition that something undesirable would happen on the trip. She told him she wished he didn't have to go and he became a bit apprehensive too because in the past she had sometimes had hunches that came true.

Then about the time he was to leave, her hunch became more specific. She told him she didn't think he would suffer bodily harm but that he would have his pockets picked. He was relieved but to take precautions he separated his money into two different places on his person and left.

Days later when he returned, he told her that before he had gone even six hours he discovered that on a rest stop his pockets had indeed been picked, even though he felt he had been careful. His wallet and checkbook were found at this rest stop later, empty of course.

It seemed, then, that a person who had a precognitive intuitive impression would be likely to realize that it did refer to an event still in the future. But if it came as a dream, it would not be known until later that it even involved a psi element. One would think, then, that people would tend to remember and report precognitive waking experiences relatively more frequently than precognitive dreams. But this apparently was not the case. Precognitive intuitive experiences did not seem to be reported nearly as often as precognitive dreams. And besides that, the precognitive dreams seemed to be mostly in the realistic form, as for example, Mr. Williams in the House of Commons, above.

Then, in addition to both these *a priori* impressions, was the one mentioned in Chapter 6, that the frequency of conviction cases varied noticeably between dreams and waking experiences. I noted there that the feeling of conviction was especially strong in the cases — all waking experiences — there referred to as "blocked." Later (see Chapter 7), when I catalogued the forms of ESP, I reclassified the blocked cases as incomplete intuitions. I realized then that conviction among them seemed to be very high even though the meaning they carried was extremely low.

What did all three of these irregularities mean and were they in any way connected with the anomaly of the distribution of dream versus waking cases in precognitive experiences? And so, with these various anomalies and questions in mind, I undertook a comparison of the precognitive and contemporaneous cases in the collection on all these topics.

On hand at the time was a total of 3290 cases suitable for study. Of these, 1324 were precognitive and 1966, contemporary (see Table I). The number of precognitive experiences was clearly high enough to confirm the impression that they now were reported much more frequently than they had been historically.

Dividing each of the two time groups into their dream and waking components, I found that 75 per cent of the precognitive experiences were dreams, leaving only 25 per cent of the group as waking experiences. At the same time, the distribution in the contemporaneous cases was the reverse, with waking experiences predominating there 60 to 40 per cent.

Next, in order to check the impression that precognitive dreams were predominantly realistic, I tabulated the number of cases in all four forms in both time groups (see Table II). Again the results bore out the impression, for the distribution of forms among the precognitive cases showed 60 per cent of them to be realistic, while all the rest of the forms were lower than their counterparts in the contemporaneous groups: only 15 per cent were unrealistic, 20 intuitive and 5 per cent hallucinatory. But the distribution of frequencies in the contemporaneous cases was quite different: 21 per cent unrealistic, only 19 realistic, 35 intuitive, and 25 per cent hallucinatory.

Of course, not only the difference in frequency of realistic cases in the two time groups called for explanation, but also those of the other forms. However, the differences between the frequencies of hallucinatory experiences did not seem unusual even though they were relatively large. This form more than any of the others is not likely to be recognized unless it coincides in time with the event — for example, the apparition of a person seen at the time of his death. If it were seen long before, the relationship of experience and event would not be clear and the experience less likely to be recognized as significant and reported. The tendency therefore would be for the contemporaneous ones to be more frequently reported. Very likely a somewhat similar explanation would suffice for the relatively slight difference between the rates of the unrealistic experiences.

In the intuitive form, however, the difference between 20 per cent in the precognitive and 35 per cent in the contem-

TABLE I
Distribution of Dreams and Waking Experiences

	Precognitive		Contemporaneous		
	No. of Cases	% of Pcg.	No. of Cases	% of Cont.	Total
Dream	993	75	784	40	1777
Waking	331	25	1182	60	1513
TOTAL	1324		1966		3290

TABLE II
Distribution of Forms of Experience in the Two Time Groups

	Precognitive		Contemporaneous		Total
FORM	No. of Cases	% of Cases	No. of Cases	% of Cases	
Unreal	200	15	419	21	619
Real	793	60	365	19	1158
Intuit.	258	20	685	35	943
Halluc.	73	5	497	25	570
TOTAL	1324		1966		3290

TABLE III
Distribution of Conviction Cases in the Forms in the Two Time Groups

	Precognitive		Contemporary		Total
FORM	No. of Conv. Cases	% of Group Cases	No. of Conv. Cases	% of Group Cases	
Intuit.	209	81	543	86	743
Halluc.	46	63	357	71	403
Unreal.	46	23	147	35	193
Real.	170	20	174	47	344
TOTAL	471	35%	1212	62%	1683

poraneous seemed possibly to be related to the earlier finding that the element of conviction was more frequent in contemporaneous than in precognitive cases. Certainly those that carried conviction would be more likely to be remembered and reported than those that did not. But whether or not it accounted for all of the difference here was a question.

Accordingly, I made a survey of the distribution of conviction cases in the two time groups (see Table III) and tabulated their distribution among the forms of each. Of the 1324 precognitive cases only 471 or about 35 per cent showed conviction, while of the 1966 contemporaneous cases, 1212 (or about 62 per cent) were convincing. Thus the overall rate of conviction was nearly twice as high in the contemporaneous as in the precognitive groups. More than that, although conviction was more frequent in all the forms of the contemporaneous cases (62 per cent) than in all the forms of the precognitive group (35 per cent), the differences between the rates of its occurence in the two time groups was greater in the dreams than in the waking experiences and greatest of all in the realistic cases of the two time groups, being only 20 per cent in the precognitive and 47 per cent in the contemporaneous groups. And so here again this form, the realistic, seemed to stand out as subject to some differentiating influence, the nature of which was not obvious. Neither was it clear whether the difference in rates of conviction in the two groups accounted for the greater frequency of intuitive cases in the contemporaneous group.

When considering the possible reasons for those differences, in my report I asked myself whether I might have had unconscious biases in collecting and accepting cases that could have contributed to them, but I concluded that I could hardly have been biased against contemporary realistic dreams, for instance, so as to have unwittingly and to so large an extent favored those that were precognitive. Neither could I have been biased in favor of contemporaneous unrealistic rather than contemporaneous realistic dreams so as to have accepted as many or more of them as of those in the realistic form (21 per cent as compared to 19 per cent; see Table II).

However, a more tenable reason for some of the differences, it seemed, might stem from the fact that certain kinds of experiences are more impressive than others to the persons experiencing them. It might be that because of this greater impressiveness their own memories might be affected and consequently their likelihood of reporting one kind of experience more than another, enhanced. For instance, a person well might be more impressed by a waking than a dream experience, by one that comes true at once (contemporary) than a future one, and especially by one that carries conviction.

Thus, the fact that the percentages of conviction cases are higher in the contemporary experiences of all forms than in the precognitive (Table III) could mean that contemporary experiences are, in general, more impressive to the person than precognitive ones and that therefore the person does tend to remember them more frequently than the precognitive. However, this would not account for the greatest anomaly of all, the excess of precognitive realistic dreams, or even for the fact that the reported precognitive cases tend to be dreams. And so it does not seem likely that either my own possible biases or the experiencing person's memory could account in any overall way for these major differences.

Another possible selective factor one can think of would be a tendency to suppress waking precognitive psi impressions more than dreams (Table I). It would be a kind of unconscious effect in the person's own process of permitting psi information to surface. It seems possible on a common-sense basis that intuitive experiences may face greater difficulty in breaking into consciousness than dreams which carry their meaning by imagery that, of course, only needs to be recalled upon waking. If so, and if, as No. 4 and 5 above illustrate, in waking experiences the person is usually aware that the event is in the future, the very element of futurity in many instances might increase the difficulty of intuitions' breaking through into consciousness. But dream imagery—especially because, as already mentioned, it usually appears as if in the present—presumably would escape this restriction.

This argument, however, merely raises another question. If it be true that precognitive dreams occur more easily than precognitive intuitions, why should fewer contemporary experiences be dreams than intuitions (Table I)? However, the larger percentage of conviction cases in the contemporaneous experiences (Table III) would somewhat offset this consideration.

Would it then mean that, in general, a greater potential for intuitions than for dreams might exist but that unconsciously they are unequally affected by the timing involved so that precognitive intuitions would tend to be suppressed more than precognitive dreams?

None of these considerations nor all of them together seem to me sufficient to explain the puzzle that these uneven percentages create, and especially the greatest one, the large number of realistic precognitive dreams, compared to the same form in contemporary experiences (Table II). The suggestion is strong that deeper-lying causes than appear on the surface may be hidden in these percentages. Could an innate tendency be showing, a tendency for the mind, in the relaxation of sleep and possibly then released from the restrictions of the present, to invade the future even more than to be preoccupied with present affairs?

However all that may be, the percentage of realistic precognitive dreams (60 per cent) when compared to any of the other frequencies (see Table II) is too great to be meaningless. In a collection as large as the one used here, it cannot pass unnoticed. In fact, it does come up again in Chapter 17 and in a context that is not touched upon by the present survey.

My study comparing the two time groups thus raised questions but did not answer them, except that I found no differences between the precognitive and the contemporary cases besides their timing and their relative frequencies. Could one then say that as far as the universe is concerned, it seems not to matter whether an event occurs in the present or in the future? On that assumption, the difference between experiences involving a present event and those portraying one still in the future would be in people, in their point of view. They, after all, live in a timed world, one governed almost entirely by the space and time of sensory experience. Can one then say that people, not the universe itself, seem to create both the contemporary and the future aspects of psi experiences? It seems a viewpoint possible to entertain from the evidence of these cases.

However, if complications confuse the ready understanding of the psi process in relation to the time element, they also confound the interpretation of one of the practical questions that arise, namely: Are precognized events unavoidable?

It is the question to be considered next.

Chapter 10

What Must Be, Must Be
Or Must It?

"I was a wreck for weeks wondering how I could have prevented it," wrote a young woman after describing the sequel to a terrifying dream which had awakened her one morning. In her report to the Parapsychology Laboratory, she wrote that she had "seen" a plane crash at the shore of a near-by lake, and the roof of a certain cottage in flames as a result. Only one man had been in the plane and he had burned to death.

She tried to write letters that morning to get the dream out of her mind, but found herself telling her correspondents about it and adding that she was sure the fire engine would go in by the canal instead of the basin road and therefore be unable to get to the plane until too late.

All day she was conscious of every actual plane that went over. Then when getting dinner that night she suddenly called out to her husband, "Robert, that plane is going to crash. Try to stop the firemen before they take the canal road. They *have* to take the basin road and they don't know it!"

Her husband went outside to listen, and put his head back in to say, "That plane's all right," but she shrieked back, "It is NOT!" Within seconds it had crashed. The firemen did take the wrong road. The cottage was only slightly damaged but the pilot in fact did burn to death.

How could she have prevented it? Could she — or anyone — have prevented the catastrophe? Like John Williams in 1812 (Chapter 9) who felt he should warn the Chancellor, many persons through all the years have agonized over this question, after having had a premonition that they felt was true. But should they, need they, have felt that way?

The first question is, can people have even a reasonable certainty that they've had a true precognitive experience? Their feeling of certainty of course does not make it so. Vivid dreams are a dime a dozen and those that "come true" are relatively few and far between. Their vividness does not necessarily signify a psi element and as everyone knows, the fantasies produced by the unconscious sometimes would do a who-done-it author proud.

ESP has no form of its own and so experiences involving it are difficult to identify (Chapter 7). On that account even the clearest precognitive impression cannot be certified as such until after the meaning it carries can be checked with the real event. But by then it is too late for warning. As Mr. Williams' friends told him in 1812, a warning to the Chancellor would likely have resulted only in making Mr. Williams himself appear as a crank. Today no more than then can people run their lives by dreams.

But another more theoretical question remains. Even if a warning were given and heeded, and if the person's feeling could be considered to have been a true premonition, could an attempt to avert the danger actually succeed? As I observed in an article on this topic in 1955, this idea of precognition "seems to challenge the concept of volitional freedom. For, on the face of it at least, it would seem that if the future can be known beforehand, then that future must in some sense already be existent. Like a roll of movie film, it must somehow be fixed and determined and waiting only to be unrolled and experienced. If such should be the case, the idea of volitional freedom could only be a delusion" (reference 19).

Naturally, the fact that many careful experiments have shown precognition to occur has led various scholars to consider and discuss again the question of freedom of will. If precognition does occur, does this mean that all is predestined, with no free will after all?

Several people, including Dr. Gardner Murphy, Dr. Robert Thouless and JBR, have found, on theoretical grounds, reason why the occurence of precognition need not necessarily imply a complete absence of freedom (reference 7, Chapter 6). But the question was methodologically difficult to test in the laboratory and no way to do so had been then, or has even yet been devised. For in a circular way, if a precognition test were given to subjects, and then an attempt made to intervene and prevent the results from coming true, the evidence that the test had indeed involved precognition would be impossible to obtain. It therefore seemed unlikely that the question would soon, if ever, be settled in a definitive way in the laboratory.

By 1955 a number of real life cases which seemed to bear on this question of the possibility of successful intervention of a foreseen danger had accumulated in the collection. With the theoretical interest in it and the unlikelihood that it could be settled by experimental research, it seemed time to survey the pertinent precognitive cases and see what they might suggest on the question.

The 1324 precognitive cases of Chapter 9 were available along with a few new ones. Many of these, however, had no bearing on the intervention question, because the person did not recognize beforehand that his experience might "come true." In fact, only in those that carried the conviction that the experience was true could the topic of intervention even be raised. The precognitive cases included 574 with conviction but in some of these the person would not have wanted to intervene, as for instance in foreseeing the winners of races and others with pleasant overtones. After removing all of those, 433 were left in which the foreseen events were such that the persons presumably would have wanted to prevent their occurrence. In only a part of this number, however, did they make any attempt to do so. In fact, in nearly two thirds of them they did not, as for instance in No. 2.

No. 2

A young naval aviation cadet, whom I will call A., in 1950 was in a preflight school in Pensacola, Florida. He had a very bad dream one night. He dreamed of another young cadet, B., a perfect stranger dressed in the regulation uniform. In the dream it seemed as if B. was an acquaintance though A. knew no one like B. at that time. In the dream B. was flying in the service-type training plane when he crashed on a strange flat field unlike any at the pre-flight school. He was killed, and to make it worse, decapitated. Cadet A. awoke very disturbed and upset.

The effect wore off as months passed. Five months later, Cadet A. was transferred to a different field for special training. The first day there he met face-to-face the Cadet B. of his dream. Somehow, almost at once, he developed a dislike for B. and a cool relationship evolved between them.

Almost a year later Cadet B. was killed, and multilated, in a diving crash on a flat plain of mud like the one in the dream. As Cadet A., reporting to the Parapsychology Laboratory, says, "It is very difficult to relate the emotional feeling I went through—and I sometimes shudder today when I wonder if it might have ended differently if I had swallowed my pride and given a warning before it was too late."

At this stage of the survey after eliminating all those cases in which no attempt to intervene had been made, only 162 remained in which the person did try to prevent the occurrence of the event. In order to increase this number, I was able to find 29 more cases of the same kind in the older literature so that 191 were available for more detailed study. In 60 of these, however, for various reasons the attempt to intervene was not successful. I could see that the reason usually was because the information the person had received in the experience was insufficient and therefore the consequent effort, ineffectual. For example:

No. 3

A girl in New York had been given a lovely ring for her birthday. It was a diamond and she was very proud of it. She had had it for several years when one night she dreamed she saw it burned, the diamond discolored and turned in the setting which was twisted and cracked.

She told her parents of the dream. They warned her to be very careful, and this she tried to be. However, one morning about four days later, she couldn't find the ring as she prepared to go to work. Her father told her he would look for it and he did. As she said, he practically turned her bedroom inside out, but he found no ring.

The next day, he examined the ashes in the small kitchen incinerator, and there he found it—as she had seen it in her dream. It seemed that the morning she missed it, her father had just started the incinerator and, as she came in, she threw some tissue into the fire.

The dream only showed the result. It did not alert the girl to the way by which the result would come about. Sometimes even with more complete information, the result still was not averted, as in the next case.

No. 4

Another woman, this one in Oregon, awoke one morning with an unaccountable fear for her 3-year-old son, and with the strong impression that he would be involved in an automobile accident. She guarded him very carefully but, still fearful and upset, she finally decided to run away from her feeling; and so she took the child and drove some miles to her mother's house.

While visiting there, the fear suddenly lifted; the relief was so great that she burst into tears. But just then came a hard ring on the door bell. A policeman with an excited crowd behind him was holding the little boy, limp in his arms. The child had been hit by a run-away car, when, as she was told, he had been sitting quietly under a tree in the yard. The car had jumped the curb and come directly at him, injuring him severely. The mother added in her report of the incident, "How he got out of the house unnoticed is a mystery. But evidently it was to be."

In such cases even though the information seemed specific, as that it would be an automobile accident, still it was not enough. This person needed to know the location as well as the kind of danger. Also, this last type of situation illustrates a kind of circularity that comes up repeatedly in that the experience itself seems to lead not to the avoidance of the foreseen threat, but to its fulfillment. Possibly, if the woman had stayed at home the accident would not have happened, or at least not in the same way. But whether in some other way is, of course, the open-ended question such episodes cannot answer. And so no one can know whether it "was to be," or whether the proper preventive measure simply was not taken.

In the remaining 131 cases in the study, an effort to evade the threat was made and was successful in as far as the person's objective was concerned. Of course, if the attempt had been such as to eliminate the dangerous situation entirely, no trace would remain to show if it had been a real threat after all. The next case illustrates this point.

No. 5

A man in Illinois who had had several dreams come true, dreamed one night that he had had a very unpleasant visit by two men to his trailer home. It left him worried and so he decided to "change the dream." His trailer was parked on the edge of a farm with the doors facing the highway. In the dream the men had approached from the highway directly to the trailer.

He decided to turn the trailer around. Even though it was heavily loaded and the plumbing and electrical fixtures had to be changed, he managed to do it.

The result—none of the elements of the dream came true. But was it a precognitive dream? Nothing remained or happened to tell whether it was or not.

But in the 131 cases in which it seemed that the foreseen threat had been averted, something did remain—or rather a part of the foreseen setting became a reality and so some reason was given to think that the impression had been precognitive. The individual situations were different of course, as were the reasons that the action was successful. In some, the person just naturally took the proper action as in the following instance.

No. 6

"My husband and I were on an excursion boat. We had saved and planned for the ride, but the gang plank was already up when I got 'butterflies.' I had our two-month-old daughter with us. I told my husband I was getting off the boat. He thought I was crazy. I said he could stay, but I had to get off and I asked the men to put the gang plank down.

"We got off but my husband didn't speak to me all the way home. The next news bulletin said there was a collision and a freighter had hit the excursion boat we had been on and that within 15 minutes all aboard were rescued and the excursion boat sunk. There was no panic; that was why everyone was rescued. I might have caused a panic had I stayed on board with a baby. I don't know."

In other cases the experience served as a warning apparently making the person more alert and so able to avoid the catastrophe, as in this experience.

No. 7

A California woman dreamed that her husband was lying jerking on the ground and that he had been electrocuted when the television antenna fell as he and a friend, who wore a green work suit, had been taking it down. She thought it had fallen over the electric wires in front of the house. People had gathered around and a bright red fire truck was there.

As a result of the dream, she begged her husband not to take the antenna down. He said she was being silly and two weeks later he started to take it down. His friend, wearing green work clothes, came to help. A wind came up and blew the antenna down but, because of the dream, they pushed it in the opposite direction.

Regardless of the specific situation in all of the cases in which intervention was successful, the experience essentially served as a warning and it was heeded, just as any other kind of warning might be. On the practical level, there was no difference because of the origin of the warning.

Of course, these instances of successful intervention do not necessarily show that precognized events can be avoided. To show that, it would be necessary first to be certain that the experience was actually precognitive and not telepathic or clairvoyant. Then, too, the impression of what would occur would have to be specific. Furthermore, the preventive action must have been taken as a result of the impression, not one which would have been taken without it.

When I checked the 131 cases to see if they conformed to these requirements, 121 of them were weak on one or another of them. Sometimes it seemed possible that the impression which served as a warning might have been based on telepathy rather than precognition, as in the next case.

No. 8

A girl whose family was living in the country for the summer was to go to the city for a day, spend the night in the family's unoccupied town house, and return the following day. The night before the trip she dreamed she was sleeping in the town house and was awakened by a man bending over her who put his hands on her throat and started to choke her. She awoke terrified. Nevertheless, she started for town the next morning according to plan.

Halfway to her destination, she changed trains and returned home. The following day, a call came from the city police saying that the town house had been robbed the night before, the night she would have been in it if she had carried out the plan.

Again, the intervention was successful because the dream was taken as a warning and heeded. An alternative, however, possibly a far-fetched one, could not be ruled out. It was that the warning could have been the result of a telepathic awareness of the robber's intention to commit robbery.

In a few cases an experience that appeared to be a good illustration of successful intervention, upon closer examination, turned out not to involve intervention of the precognized event at all, as for instance this next case.

No. 9

A young woman in Florida dreamed that her mother, who lived in a distant state, was almost bitten by a rattlesnake, and that she pushed her mother away before the snake could strike.

About a week later, her mother came to visit. That night, a neighbor's house burned down. The next morning her mother said she was going over to see if she could lend a helping hand. She started across to the burned dwelling when suddenly the girl remembered the dream and ran after her. Her mother had just reached the area of the burned house and at that moment the daughter caught up and saw a large rattler coiled in the warm ashes ready to strike. She gave her a frantic push and caused her to fall head over heels, but out of danger, just before the rattler struck.

In that case, the dream actually did come true as dreamed, In the dream the mother had not been bitten. Without the dream, she well might have been. But still, the precognitive experience did come true and so the case does not count as evidence of intervention.

In some instances, the danger was not clearly or specifically foreseen, so that any calamity which may have occurred could have been taken as a fulfillment. Or sometimes, such as in No. 9, no specific information was received to indicate that the person would actually be involved in the catastrophe and therefore his escape from the danger would not actually mean that a foreseen danger had been avoided.

After all of the cases that involved any of these defects had been eliminated, only nine were left. In them I could find no reasonable alternative to the successful intervention of a potentially precognitive experience. One of these is the following.

No. 10

A woman in New York dreamed that she heard a scream, turned around and saw her two-year-old son falling from an open window. She then heard the siren of an ambulance in front of the house.

Frightened awake, she checked the baby and then the window. Everything was in order. A couple of days later, she put the child's mattress on the window for airing and pulled the window tightly down on it. She was busy in the next room when she suddenly remembered the dream. She ran into the baby's room. He had managed to push the window up and had climbed onto the window sill. She grabbed him the minute he was about to fall. The mattress had already fallen.

The only possibility that the case was not an instance of a true intervention would be if the child would not have fallen anyway, even if his mother had not rescued him, and that his fall in the dream was an inference and not part of the precognized situation that he would fall.

Far-fetched as that alternative may seen, I found three cases of the nine in which even such a remote alternative did not seem possible. The one most convincing of all on this point was the following.

No. 11

A streetcar conductor in Los Angeles dreamed one night that, headed south, he pulled into a certain intersection on his ordinary route, near which was a one-way exit for auto traffic. At this intersection cars sometimes made an illegal left-hand turn. In order to do so, the car would have to cross both the north- and south-bound streetcar tracks.

In the dream, he crossed the intersection at the point of the exit and just then a north-bound trolley, No. 5, passed him. He waved at the motor man, and suddenly just ahead and without warning, a big truck painted solid bright red cut in front of him coming from the exit. The other car had obstructed his view of the exit and the truck making the illegal turn could not see his car for the same reason. There was a terrific crash. People were thrown from their seats and the truck was overturned. Three people were in the truck, two men and a woman. The men were sprawled in the street dead and the woman was screaming in pain. The conductor thought that he walked over to the woman and she looked at him with the largest blue eyes he had ever seen and shouted at him, "You could have avoided this."

He awoke with a start, soaked with perspiration. It was nearly time to arise, which he did, quite shaken by the dream. He reported for work and by his second trip that day had put the dream out of mind. But then, at the intersection of his dream, he became sick at his stomach and as he left the intersection when the signal changed, he saw the north-bound car, No. 5. He at once felt definitely sick and nauseated, but it was when the motor-man on No. 5 waved to him that he remembered the dream. He at once applied the brakes and shut off the power. A truck, not a big truck completely red as in the dream, but a panel delivery truck with space for advertising on the side painted over with bright red, shot directly into his path. Had he been moving at all he would surely have hit it.

Three people were in the truck, two men and a woman. As the truck passed in front of him, the woman leaned out of the window and looked up at him with the same large blue eyes he had seen in the dream. He was so upset he had to be relieved from work.

The account seemed to pass every test. The event as dreamed occurred hours after the dream and so it was clearly precognitive. It was specific in all essential details and presumably the collision of the dream would have occurred if the warning had not been heeded and if the attempt to intervene had not been the proper one. (Besides being a perfect example of a precognitive experience prevented from fulfillment, the case, incidentally, was a good example of the occasional intrusions of incorrect details into true and realistic dreams — the description of the truck and the action of the blue-eyed woman — a topic which will be discussed further in Chapter 14.)

These nine cases among the 131 instances of a successful escape from a threatened calamity, of course, are not final proof that a precognized calamity can be avoided. However, they are the best examples in my collection and at least tend to show that what might seem to be a precognized danger can be avoided if the proper preventive action is taken. The situation can serve as a warning and can be treated accordingly, just as if its source were not an extrasensory one.

But should outsiders be warned? Should John Williams have warned the Chancellor? Because of a dream? Need a person feel guilty if he does not do it and the calamity occurs? Hardly, at least not yet. The world still knows too little about the possibility of precognition and has been misled too often by misdirected cranks and fanatics to be able to discriminate. And so, on the practical level, no. My survey at least shows that an individual need feel no necessity to issue public warnings, but for himself, he can be on the alert for the possibility that he has glimpsed the future truly and that by his own free will he can avoid catastrophe.

By his own free will? For the present the possibility of free will can at least be a good working formula, even though the theoretical question may still be open and remain so until the phenomenon of precognition is understood. This, I believe, can be considered a working formula in spite of the frequent and ancient conclusion, "It was meant to be."

This idea, that attempts to intervene in precognitive warnings must be futile, seems to have been a prevalent one in ages past. Often then, it well may be that man's preoccupation with the question of his destiny may have led to the preservation of those narratives in which a precognitive dream or vision came true in spite of his every effort to escape his "fate." Even Webster defines fate as "that which unavoidably befalls one."

However, I believe such older material may be suspect, for even if the incidents themselves be taken as authentic, it can be suspected that a kind of selectivity preserved a disproportion of those in which it seemed an inexorable fate was shown. At any rate, the cases in my collection seem to me much less suggestive of an unyielding and inescapable destiny than simply of a *human capacity* that is limited in conscious scope and function. The suggestion then is not for a supine acceptance of the idea of predestination, but for a vigorous search for the nature of precognition — which means, of course, a search for the nature of the psi ability in all its types and operations.

In this search the problem is not only that of digging out the actual facts, however slow-going and recalcitrant the process may be, but also of clearing away the misconceptions and misunderstandings that have accumulated over ages past. Of these, the one that involves the telepathic process which comes up next is one of the most far-reaching.

Chapter 11

Who's Who in Telepathy?

Nineteenth-century England knew nothing of psi. But the early psychical researchers did suspect that telepathy somehow does occur. Their interest in proving it led, as Chapter 3 shows, to the publication of *Phantasms of the Living*. Because of this background, one can say that this one type of psi has a much longer history, at least in the English speaking world, than clairvoyance or precognition. Even so, however, the telepathic process still today remains more of a puzzle than that of either of the other types. Even among parapsychologists themselves, no general agreement has been reached as to just what goes on in telepathy, except that it is a process by which one person becomes aware of the thought of another when no outward sign has been given.

In telepathy, and in telepathy only, two persons are involved. One of them, the agent, has the thought that is transferred. The other is the person who receives it. He is the experiencing person, the percipient. The situation is complicated by the fact that telepathy may occur in many different kinds of situations. The underlying process consequently is often obscured and the superficial impression that is given may be misleading. In some cases, for instance, the process may appear to be quite self-evident and frequently has been taken too simply at what seems to be face value. Take a case like this, for instance:

No. 1

"Since I hate writing," reported a woman from Indiana, "when I had gone on a visit to St. Louis to see my sister, I failed to write my husband when I would be returning home. I was on the train headed for Indianapolis when it dawned on me that I had not sent him a telegram as I had intended. The train would arrive at two a.m. and there would be no one there to meet me. So I decided to try telepathy. I kept saying over and over, 'Meet the two a.m. train, meet the two a.m. train from St. Louis.'

When I got off the train, my husband was there to meet me. His first words were, 'Why didn't you tell me you were coming home?'

"I asked him how he knew I would be on this train, and he said, 'I don't know. I was sound asleep when something kept telling me to meet the two a.m. train from St. Louis. So I got up and called the station and was told there was a two a.m. train from St. Louis — so I met it.' "

The initial impression is that because the wife, the agent, "sent" her thought to her husband, he received it in the form of a realistic dream. Granting the extrasensory ability, what could seem more obvious? Then take an experience in a different form, a case of a visual and auditory hallucination:

No. 2

"Don't worry, Mom. Everything will be all right," a man in Pennsylvania kept saying over and over as he lay, still sleepless, at about 2 o'clock after a hard and busy day and late retirement. But grief and worry about his mother, desperately ill in a distant hospital, was defeating his need for sleep. His vacation was coming up in about a week. But would she last that long?

She did, the vacation came and he and other members of the family were visiting in the sick room. He greeted his mother. She said he had been to see her about a week before. "Yes," she declared, "You stood right where you are standing now and you said, 'Don't worry, Mom. Everything will be all right.' "

And then he told them all about the night he couldn't sleep and that he had kept saying those very words. His mother said it was about 2 a.m. that morning when she awoke from sleep to see him standing there and hearing his words. The night nurse had come in and wondered what was going on.

"My son was here," she told her, but the nurse just said, "You were dreaming. Now go back to sleep."

Several years later the man reported the occurrence to the Parapsychology Laboratory. The nurse's explanation had not satisfied him. "How can such things be?" he asked.

The form in No. 2 was different from that of No. 1, but again, the agent, the son in that case, seemed to send his thought. Then his mother, the percipient, picked it up. The next experience is similar, though in this one the experiencing person was awake and her impression, intuitive.

No. 3

A young woman in Missouri was preparing breakfast for her husband one morning about seven when she suddenly knew that something was wrong with her mother. She told her husband she had to drive to Kansas City at once and find out what the trouble was. He suggested that a phone would be cheaper and quicker, but she insisted that it wouldn't do.

An hour later she drove into her parents' driveway. A young girl who worked for them came running out to meet her saying, "Your mother had a small heart attack a few minutes before seven and I wanted to call you but she said not to bother, that you were coming."

When the daughter walked into her mother's room, she was greeted with, "I thought you would make it about now."

The agent in that case was the mother and she needed to get a message to her daughter. Whether or not her thought actually caused the percipient, the daughter, to get it, she obviously somehow knew the significant part of it, "Come at once."

Or take a variation in the part of the agent, along with a still different form of the resulting experience, as in this instance from a Texas college boy.

No. 4

His roommate had asked to be awakened at a particular time one Sunday afternoon. When the time approached, he decided to awaken the roommate "in the most devilish manner possible." He would drip one drop of water after another on the sleeper's eyelids until he awakened.

He went to the bathroom to get a glass of water and just as he re-entered, the roommate sat up suddenly, rubbed his eyes, shook his head and said: "Oh, oh, what a dream I just had! I dreamed I was in a terrible rain storm with the water beating down on my face."

The agent was awake, his roommate, the percipient, asleep. The agent had no intent to send his thought, but nevertheless it apparently was received, and incorporated into the percipient's dream, this time in the form of a little fantasy, an unrealistic experience.

Still another variant occurs when the agent and percipient are both asleep, as in the following instance.

No. 5

She and her husband were "animal people" and for twenty years had had an animal show. That fall they had tentatively booked a tour to a northern sportsman's club. She and her husband had talked it over and had about decided to take the offer, even though it was different from their regular routine in that the request was only for their gorilla, Jock, to be on display. The offer had created the problem of knowing how to manage their six chimps in the meantime.

She was thinking of it as she fell asleep that night, and she dreamed they had moved to some big arena—maybe New York—and were showing Jock in their portable rope arena. Her husband had to go back to check on the chimps, leaving her alone with the gorilla, but she knew she could handle him.

She had to take him from a back room on a collar and chain and bring him out to the rope arena. All went well until she started to take off his chain. And then, in the dream, he suddenly started biting her forearms, from wrists to elbows. She was covered with blood. She thought she managed to get out of the arena and close it with the animal inside and that a policeman rushed up and pulled his gun. She stopped him from shooting the animal—and woke up.

As she lay in bed thinking, "My God, what an awful dream! Maybe we'd better cancel that date," her husband beside her groaned in his sleep, "How awful." She woke him.

"What's the matter, Bill?" Still half asleep he muttered, "Jock was biting you."

Of course, in this experience the agent apparently did no sending. She reported no thought whatever about her husband, yet he responded.

Through all these seeming variations in which agents and percipients were sometimes both asleep, sometimes one or both awake, whether the agents consciously sent their thoughts or not, it seems the percipients became aware of them. In cases when the thought was sent, the process appeared to be like that of auditory sense experience as when an individual calls another person to tell him his thought. But in instances like that of the animal trainers and the college boy in the dormitory, the process would seem more like thought reading than like thought sending, because the message was picked up when the agent had no conscious intent to send it.

As processes, thought-sending and thought-reading would be essentially different. Thought-sending would begin with the agent, thought-reading with the percipient. Could this mean that not one kind of process, but two, may go on in different telepathy experiences?

This question about the process in telepathy is almost as old as the idea of telepathy itself. It was formalized in a way in 1886, when in *Phantasms* Gurney decided that it had better not become known as "thought-reading," the name that "we first adopted; this had several inconveniences," he said. "Oddly enough, the term has got identified with what is not *thought*-reading at all, but *muscle*-reading.... But a more serious objection to it is that it suggests a power to *read* anything that may be going on in the mind of another person ... which raises a needless prejudice against the whole subject" (reference 2, page 10).

And later, "It is clearly important to avoid such an expression as thought-reading.... It is for the sake of recognizing this that we distinguish the two parties as 'agent' and 'percipient' and that we have substituted for thought-reading the term thought-transference."

Thus, way back then the nature of the telepathy process was decided. And the decision was a simple matter of strategy. It was not the result of analysis. The decision was that the telepathic process should not be considered analogous to reading, which puts the initiative on the percipient, but rather as analogous to hearing, which puts it on the agent. Of course, for Gurney, it was not the *nature* of the telepathy process which he was trying to establish, but the *reality* of telepathy itself. The process as such was not of primary concern to him. He therefore decided to use it arbitrarily in the way that then seemed most acceptable or diplomatic, but in line with the general purpose of the study in which he was engaged. Of course, in cases like the life situations with which he was dealing and like these reported here, it may not matter which of the two individuals exerts the initiative in the transfer. But it is important in trying to understand the psi process. In an attempt like mine it was necessary to know whether the telepathic process is the same as that of clairvoyance and precognition. If so, differences in type would be only differences in the kind of target, whether a thought, a thing, or a future event. In clairvoyance and precognition, the experiencing percipient must take the initiative in securing the information, for no second person is involved. Only in telepathy, then, does this quesiton of the role of the second person, the agent, come up, and then only when agents seem to send their thoughts to the percipients. In such instances the initiative for the transfer has seemed so obviously to come from the one in need that Gurney's decision to name that person the agent has been generally accepted, for it did seem quite naturally that the agent "sent" his or her thought to the percipient.

This idea of the way telepathy works also filled a need of those concerned in the early days with the survival question, which in the background was the main basis for interest then in psychical research. As discussed in Chapter 3, a telepathy-like experience was interpreted to mean that the dying one had come to say good-bye. If so, the deceased was the agent, the active party, in the exchange. And it was the agent's active part in it that made the experience seem meaningful for survival.

At that time the actual occurrence of telepathy had not been proved, but by the middle of the twentieth century, extrasensory thought exchange between two people had been shown by well-controlled laboratory tests to occur. In these, the set-up usually was a bit like the situation in No. 1 when the woman sent her husband the thought of meeting her train. A test subject having a target thought in mind tried to "send" it to a percipient. The difference was that in the test the percipient, the subject, was aware of the situation and tried to guess it. If the percipient guessed correctly, was it because the agent sent it? Or was it because the percipient chose the correct target just as he or she would have if the situation had been one of clairvoyance or of precognition? The laboratory tests did not answer this question nor did spontaneous cases. In fact, it seemed that many of the cases in my collection, as in the call cases of Chapter 8, failed even to suggest that the agents actively sent their thoughts. However, I thought perhaps they were not truly representative of telepathy cases in general and so I felt the need for a more inclusive study in which to observe again the actual nature of the telepathic process.

Then a survey of the general telepathy cases in the collection seemed to be in order. It was time to do it not only because parapsychologists were interested in the nature of the psi process, but also because of the central role which telepathy had been given in the earlier speculations about survival (reference 21). Interest in that problem still existed although it no longer was so intense as it once had been. Even JBR and I were still concerned with it, though none of the discoveries about psi ability over the years had encouraged the idea that experiments with mediums could answer the question.

With that reason for trying to understand the telepathy process in the background, and the newer need of parapsychology to understand its own processes in the foreground, I assembled all available telepathy experiences in the collection. I found that all of the four standard ESP forms were represented among them although in widely differing frequencies. For some unknown reason the hallucinatory form predominated. Of these, auditory hallucinations which included the call cases, were the most frequent, while the intuitive type and then dreams followed in order. But since so many of the telepathic experiences were hallucinatory they seemed to deserve special treatment, which would have to come later so I did not include them in this study. Here the objective was only to study the roles of agent and percipient in obviously telepathic experiences.

The first precaution I had to take in assembling cases for the purpose of this study was to be certain that the identity of the agent and percipient in each instance was clearly defined. A few cases were ambiguous on this point. For instance, No. 6.

No. 6

A now retired school teacher from Southern California at one time drove back and forth from Walnut Creek to Richmond and on the way picked up a passenger, a woman named Nancy who worked in a laboratory along the way to Richmond. She was a quiet, pleasant companion who did not volunteer much about her personal life or ask questions of a personal nature.

As the   teacher reported to the Parapsychology Laboratory, "One late afternoon, I left school in a state of exhaustion. Mentally I was tattered and torn by a hectic day with the younger generation and on top of this I had attended a boring faculty meeting. Nancy was waiting for me when I drove up to the laboratory. She volunteered that she had had a bad day too and as she entered the car, asked, 'Would you mind if I don't talk, but just lean back and close my eyes?'

"I glanced at her and thought she certainly looked very tired and her face in repose looked sad as she slid back into the seat and shut her eyes. Then I pulled out into the freeway traffic. That is all I remember until the car came to a stop and I was surprised to find my foot on the brake and my hand on the gear shift, the car in neutral. I looked around and discovered I was on a street I had never seen before, a very quiet one without a human being in sight. I was parked in front of a rather ugly brown house with brown pillars and a diamond shaped glass in the front door. How had I left the freeway and where was I? Ordinarily my route home never varied—a left turn off the freeway and then straight up that street a mile, through the tunnel and home.

"I felt bewilderment and fear. I leaned over and touched Nancy and when she opened her eyes, I said, 'Nancy, I seem to have made a wrong turn somewhere. I think I am lost.'

"She looked at the brown house and the street and a look of joy came over her face. She exclaimed, 'It's exactly the same as when I was a child. I was born in that house and spent my early childhood here, the happiest time of my life. I was sitting here thinking about it and longing to see it again. I've never been back since I was a little girl and when I opened my eyes here we were in front of it. How could you possibly know?'

"We stared at each other and finally I said, 'I must have read your mind and followed the directions for reaching it that you knew.' But she said, 'When I was a child there was no freeway and I didn't know or remember the streets. Besides my eyes have been closed since we left the laboratory.'

"In a few minutes I drove on. My hands were trembling. Then I reached a little store where I asked how to get back to the freeway. I later figured I had driven between 15 and 20 blocks off my regular course. I drove very slowly and carefully back to Walnut Creek. Later when Nancy was not along I tried to retrace the route I must have taken to reach the house. I went up and down street after street. I never found the brown house on the quiet street again."

Besides telepathy, this case illustrates other puzzling aspects that occasionally are presented in life experiences. Here they were the unusual mental state of the presumed agent, and the fact that neither person, consciously at least, had the information. Therefore, with no individual from whose conscious mind the directions for finding the brown house could ostensibly have been drawn, the case was unsuitable for the contemplated survey and so it and all other instances with comparable complications were removed from consideration. This left 328 items suitable for the study.

In analyzing these cases, I took it as my first objective to select and isolate all those in which the agent appeared to send the information to the percipient. The second, to observe also the attitude of the percipient toward the agent to see whether the percipient, rather than the agent, could have had a motive to initiate the transfer.

As already mentioned, when the cases were classified originally as telepathic, I had noticed that the agents had not always been consciously aware of the percipients or even thinking of them and wanting them to get the thought. But that did not necessarily mean that the agent might not unconsciously exercise the necessary initiative. Therefore, possible unconscious attitudes had also to be taken into consideration.

The first question thus, was, did the agent consciously wish the percipient to know the item, as in cases like 1, 2, and 3? I found that in 107 instances, the agent obviously did. In all of these, however, the persons were close relatives and the percipients presumably would have been equally oriented toward the agents. For instance, in No. 3 the percipient, the daughter, would presumably have been alert at any time to a crisis involving her mother, whether or not the actual securing of such information was consciously in her mind. In this first group of cases, then, no basis appeared on which a discrimination could be made between the roles of the agent and percipient. Presumably, either or both could have initiated the transfer.

The next question was whether in cases of less apparent motivation (Nos. 4 and 5) the agent could be assumed to have initiated the exchange. Certainly the prankster in No. 4 did not intend to do so. Yet, he was strongly oriented toward his sleeping roommate and it might just be possible that that orientation, rather than specific motivation, was all it would take to stimulate the transfer. Even in the animal trainer case, No. 5, since the husband and wife were a team, the wife might have sent unrecorded thought to her husband in her dream crisis. If so, even in such cases, the possibility that the agent was responsible could not be discounted. One hundred and sixty-nine cases were of this mixed or questionable kind. In a few of these, like No. 4, the agent was consciously oriented in some way toward the percipient but in the rest he could only have been so oriented unconsciously. And so, in this second group, too, the judgment of initiative could not be made with certainty because the two individuals knew and were interested in each other at least on the unconscious level. It therefore was just possible that either one could have taken the initiative.

But 52 cases remained in which the agents would not have been oriented toward the percipients either consciously or unconsciously. Usually the two were only casual acquaintances or strangers. Besides, the situations were usually such that the agents would have had no reason to send the particular thought to the particular percipient, as in this case:

No. 7

A girl was working in a linen shop in Chicago during the Christmas shopping rush one year. The shop was embroidering handkerchiefs with monograms in several patterns. The girls who were taking the orders were not being sufficiently explicit and some orders were refused resulting in a loss to the shop. And so when a customer came in one day who didn't seem to understand, this girl used for an example the first name that came to mind, "James Allen Beck." It turned out that it was almost the exact name (Beck for Buck) the customer wanted to have embroidered on the handkerchief, and she became quite indignant asking the clerk how she could possible know her sweetheart's name when it was her first visit to the shop.

Certainly the agent (in this case, the customer) would not have sent the name to the percipient (the clerk) either consciously or unconsciously. The percipient, however, was interested in the customer and her order and on that account it is not too difficult to suppose that she exercised the initiative necessary to get the name from the other. Similarly in the rest of these cases, agents were uninterested in the percipients or often had never heard of them. But the percipients always had some reason for interest in the agent, even though sometimes it was quite casual.

Sometimes, too, a situation occurred that seemed to preclude any acquaintance at all between the two persons, as in the next case:

No. 8

A woman from Atlanta who characterized herself as naturally of a cheerful and happy disposition had an unusual, and she thought, atypical experience one night which seemed to be a sort of sleep-walking nightmare. She wakened her husband by crying and walking the floor and he couldn't at once bring her back to normal consciousness. She kept saying, "I've killed a man." And then, "Run and keep running." Finally by slapping her and even throwing water on her, he awakened her and, as she said, "I immediately went down on my knees to thank God that it was just a dream."

Then she told her dream. In it she thought she was a small boy driven to do a crime. And then she was a woman talking to the boy. "I told him to run to a jail and be locked up."

When the *Atlanta Journal* came out the next day, she read a column on the front page which told of a 12-year-old boy who had fled 18 miles to a sheriff's office to ask the sheriff to lock him up to keep his uncle from killing him. The boy lived with an uncle in another county. The uncle was a moonshiner and had killed a man and stolen his car. The boy told the jailer that a woman told him how to get protection.

Cases with the implications of No. 8 naturally are infrequent, but are reported sufficiently often to suggest rather strongly that even entirely on the unconscious level, the ESP ability permits a possibly wide range of contact with the objective world so that a sufficiently sensitive person, the woman with the "nightmare" in this instance, can be affected by a situation of which she has no sensory knowledge nor even unconscious information until by ESP the gate is opened, as it were. In fact, such instances again suggest a kind of "leakage" or contagion of thought but even so, one in which the experiencing person could exert whatever minimal initiative is necessary. The initiative would not be unlike that which led the woman to read the article in the paper the next day, a kind of humanitarian interest in items of the outside world.

To what, then, did the cases of these three groups add up as far as the active involvement of the agents was concerned? In the first group, the agents had been strongly oriented toward the percipients and either consciously or unconsciously could have been the ones to initiate the transfer. In the second group the agents could have been unconsciously aware of the percipients but not actually thinking of them. Still the possibility that they did somehow cause the transfer could not be entirely ruled out. But in the third group, the agent had no knowledge whatsoever of the percipient. The two were entire strangers. In these cases, it could not be assumed that the agent caused the transfer.

But what of the experiencing persons in these three groups? In the first two groups, the relationship between the two was reciprocal. The motivation for an exchange of thought could have come from the percipients if they became aware by ESP of the crisis of the agent. Even though they did not appear to be seeking information about the agents, they might have been able to acquire it in much the same way that percipients in clairvoyance and precognition cases get information about things and events. But in the third group when the agents and percipients were strangers, the percipients still had at least a minimal degree of interest in the agents. They were always involved since they had the experience, and even in cases like examples 4 and 5 when the agents were oriented toward the percipients, the latter could still have been the ones who caused the transfer in spite of the appearance that they were playing inactive parts. But take No. 2, for instance, in which the son was worrying about his ill mother. In a case like this, one can assume that the mother was naturally also, at least unconsciously, oriented toward her son. It was she, of course, who constructed the pseudo-sensory (hallucinatory) image of him. The mother's role as percipient thus would not have been a passive one; instead her active part was obscured by the activity of the son, the agent, which was much the more obvious of the two. This kind of situation existed in all of the telepathy cases, regardless of their form.

By analyzing telepathy situations in this way, it seemed to me that the process involved was analogous to thought-reading rather than thought-sending. But when thought-sending by the agent also occured it would be a complementary factor, as in the call cases of Chapter 8, where too it seemed to be the percipients that "did it," with the agents being, as it were, only accessories after the fact.

If this idea of the psi process proves to be correct, when and if sufficient experimental work confirms it, then the telepathy process will be shown to be of a single kind and not basically different from those of the other types of psi. All types of psi then could be defined as non-sensory methods by which individuals (percipients) acquire information about the world.

The thought-reading model of telepathy, however, is one that undermines the early pre-experimental concept of telepathy which seemed to support the survival hypothesis. Without a necessarily active agent who initiates the exchange, telepathy would be as useless to that thesis as any of the other types.

However, the form of experience that, in the past, most strongly suggested the survival of the personality after death was the hallucinatory, and especially instances of apparitions of a dead or dying person. But the experimental work of the first half of the twentieth century throws a considerably different light on the old interpretations and especially on those concerning apparitions. Realizing this, I therefore made an appraisal of the hallucinatory experiences next.

Chapter 12

Hallucinatory Psi Experiences

No. 1

During World War I a corporal in the Canadian Expeditionary Force was captured in Germany after a mine explosion. After an abortive attempt to escape he was treated rather badly by the Germans, sent to a farm to recuperate, and then escaped again. He walked some 200 miles through Germany to the Dutch border. It was a hazardous tramp of many days. He had little to eat. He reached the border in a state of exhaustion. It was night and snowing.

He came to a crossroads about which he had some information. He knew that if he took the correct way he would be in friendly Dutch hands. If he took the wrong way he would walk almost certainly into a German post or patrol. He did not know which was which and he was much too exhausted to try walking at random over plowed fields in the dark and in a heavy snowfall. He hesitated, badly lost, and then started up one of the roads.

His brother, a man now living in Washington state reported the story to the Laboratory in 1956, saying, "At this time I was probably asleep in an officer's quarters in the south of England. My brother says that this happened to him, as clear and well-defined as any actual happening. He says I stepped in front of him, and said, 'No, Dick, not that way. Take the other road, you damned fool!'

"He did so and shortly after was in Dutch hands in kindness and safety. They sent him back to London and a few days later he told me all this with the clear conviction that in some extraordinary way I had been there and saved him. But I had never

135

been in Holland nor Germany and I did not recall any dream or thought about it until he told me the story.

"Can ESP fit into this picture at all?"

The question cannot be answered with finality, of course. It could have been just a coincidence that the man chose the safe direction on the basis of what one would have to call a fantasy produced by his own subconscious mental activity. But, on the other hand, ESP *could* have been involved. It could have guided the construction of the fantasy, which since the man was not dreaming would have to be called an hallucinatory effect. He could have perceived the correct way clairvoyantly and then projected a pseudo-sensory impression of his brother's giving him the direction. It was a form of expression in which the percipient saw and heard his brother *as if* by real sight and hearing. But it clearly was a mental construct which must have been based on memory, imagination and the ability to have pseudo-sensory impressions.

By 1956, after the study of the telepathy experiences of Chapter 11, the Duke Collection included a total of over 8,000 cases, of which 825, or about 10 per cent, had been classified as hallucinatory. I had accepted these cases, it can be emphasized, without any other selective criterion than that they seemed possibly to be instances in daily life in which people had received information without the use of their senses. I now selected them for further study and classification (reference 20).

The hallucinatory experiences had been classified originally as a separate form on the basis of their imagery, which was distinctly different from that of dreams. They occurred when the person was awake or at least thought he was awake, and the imagery accordingly was that of sensory experience. The person, therefore, did not necessarily recognize that the experiences were not real since they came by way of the familiar sense modalities, visual, auditory or combinations of them, with an occasional olfactory or even tactile or somatic effect.

Among these modalities, visual hallucinations were usually the most impressive, although not the most frequently reported. Auditory effects much outnumbered them, especially since they included the already mentioned call cases. In the collection, only 231, or 28 per cent, were visual hallucinations, to

435, or about 53 per cent, auditory. A visual experience was reported by a girl in California:

No. 2

She had just retired and was lying wide awake, as she thought, when she heard a rustling sound coming from the adjoining bedroom door where her parents were sleeping. She looked toward it and saw the "living image of an aunt of mine," as she reported it.

"The image was standing as if suspended in mid air. She was dressed in a white flimsy sheer costume, her body slowly moving. She was smiling and motioning to me with both hands. Even her gold tooth was natural and bright."

The girl woke her parents and told them. They said she was dreaming, but she insisted she had not had time to go to sleep.

The next morning before daylight a knock came at the door. It was a neighbor who worked at the little telephone office. He had a call saying the aunt had passed away. It was about the time of the girl's experience.

Besides the call cases of Chapter 8 in which the human voice was heard, the auditory hallucinations included others in which the nature of the impressions heard varied over a variety of mechanical sounds such as knocks, raps, footsteps, even shots, as in the next example:

No. 3

A woman in Tampa, Florida, had an uncle in Battle Creek, Michigan. She knew he was having domestic trouble, and on account of it he had told her where he kept his will and that he was leaving everything he had to her.

One morning about 6 a.m. she heard a loud shot. She could find nothing whatever to account for it. At noon that day she received a telegram saying that her uncle had been found shot through the head, and that outsiders had heard a shot at 6 a.m. The death was never solved nor was the will ever found.

In addition to these more familiar modes of hallucination, the few olfactory cases were instances when, for example, smoke was smelled at the time of a distant fire, or the aroma of a familiar pipe or perfume at times that proved significant. There were, in addition, 36 somatic cases (about 15 per cent of all) that also seemed to be hallucinatory. These were not referrable to a single sense modality but involved bodily sensations, although they did not have an ascertainable physical basis. In *Phantasms of the Living*, the author had defined such experiences as instances "where the experience of the percipient is sensory without being an external-seeming affectation of sight, hearing or touch—for instance a physical feeling of illness or malaise." He placed such experiences "with the emotional" (reference 2, page 187). However, by my present standards, experiences seeming to involve only emotions without any information were classified as intuitive while those featuring bodily sensations now seemed to fit more logically under the hallucinatory classification. The following from a woman in California is an instance:

No. 4

In 1955, she had a 23-year-old son serving in the armed forces in Germany. She wrote, "One Thursday morning about four a.m., I jumped out of bed, feeling I was dying. I felt as if blood or something was pouring down from my head choking me and I was trying desperately to get my breath. My husband got up to help me. He tried to get me to the bathroom for some water to drink to stop the terrible choking spasms I seemed to be having. They soon diminished and I grew very weak. I thought I must be really dying. My husband put me down on the bed where I rested but felt so 'all gone.' Then I thought my son had called, saying, 'Oh, Mama help me,' in such anguish.

"Later in the day I went to the doctor for an X-ray of my chest. I thought with such acute pain that something must be wrong. But the doctor could find nothing. That was February 10th and on the 12th we received a telegram saying our son was killed by gunshot in the head at one o'clock on February 10th. There is nine hours difference in time. I feel he called me as it happened, and I heard his groan and felt his dying."

A point of special interest was that all of the types of ESP, clairvoyance, and precognition, as well as telepathy, were represented in these hallucinatory experiences. In older studies, as already mentioned, apparitions had tentatively been considered as involving telepathy. However, now that clairvoyance and precognition are also recognized as types of psi, it was obvious that some apparitions might not necessarily involve telepathy. Instead they would have to be considered as indeterminate in type, general ESP (GESP).

Out of the total 825 hallucinatory experiences, 268, or nearly a third, fell in this GESP category. They were mainly either visual or auditory with a few somatic experiences, as in No. 4 in which the percipient, the mother of the dying soldier, seemed to experience his total death struggle.

I found some basis, however, for the historical impression that hallucinatory experiences tended to be telepathic, for the majority, 431 of the total 825 (or a little over half), could be so classified. And over half of these telepathic experiences were auditory and best illustrated by many of the call cases of Chapter 8. The next most frequent modality was the somatic, in which the entire experience seemed to be confined to the feeling and sensations of the agent, or target person, as in this instance:

No. 5

A man in New York reported that one morning in the preceding November he arose like any other day, shaved, showered and started to dress when suddenly he felt what seemed like a blow on the head although he had not bumped himself and was alone in the room. It was painful and then his mind seemed confused, thoughts jumbled, disconnected, and only with effort did he manage to get dressed and to work. The jumbled confusion in his head continued and he finally became frightened and was about to call the doctor, but then it ceased. It had gone on from about 8:30 until 9 when he then was able to go about his work normally.

A few hours later he had a phone call from California. His mother had had a stroke, a blood clot in the head. She was in a coma. He flew out at once. He met the doctor in the corridor and told him the way he had felt that morning.

The doctor looked a little startled and said, "Those were exactly the symptoms your mother felt." A day or so later when talking to his mother, who at first had had difficulty remembering, but who then had regained her memory, she said she had awakened at 5:30 feeling ill and started for the bathroom when she felt something like a blow on the head, and fell to the floor. Frightened, as she fell, she called his name. With the three hours time difference, apparently the two experiences were simultaneous.

In some instances both a visual and auditory component were present. The combination, however, was relatively infrequent, only 81 or less than a sixth of all being so classifiable. An example of a visual and auditory instance was the following:

No. 6

A man on a business trip through the northwest had arrived in Butte, Montana, when it became necessary to have a tooth extracted. He was in a dentist's chair; the dentist, with needle in hand, was holding it before the patient's face when suddenly he stopped talking, stepped back and went into his laboratory. A few minutes later he came out, stood before the patient and asked him why he hadn't warned him that he was unable to take Novocain.

The patient replied that he didn't know it for sure, although some years before in Chicago he had had a tooth extracted and when the needle had been inserted in his jaw, he had blacked out. It had taken three doctors several hours to bring him back to consciousness. The dentist asked what he did then. He said he had gone back a week later and had it pulled "without any extra frills."

"Well, said the dentist, "here is another you are going to have pulled without any extra frills, and NOW!"—and it was. Half an hour later when the patient was ready to leave, the dentist told him he had just had the "strangest experience in my life." He said that when he stopped talking and went into his laboratory, it was because his mother, who had been dead for twelve years, appeared in his laboratory door and spoke to him. She said, "No, John no. He thinks the narcotic will kill him. He wants to die in your chair so you will be blamed and his family will not lose his life insurance."

The man reporting the case said after discussing the incident with the dentist, that he was convinced that the dentist had never had any other experience of the kind and that he was completely convinced that the dentist had seen his mother and heard those words. Then he added,

"And this is the stinger. The message he received was completely and wholly true and correct. But it had come from *my* brain. No other living person could have given these facts."

The above incident, of course, has overtones for the survival issue which will come up again in the following chapter, but it also presents a situation comparable to that discussed earlier, for the dentist as the percipient, could have obtained his information by ESP and hallucinated it into the form of a warning from his mother.

In addition to the GESP and telepathy cases, 66, or a little more than a sixth of the total number of hallucinatory cases, I had to consider as probably of the clairvoyant type. The majority of these, 46 in all, were auditory hallucinations. No. 3 above, in which the person presumably heard a "significant" shot, was one example, with a few that were hallucinatory in various other ways. An instance of the latter, apparently olfactory, is reported by a woman from California:

No. 7

In 1957, she was in the early months of pregnancy, half ill and with two small children to care for, when her husband, as she said, "seemed to go wild." For about two years he drank all the time and he would abuse her so violently that she feared for her own life and while still pregnant, that of the unborn child, as well as the other children. He allowed her no money so she couldn't leave. She could only watch for him to come home and hide until he was asleep, then slip back into the house and get what rest she could before he wakened. Desperate, she considered suicide, but couldn't leave her children to the fate that would have meant.

Worn out one night, she propped herself up in bed determined to watch out the window for his return. But she fell asleep and about 4 a.m. suddenly found herself awake, not knowing

what had awakened her. Then she got a whiff of beer so she slipped out of the house to hide. He didn't come and she decided she
imagined it and slipped back to bed. This was repeated several
times, each time the smell of beer a little stronger, and finally he
came home about a half an hour after she had smelled the beer.
It happened so many times that finally she started going to bed
confident that the smell would awaken her before he returned,
and thus got much needed rest.

As she added, "It is my belief that it was God answering
my frantic prayers. I was desperate and without this help, I'm
sure I would have done something I would have been sorry for."

The remaining cases, 60 in all, involved precognition. The
majority of these, 32, were auditory, and frequently call cases,
often bringing a warning of coming danger, as in this instance:

No. 8

A number of tourists, Labor Day 1920, were waiting their
turns at Niagara Falls to board the *Maid of the Mist.* One girl
was about to step on the plank when she heard the voice of her
dead sister saying to her, "Don't go, don't go." It was as clear as
if her sister had been standing next to her, but she had not been
thinking of her sister for days. Along with the voice the girl felt a
pain in her right arm and leg, and as if paralyzed, she watched
the ship pull out.

A short while later, the *Maid of the Mist* returned
bringing in some injured passengers. It was the first time an accident had occurred to the ship. High wind and waves had
separated the mast which fell and cut the faces of some of the
passengers.

The rest of the precognitive hallucinatory cases were
visual, somatic or olfactory, and most of them were warnings of
coming danger. Further discussion of this kind of case will come
up in the following chapters.

In general, then, the survey of hallucinatory cases showed
them indeed to be a varied lot. While telepathy seemed to be the
most frequent type, it was by no means the only one. The variety
of types and of modalities showed the form itself to be adapted

to a wide range of situations and variations. Just as with dreams and intuitions, the total kinds of hallucinatory cases give a wide perspective over situations that could be expressed in this way and show that the situation itself does not dictate the form. As with the call cases of Chapter 8, it would seem that the form of the experience must depend on the personality of the person having the experience. Since hallucinatory experiences made up only 10 per cent of all the cases in the collection, the suggestion is that only a few people experience the hallucinatory form even without psi, while practically everyone of course can dream or have an intuition.

However, mixed in among all the varied types and modalities of the hallucinatory experiences were those special apparitions that in the early history of parapsychology stood out so prominently because of the bearing they seemed to have on the survival question. Against the background of the accumulating knowledge of psi in the 1950's, the question whether such experiences still had special significance was the next one I had to consider.

Chapter 13

Apparitions — Old and New

"We come now to examples of the most important class of all, Class A — externalized impressions — occurring to persons who are up and manifestly in the full possession of their waking senses. Of this field, the most important examples are visual impressions or apparitions" (reference 2, page 208).

In those words, in 1886, in *Phantasms of the Living*, the old view of psychic hallucinatory experiences was clearly expressed. The reason why they were considered "the most important class" of all psi experiences then was summarized briefly in connection with hallucinatory experiences that occur at the time of death of the agent: "... there is difficulty in understanding an abnormal exercise of psychic energy at such seasons. The explanation may possibly be found in the idea of a wider consciousness and a more complete self which finds, in what we call life, very imperfect conditions of manifestation, and recognizes in death not a cessation but a liberation of energy."

Perhaps if one has never seen an apparition one cannot fully realize how great a mystery such a phenomenon can pose. To see a figure that "isn't there" has in all ages impressed the percipient as unexplainable in ordinary terms and therefore mysterious, even miraculous and in the past (and largely still today), with no idea of a normal process that could produce such a manifestation, the individual was likely to be completely overwhelmed. Unfortunately, but understandably, the conviction that a figure *was* seen was not so convincing to others as to the percipient — few friends or relatives believed it was what it seemed. It must have been a dream, perhaps imagination induced by suggestion, or even a fabrication.

144

As the above quotations show, in the nineteenth century the early psychical researchers thought they saw a possible meaning for such occurrences. They, of course, knew of no normal process to explain them, except possibly telepathy if it existed. Naturally, apparitions then were of special interest to the members of the committee appointed by the Society for Psychical Research to collect cases that could give evidence of telepathy. It should always be remembered too that this committee was not trying primarily to understand the process by which apparitions are produced (although Gurney in *Phantasms* undertook an explanation of apparitions). Instead, as mentioned in Chapter 3, the immediate objective was to obtain proof of the occurrence of telepathy, on which it seemed depended the interpretation of apparitions of the dying and the dead as evidence of post mortem survival.

The first question then was whether apparitional experiences did actually occur as reported. It was a question that called for the most careful documentation. If the accuracy of the reports could be established, the unspoken assumption seems to have been that then the experience could be interpreted at face value and be evidence for survival.

As mentioned in Chapter 2, other evidence on the same point had appeared to come from mediumistic utterances, cases in which special "sensitives" seemed to give messages from the dead. In the mediumistic studies the first objective was to show that the medium could have no normal knowledge of any correct facts he or she reported; that no sensory leakage of any kind had occurred. After that, the question was how these messages could be interpreted. This was still an unsettled question when the Parapsychology Laboratory was established. A direct experimental attack on it was made there in the 1930's involving a well-known medium, Mrs. Eileen J. Garrett (reference 11, page 308).

Carefully controlled mediumistic sessions were held with Mrs. Garrett and they showed that she had given correct information about people acting as "sitters," of whom she could have no possible sensory information. Her reputation as an unusual medium was thus confirmed under laboratory methods developed especially to guard against sensory leakage. This involved objective evaluation of the messages she gave for sitters whom she did not know and whose identity she never learned.

Mrs. Garrett was also tested for ESP when she was in trance as well as under the standard conditions used for other subjects. Her regular ESP test scores were quite high. They compared well with those of the better student subjects and showed that Mrs. Garrett was a person gifted with considerable ESP ability. Even though the messages which she produced in trance purported to come from an external, presumably spiritual source, her success on the regular ESP tests showed her so capable of ESP itself that it was reasonable to assume she also might have secured the mediumistic material by the mundane ESP ability rather than from a deceased personality. No way has yet been found in mediumistic research to distinguish between the two possible sources.

In scientific research a technique that can yield results which have two or more possible interpretations is not good enough. A problem cannot be considered solved if only an either-or conclusion can be reached. This dilemma has confronted the techniques for studying survival to date and has delayed any well designed attack on the problem. At the same time, it seems that if the full reach and meaning of psi ability in living persons could be discovered it would probably throw light on the best approach to the survival problem as well. Thus, a sort of stalemate developed regarding the research on the survival question. The methods of ESP research were already developed, so that progress could be made on that front, while the other topic had to wait for a satisfactory method. This was in general the outlook at the Parapsychology Laboratory in 1956 which I summed up in an article on hallucinatory experiences, saying, "In the course of recent decades the attempt to solve the problem of survival by direct experimental attack has been almost entirely abandoned, leaving in its place the objective of first securing an understanding of the living personality through an extended investigation of its hitherto unrecognized capacities" (reference 20, page 231.

The years of experimental work at the Parapsychology Laboratory and elsewhere by which the nature of the psi process was gradually being disclosed had the objective of securing a more complete understanding of the human personality. My own case study project from the start had explicitly shared that objective. But now it was producing what seemed to be a discrepancy between the older concept of the nature of apparitions and the newer view drawn from the hallucinatory experiences in the Duke Collection, in particular from the visual experiences involving the figures of dying or deceased human beings. The discrepancy specifically involved the role of the agent and the percipient in apparitional experiences.

The meaning for survival which was earlier seen in apparitions of the dying or the dead was based unmistakably on the idea that in such cases the agent was in some way the active party, that he "came" to the percipient who was a more or less passive receiver. It was this presumed activity of the deceased agent that could show that the spirit was separable from the body and did not terminate with it.

But in the telepathy study (Chapter 11) and in the analysis of the hallucinatory experiences of the Duke Collection (Chapter 12) the weight of evidence had suggested that the percipient was generally the active party, regardless of the part the agent did or did not play.

The next study I undertook concerned the process that produces apparitional experiences (reference 22). The question specifically concerned the role of the agent and the experiencing percipient. I wanted to observe whether it appeared to be the same as in telepathy-like experiences that did not involve the dying or the dead. I could at least compare the probable role of deceased agents with the role of living ones and whether they seemed to be significantly different. Such a comparison, however, was difficult. Even in the telepathy cases, I found that the basis of differentiation between roles depended mainly on situations in which the agent and percipient were strangers to each other. But now it was all the more difficult because in the cases with dying and deceased agents the two were nearly always close relatives or friends.

The first step, however, seemed to be to separate the cases according to the state of the agent, A: living, B: dying, and C: dead, to see if any group characteristics might offer a basis for comparison. This separation resulted in Group A's having 444 cases, which were nearly half of all. Case No. 11 in Chapter 7 is an example. It is the experience in which a daughter "saw" her mother being held up in the parking lot. Group B included 297, nearly a third of the entire number. Examples are cases No. 3 and 4 in Chapter 12. No. 3 is the instance when a woman in Florida heard a shot about the time her uncle in Michigan was killed. No. 4 was the case of the mother who seemed to suffer the physical symptoms of her son as he died after being shot in the head. Finally, in Group C the remaining 88 cases were those with *deceased* agents. Examples, also in Chapter 12, are No. 6, the case of the dentist whose deceased mother seemed to warn him of a dangerous situation involving a patient, and No. 8, the case of the girl about to board *The Maid of the Mist* at Niagara Falls, who was warned by an auditory hallucination in her dead sister's voice not to go on the boat.

When searching for an angle from which to compare these three groups, and taking them in reverse order, those with deceased agents first, it was evident at once that the group was not only the smallest but also the most restricted in type and modality. Although the cases were telepathy-like in that they involved two persons, potentially an agent and percipient, the type could only be labelled GESP because the question to be determined was whether a deceased person can act an an active agent. In a few instances a suggestion of futurity was involved, as in a warning of impending danger, but the situations were not distinct enough to permit a definite precognition classification. In modality, these cases were all either visual or auditory or a combination of the two.

The cases of Group B were limited of course to situations in which the percipient's experience was considered to have occurred at the time the agent was dying. This eliminated the precognitive type of experience from this group. They were also mainly visual or auditory experiences but with a few somatic instances like No. 4 in Chapter 12, above, the case of the mother who seemed to feel her dying son's sensations.

The group A cases, with their living agents, were not only the most numerous, but also the most varied. They included all types and modalities. But in order to compare cases in this group with those of Group C, of course only those comparable in type and form to those of C could be used. It therefore was necessary to exclude all but the telepathy-like cases (telepathy and GESP) and only those in the visual and auditory modalities. But since I had already examined the call cases in Chapter 8, to simplify the study I decided to omit them from all of the groups, leaving only visual or visual and auditory experiences to be compared. After all these eliminations, 45 cases remained in Group A, 114 in Group B and 49 in Group C, a total of 208 altogether.

In working over this material, I had noticed an outstanding variation in the degree of realism of imagery. It varied all the way from one extreme so realistic that the percipient did not at once recognize that the person seen was not actually present, to other effects that could only be construed as "signs" of the person or event to which the percipient associated them. And so I thought it might be possible that the three groups would show meaningful differences in the degree of realism of their imagery.

In Group A, the imagery in 16 cases was so realistic that the experiencing person did not at all realize that it was hallucinatory. An extreme instance is the following:

No. 1

A college girl off at school was called home quite unexpectedly by the tragic death of her younger brother. She was able to get the next train which should have brought her home by midnight. But the train was delayed and the one with which it should have connected at the junction city had gone on. Knowing no one, she scarcely knew what to do. But then out of the crowd emerged a close personal friend of her older brother. He said, "There is no other train tonight. There's a good hotel across the street. I'll take you over and tell them to call you in time for the five o'clock in the morning."

As she reported to the Laboratory, "This he did exactly. I sat in that hotel room full of grief and loneliness and grateful that this friend had happened to be there. The next afternoon he came to our house and I said, "In all my life I never was so grateful to see anyone as I was to see you last night."

He said, "But I didn't see you — I was coming to that same junction to meet you as I knew you'd be coming in on that train and I knew you couldn't make connections. But I never got there. My train was late too.

"I knew this young man well. I have not the slightest doubt that it was he who helped me. What I don't know is how?"

In each of these 16 cases as in that example, the agent (the young man), was thinking strongly of the percipient (the girl at the railroad station), but apparently was unaware that he had appeared to her, nor did he give any evidence that he even intended to do so. Presumably, then, the explanation was that the percipient, in each case, had an ESP message of the agent's thought and responded by projecting the appropriate hallucinatory effect. While other personalities might have responded to the ESP message by a significant dream or intuition, for these individuals it was by an hallucination. The resulting impression was as if, unconsciously, the percipient had created a little drama in which, as it were, she said to herself, "the agent is thinking of me so strongly that I can see him." The experience then was a simple one-character dramatization and as far as ESP is concerned, no more surprising than a dream covering the same situation would have been. Since in the experience the agent appeared in an environment where the percipient could have expected him to be and one which overlapped with her own, nothing about the situation actually seemed unusual. The result was a realistic reproduction of the reality and the percipient rather than the agent obviously created it.

Then, in 23 other cases of Group A, the imagery was only semi-realistic. That is, the figure itself was realistic, but not the place where it was seen, as in this example:

No. 2

The husband of a woman in Colorado was in Denver Veteran's Hospital very ill with pneumonia. To complicate the situation, he was allergic to drugs and his wife was very concerned and worried about him. She left him at the end of the visiting hour for the added strain of notifying relatives and caring for their small son. She knew that his condition was grave still, although it had been thought that he was improving. Completely exhausted, she fell asleep about 10:30 p.m.

About 2 a.m., she found herself sitting upright in bed. She was looking at her husband standing in the doorway of the room, But he could not possibly be there. As she said in reporting the occurrence, "I felt like a complete fool, but I couldn't get back to sleep so I called the hospital. Sheepishly, I told the floor nurse what had happened so she graciously said to wait while she checked up on him."

Minutes, then half and hour went by, when all she could hear was the sound of running feet, wheeling carts, etc. But finally the nurse came to the phone out of breath, but happy. It seemed that when she went to the sick room the patient was in a crisis. He was choking. The delay had been while the nurse got two doctors and another nurse. It took all four to keep the patient alive. The nurse said if the wife had not called, by the time the intern made the next check it would have been too late.

In these semi-realistic cases the percipient, as the wife in that instance, knew at once that the agent was not actually where seen because it was impossible. The environment of the percipient and the known environment of the agent were different. Memory could create the figure realistically but because of the circumstances not in a realistic place. In these cases the percipients, of course, projected their own mental constructs, again one-character dramatizations, within their own frames of reference. But they knew the agents could not be there. And, on the other hand, whether or not the agents were thinking of the percipients, they were not attempting to project themselves or their thought to them. Again, the initiative for the experience must have come from the percipient who then dramatized the impression into his or her own visual perspective.

In the remaining cases, the percipients' experiences were entirely unrealistic and in no outward way resembled the agents'. The percipients however felt that their experiences applied to the specific agents even without an ostensible reason for doing so.

No. 3

A Canadian soldier, a farm boy, 21 years old, was stationed in Toronto. He went to a movie one afternoon and the girl in the next seat began to touch his knee under cover of her rain coat. He got up and moved to a vacant row of seats, but soon there she was again and she whispered a provocative invitation to him.

He was shocked even though he had heard barracks room stories. Confused, he asked her if she wanted some supper, and, of course, she said yes. So he took her to a nice restaurant and as her advances continued, he decided he might as well forget his morals and scruples. Just then a blaze of light enveloped their table. It seemed to him as if every light bulb was suddenly 1000 candle power. But no one else seemed to notice. The light apparently was visible only to him. It was about 8 p.m.

As that happened his view of the girl changed. She lost all attraction for him. Cool and passionless, when the meal was finished he "saw her home," but her entreaties for him to come into her flat were only amusing as he left her and went back to the barracks.

About a week later, he got a letter from his mother. She said, "About milking time last Monday I had the most frightening feeling that you were in great danger of some kind. I prayed and prayed and suddenly all my nervousness vanished and I was sure you were safe. Please tell me where you were at 5 a.m. prairie time and what you were doing."

Apparently it was at the moment of blazing light in the restaurant that the mother's fears were lifted. But she knew nothing of the blazing light. As the agent of the telepathic message, she did not send or create that impression. It must then have been the percipient's (the son's) own creation.

Turning next to the Group B cases, the so-called death coincidences, they too proved to be of the same realistic, semi-realistic and unrealistic forms as were those of Group A. In the realistic, the agents were seen in a place where the percipients might have expected them to be; in the semi-realistic, in a place where the percipients knew they could not be, and in the third, the hallucinated effect was not the person of the agent, but an unreal one which to the percipient represented the agent.

The only difference between these Group B cases and those of Group A was that in these the agent was dying instead of undergoing any of the varied crises of the agents in Group A. And since the timing in such experiences is necessarily inexact, the percipients could have had their experiences while the agents were still living. The Group B cases thus seemed not to be essentially different from those of Group A, the degree of realism depending on whether or not the hallucinated figure was seen within the percipient's ordinary frame of reference.

The older view of these Group B cases would have been to consider them as carrying the same meaning for survival as those of Group C in which the agents were already deceased. But now it seemed clear that they more rightfully belonged with the Group A cases. In the earlier time, when no one had actual knowledge of psi as an ability of the living, the explanation hinted at in the quotation from *Phantasms* cited at the beginning of this chapter was that at death "a wider consciousness and a more complete self" is achieved. The person who was no longer living was, of course, not limited to the sensory range then assumed to limit the living and therefore it was possible to assume that unusual extrasensory faculties might be unleashed at the point of death and afterwards. And it well may have been that because death coincidences were striking and unforgettable, they were reported relatively frequently. On the other hand, the experiences involving living agents (which in this later more unselected Duke Collection were the most frequently reported of all) did not raise the suggestion of survival and so no doubt in the earlier days they were easier to overlook or ignore. Some such explanation could account for the differing frequencies of reported kinds of hallucinatory experiences in the older compared with the newer collection.

The situation in the 88 cases of Group C was complicated by the fact that in all but five instances the percipient already knew that the agent was dead. In those five nothing betrayed the fact that the figure was not actually "there." No. 4 is one of these cases.

No. 4

A woman in California went to the local hardware store where she often traded to get a fishing license just before the season closed at the end of February. The elderly clerk who usually waited on her was not behind the counter as usual, however, but was wheeling a hand truck to the back of the store. She called a greeting to him but he apparently did not hear her. The clerk behind the counter took her order.

A month or so later she went to the store again and not seeing her old friend, inquired about him. She was told he had passed away in January. She said it must have been February because she had seen him when she bought her license. But no. She was shown a newspaper clipping of his funeral notice taped to the counter.

She was so upset, she left the store and did not shop there again for years.

No reason appeared in any of these five to indicate that the agents necessarily had anything to do with the experience since the percipients could have projected the figures as one-character dramatizations just as they obviously had done in the cases above with living agents.

But in the remaining 83 cases, since the percipient already knew that the agent was dead the criterion of degree of realism could not be used directly because to see a person known to be dead could never be considered realistic. However, since that criterion had depended on the percipient's knowledge of the location of the agent, the cases here could still be divided on the basis of the locations of the two.

On this criterion in 19 instances the customary locations of the two individuals overlapped. (This was true also for the five instances like No. 4 in which the percipient did not know that the agent was dead.) The situations varied considerably as to the relations of the agent and percipient. In some they had never known each other but the agent, when alive, had inhabited the present environment of the percipient, or in other words the per-cipient was then present presumably in what had been the life-time environment of the agent. This produced situations typical of haunting cases, as for instance No. 5.

No. 5

Two elderly couples in Vancouver had gone for a picnic on a woodsy spot beside a stream and afterwards the two women went for a stroll. Presently around a bend in the road, they saw a large house with a wide veranda around it. It looked deserted and so they went up on the veranda and peeked into a window. To their suprise they saw an elderly woman walk through a door inside the house and cross to a rocking chair where she sat down and began to rock.

They crept away ashamed at having peeked into an occupied house. But they thought it strange that the red dress the woman wore was a very old-fashioned one. The following week, again after a picnic, they walked up the same road intending to walk past the house. This time a young woman and a child were near the house. So they stopped and apologized for looking in the week before and inquired about the "grandmother" they had seen.

Immediately the young woman asked, "How was she dressed and in what color?" When they described the dress she said, "You know, nobody lives in this house but my husband and myself and the children. But so many people have told us that they have seen this old lady in the house and have described the clothing as you have." (Upon further inquiry no one was found who recalled such an old lady having lived there.)

In a final 16 cases with deceased agents, the percipients knew the agents and knew they were dead. The criterion of overlapping environments therefore lost significance since the agents no matter where they might have been located in life were, of course, hallucinated within the percipients' visual perspective. These cases were the most convincing of the traditional kind of experience bearing on survival, for in them the deceased person seemed to "come" to the percipient and to bring a message.

The nature of the messages showed an element not clearly observable in any of the other kinds of hallucinatory experiences. That element was the seemingly strong motivation of the agents to communicate, as in:

No. 6

A man who owned a tow boat died and his 17-year-old son took over the running of the boat to help support the family. Every few trips a certain part of the engine would break. One night getting home about 2 a.m., the son was lying in bed trying to figure out what caused the breakdowns.

His bedroom door was closed but he saw his father enter through it and he came and sat on the bed. He said, "You're worred about the engine, aren't you, son?" And the young man agreed. The father then told him to adjust a certain part and his troubles would be over. The son got up out of bed, drove the five miles to the boat, carried out the suggestion, and that part never broke again.

The messages in all these cases were either advice or warnings to the percipients. The initiative of the agent, consequently, looked quite obvious. But in each case, the agent was a person who, in life, would have warned or advised the percipient as, for instance, did the father in No. 6.

However, by the same token, the percipients were persons experienced in being warned or advised by the agents when those agents were alive. And in these cases, the percipients were in need of the advice, as in the above experience, or would have wanted the warning of the impending danger. But in either situation the necessary information could have been available to the percipient by ESP. If so, it could have been dramatized by the percipient into the form of a message from the agent, the personality who, in life, might have performed just that helpful function. And so, even though the motivation of the agents appeared obvious, still the percipients were interested in and needed the information. Therefore, the possibility that they were responsible for getting it by the projection of rather simple one-character dramatizations could not be ruled out.

The study thus showed the weight of evidence as questioning the old assumption that the agent was the active party. In the cases with living agents, the percipients seemed almost necessarily to have created the hallucinatory effect themselves. If so, it was simply the form or vehicle by which psi information was evidenced in their consciousness. In spite of appearances in some instances, I found nothing to conflict with this idea in the cases with deceased agents.

However, it seemed possible that the method of approach I had used might not have done full justice to the older explanation, especially in those instances like No. 6 in which a deceased agent seemed to help, sometimes to warn, the percipient and seemed to show strong motivation to communicate. To explain them it was necessary to suppose that the percipient must have created a more involved fantasy than in the others. If the others were one-character creations, these involved two characters, as one might say, the deceased individual and the percipient whose crisis was involved. In No. 6 it would have been as if the son, getting the information by ESP, would have said to himself, "My father would have told me this and it is as if I can see and hear him telling it to me."

Or in a few examples, the response might take the form of a psychokinetic (PK) effect instead of a dramatization, as in this case:

No. 7

A young woman had been recently widowed and was still in the first agonies of grief. Her husband had been killed suddenly. She and her sister had been talking about it one day and afterward she felt she just had to know about him and "the great beyond."

After her sister went to her room, she threw herself on the bed and cried, "Oh Glen, Glen, if you are still alive somewhere, please, please let me know. Reach me someway. Give me some sign." And she prayed. "Dear God, help me to know. Help me to be sure."

As she finished speaking, a note was struck loudly on the piano downstairs, a pause, then the same note twice again. She thought one of the children who had been playing outside might have come in, but then her sister called and asked if she had come down to the living room.

"No, I'm upstairs."

"I thought so." Then her sister went into the living room, and called up to her. "I heard a note on the piano, a pause, then the same note twice. There is no one here and I know I heard the piano." Her sister found the note on the piano which she said still rang in her ears.

"It was the same one that was still ringing in my mind," she reported. Then I told her I had just been praying for a sign. She laughingly said, "Well, you were asking if he were A-live and A-ll right and the note we heard was A. That means he is."

Again a two-character effect. It would have been as if the percipient said to herself, in effect, "My husband would want to assure me. I must have him to do so by sounding the piano key."

Sometimes a warning of danger to the percipient took the form of a visual apparition, as in the next case, No. 8:

No. 8

A woman in New Jersey reported an occurrence that happened on her parents' wedding day, of which her mother had kept a memoir. The young couple had driven though mountains to a town in Utah for a wedding dinner. While there the husband was given a telegram stating that his wife's mother had died.

He did not tell his wife about the death, but only that they would have to return at once. Although it was dark and overcast, they were given a fresh team and started on the long drive back.

They were deep in the mountain area when a furious storm broke. From her mother's memoirs, the daughter, reporting to the Parapsychology Laboratory, quoted, "The rain came down in torrents amidst deafening bursts of thunder and piercing flashes of lightning. I was horribly frightened and somehow in the darkness we got off the road. Suddenly the horses lunged backwards and stopped still. At that moment a blaze of lightning emblazoned the scene and I saw my mother standing in front of those horses with her arms outstretched. We were at the very brink of a precipice which dropped straight down to the river far below.

"Now, I do not think this is to be an idle dream or fancy. I did not then know my mother was dead, but just as firmly as I have ever believed anything in my whole life I believe that Mother — in spirit — stopped those horses, thus saving our lives."

The daughter, in reporting her mother's story of the warning, emphasized that in all the time she had heard her mother recall the experience, she never once deviated from the account as given.

Another two-character dramatization, which seemingly had overtones for survival as interpreted by the percipient. She did not consider the possibility that she could have had the same experience if her mother had been living. Nor did she consider the fact that the horses might have become aware of the danger and "lunged backward and stopped still," without any kind of human warning.

However, the reason I made these distinctions regarding the complexity of dramatizations on the part of the percipients was that some of the experiences with deceased agents were still more complicated. They were three-character dramatizations, the third person usually being one in whom both the agent and the percipient were interested, as in this example:

No. 9

The father of an 18-year-old girl in training at a local hospital was taken very ill, so she was allowed to come home and care for him until his death. In the course of this period, she became even closer to him than before.

One night about three months after his death, the girl awoke from a sound sleep, she thought, and, as she reported, "Very much at ease, and I knew my father was going to come to me." She waited, she said, for about a minute, and then he stood in the doorway, smiled and said,

"Don't worry, Caroline, everything will be all right. Mama is going to the hospital, but she will be fine."

She called to him, but he smiled and left. She was very confident that she had actually seen him. At the time, neither she nor her mother knew that her mother would need to go to the hospital, but about two months later, she did in fact have to go and a very serious operation had to be performed. She recovered from it completely and was still living when her daughter reported the experience.

In some of the three-character cases, the situation was even more complicated and in ways too diverse to generalize here. But, after careful analysis, I realized that all of them still were open to two possible interpretations: first, that the deceased person did influence the situation and cause the percipient to have the specific hallucinatory experience or second, that the percipient had ESP information of the situation of the third party — the mother in the case above — and it was manifested in consciousness dramatically by having the agent (the deceased father) "come" and report to her.

This second interpretation was in line with the impression of all the cases of Groups A and B. The dramatizing ability of the mind varies greatly among individuals, both on the con-

scious and the unconscious level. This, of course, is shown quite
clearly in the variations in complexity of dreams, and dreams after all are not entirely different in origin from the dramatizations
of hallucinatory experiences. This will be discussed further in
Chapter 14. One observation to make here is that the state of
mind of a percipient, like the person in No. 9 above, may actually
by removed only slightly from that of dreaming. It may bear
repeating that the distinction is in the kind of imagery. When
the person thinks he or she is awake, the imagery tends to be like
that of sense experience, and this, of course, is different from
that of actual dreaming.

This final study of hallucinatory experiences thus did not
lead to a definite conclusion. It did show that hallucinatory experiences, when they involve someone the percipient knows is
dead, usually show a more complicated level of dramatization than
when the percipient is unaware that the agent is dead, for the
three-character dramas only appeared among the cases with
deceased agents.

Here again, two explanations are possible. One, that such
dramatization requires the influence of the discarnate, the other
that only those persons whose unconscious dramatizing ability is
great enough to create this kind of hallucinatory experience have
them.

And so, the question must be left. The survival question
never could be settled by an anecdotal method such as this one.
But I hope these studies serve to show that if the deceased do
play a part in experiences such as these of Group C, it cannot be
so determined because of the apparitional form, which in any
event is only one of those by which psi may be expressed in consciousness.

* * * * * *

Addendum on Survival

In 1959 a symposium on the question of post-mortem survival was held at the Duke Parapsychology Laboratory. Its purpose
was to give a critical examination of the research to date dealing
with the problem.

I was asked to prepare a paper for this symposium

covering the evaluation of spontaneous psychic experiences that seemed to bear on survival (reference 24). Accordingly, I attempted to formulate a set of criteria, in light of the knowledge of psi now available, for judging the relative value for the survival issue of such experiences.

In consequence, I tried to grade the cases that bore on the question. This time I decided to use the criterion of the relative level of motivation that could be ascribed to the percipients versus the agents. The supposition for this was that the stronger the agent's motivation to communicate to the percipient seemed to be in relation to the presumed motivation of the percipient to get the information, the stronger would be the bearing of the case on the survival hypothesis.

As a result, four different levels or grades of bearing seemed to cover all the possibilities. There were on hand for the study at the time 258 cases with deceased agents. In some instances it was clear that the percipients and agents would have been about equally interested or uninterested in communicating. When this seemed to be the situation, the case would have no compelling weight for survival since the percipient could have received the information himself by psi. Such would have been true in cases like that of the woman in the hardware store, No. 4 above, when no strong motivation could be ascribed to either party, the experience being like a casual meeting between acquaintances. If any difference could be ascribed, it would probably be in favor of the percipient because she expected to see the clerk. At any rate, such an experience would not have any great bearing on the survival question. The same judgment would also hold if the two persons were closely involved emotionally, as in the hearing of the piano note of No. 7. Presumably, the husband and wife would be equally motivated, and therefore, that case would also belong in the same category, Grade I.

The next category, Grade II, included all instances in which motivations would have been strong for both parties, but that of the agent could be considered stronger. The distinction between these cases and those of Grade I was difficult, but can best be illustrated by instances when the percipient was a child, and the agent was a parent or other protector of the child, as in the case given in an earlier chapter of the daughter who was saved

from being run over by a street car by hearing her deceased
mother call, "Harriet, Harriet, look out!"

Then came the Grade III cases in which the agent's interest was very strong, the percipient's weak. One example is No.
10.

No. 10

A Mrs. A. dreamed of a former neighbor's son and
thought he asked her to take a message to his mother. The
message was nothing significant and as Mrs. A. awakened she
thought it a silly dream since the boy would not need anyone to
take a message to his mother when he could tell her himself.

Some time later, Mrs. A. met her former neighbor and
asked about her son because, as Mrs. A. told her, he had figured
in a recent dream of hers. Mrs. A learned then that the boy had
died some time earlier. His mother felt that the dream had been
an attempt by him to communicate with her.

A final Grade IV concerned cases in which the agent's
motive would be considered very strong and the effect one which
presumably the living percipient could not produce. Four cases
were tentatively placed in this category mainly for illustrative
value, for each one was a solitary instance of its own particular
feature. Since the case method I was using was based on numbers
rather than on the value of individual instances, these four could
serve only as illustrations of kinds of experiences that could speak
strongly for survival if they were ever supported by adequate
numbers of similar instances. And even these four cases varied in
their possible strength as evidence for survival. The best of the
four, No. 11 below, was one submitted by a college teacher to
whom it had been offered in fulfillment of a class assignment.
My attempt to reach the student and possibly get verification
was not successful. But this is the account:

No. 11

"When I was a boy of four, and before I knew anything of
school or alphabet, I got hold of a call pad one evening while my
mother was working at her desk in our hotel, and was busy
making marks on it. This kept up for three or four small sheets

of paper, when Mother, noticing what I was playing with, told me to stop and play with something else. I put away my pencil, folded the papers I had written on and stuck them in my mother's mailbox and went away, the incident forgotten.

"The next morning Mother found the papers in her box and was about to throw them away when the day clerk, who had taken shorthand in night school, told her they looked like shorthand. Mother explained that they were just my scribblings, but the clerk insisted on taking the papers to her teacher for examination. They were shorthand. The entire scribbling made sense and there was not one mistake or extra mark on the papers. It was written in the old fashioned square-type shorthand, something I had never heard of, let alone had the slightest idea of how to write. It was a message to my mother. It started, 'Dearest Beloved,' and spoke of a letter that had not been posted. It was an urgent letter concerning my father's safe deposit box in the East.

"My father had died two weeks before. He had died in New York while my mother and I were in Oregon. His death had been sudden and mother hadn't known the location of the box. Moreover, my father had always called my mother 'Dearest Beloved,' and while he was a young man had learned shorthand, the old-fashioned method. Mother still has those pieces of paper, and the message has been translated by other people and is actually there. It was years later, when I was old enough to understand, that Mother told me the story and showed me the papers."

Naturally, experience in Grade I and II had no compelling weight as survival evidence. The majority of the cases fell into these two categories, 181 cases in Grade I and 43 in Grade II. The 30 cases in Grade III could be interpreted as fairly strong evidence of survival, but still within the range of psi of the living (not limited by space or time). The four Grade IV cases seemed to bear most strongly on the survival question and constituted the most conclusive kind of evidence that could be given by the spontaneous cases in the collection.

The decreasing numbers of cases going from Grade I to IV showed that the value which can be ascribed to spontaneous cases on the survival question is much less, now that psi in the living has been established. For although all of these cases could involve the deceased person to some degree, their value as evidence of survival thus turned out to be minimal. Also, in 1960 when the study was published, the possibility could not be excluded that succeeding years might bring new cases that could be classified as Grade IV. Such has not happened. As far as case material is concerned, then, from my collection at least, it must be concluded that its relevance on the survival question is problematic at best.

Chapter 14

The Psi Process in ESP

"The first thing to be noticed is that paranormal cognition is not a conscious process. No percipient of telepathy, clairvoyance, or precognition has even been consciously aware of a telepathic, clairvoyant, or precognitive *process* at work within him. No one has been able to say: Now I am conscious that a telepathic message is coming to me from origin X; or, now I am aware of the process of clairvoyantly perceiving an object Y; or, now I am conscious that knowledge of a future event Z is reaching me. It is always the *product* and never the *process* of paranormal cognition of which the subject is aware. In this respect, paranormal cognition resembles normal sense perception and also memory" (reference 37, pages 67-68).

Dating back to the 1940's, this quotation from the English psychical researcher, G.N.M. Tyrrell shows that he (more than those who preceded him) was concerned especially with the process by which ESP impressions, or paranormal cognitions, as he preferred to call them, are created. He not only recognized their unconscious origin and resemblance to other psychological processes, but also that the process that produced them could be thought of, in general, as occurring in two rather distinct stages, even though it functioned as one.

Tyrrell considered the first stage to be parapsychological, the second entirely psychological. In Stage I, information from the external world was received on an unconscious mental level without the use of the senses. In Stage II, that information was "processed" by the use of mental constructs, or "vehicles," as he called them, which permitted the information to be recognized in consciousness.

165

At the time Tyrrell wrote, the different vehicles had never been concisely specified, but were recognized only as widely differing phenomena covering the kinds of experiences generally called psychic. It was soon after this (1956) that my own study (Chapter 7) indicated that only four basically different vehicles or forms were used.

As the years passed, and as I have already noted, investigators in the laboratory, as well as Tyrrell, had come to recognize that psi operates unconsciously. In my own study, in trying to understand the process that produces an ESP experience, the first assumption had to be that somehow the particular objective event must become "accessible" to the person, or the *psyche*, as one might say, must come in contact with the item of information that will be the subject matter of the person's psi experience. Somehow the experiencer selects that specific item or event from all the world's events for the fact of psi experiences means that such selection does occur.

But how then can such selection be accounted for? One possibility would appear to be that all the world's events are in some sense "accessible" to the human mind and that like a search light it scans the horizon to pick up and select those items that are of personal interest or concern and disregards all others. This supposition implies a potential omniscience, an idea which would seem too startling to be easily accepted if any less grandiose one could be conceived.

The other possibility in Stage I is that the only items accessible are those that have some degree of affinity or relevance for the percipient. This idea, too, seems difficult to envisage for it implies a connection between the psyche of the percipient and the event for which it would seem difficult to account. Besides that, often the item that is selected is only one of many that would seem of equal or greater concern or interest to the percipient. And so, both theories raise questions as difficult as the one they are designed to answer.

A recent résumé of philosophical attempts over past years to come to grips with this central problem of the ESP process has been made by the English psychologist Alan Gauld (reference 1). But these attempts yield no easy explanation either. So, at the present time, this Stage I, the essential parapsychological stage of the process is still unexplained and without even an adequate theory; none of the alternatives settle the question but instead only introduce further unknowns. The presumption at least seems safe, however, that the particular event is selected because it is of interest to the person (although how slight that interest may be will be demonstrated in Chapter 17). At any rate, the information about this event then constitutes the meaning, the message of the ESP experience. This Stage I of Tyrrell's, thus, is an inferential but necessary and wholly parapsychological stage.

Stage II, however, is then a psychological one which takes up where Stage I ends. The message from Stage I must be processed by the use of the mental constructs or vehicles by which it arrives at the level of conscious attention, where it can be recognized as one of the forms of psi experience categorized in Chapter 7.*

The main and practically the only one of these four forms of ESP used in the experimental laboratory for long, was the intuitive. (More recently, research using dreams instead has been carried on primarily at Maimonides Hospital, Brooklyn, N.Y. — reference 39.) Consequently, in my study the cataloguing of the spontaneous forms revealed for the first time the actual number of vehicles of psi. They could now be studied in detail as to the processes which they involved.

Therefore, in 1962, I undertook a study to find out what the experiences themselves would show about the Stage II processes that had produced each of them (reference 25). One strong hint as to a way to gain some insight on the topic had emerged repeatedly as the cases were classified in the making of the collection. This hint came from the fact discussed in Chapter 6, that the relative amount of information the percipients received varied greatly in different instances. Then, in Chapter 7, variability in completeness of information was shown in connection with the different forms. For example, in No. 1 of Chapter 7, in a realistic dream, a father foresaw in detail his little daughter's injury that would occur when he was playing tennis. In contrast, in No. 4, in an unrealistic dream, the death of the

*It will be recalled that two forms of dream and two of waking experience were shown to account for all the ESP experiences in the collection; two kinds of imagery, realistic and unrealistic, for the dreams; no imagery for the waking intuitive cases, pseudo-sensory for the hallucinatory effects.

neighbor's Marine son was only hinted at. A similar range of variability in amount of information was also shown in the intuitive experiences. For instance, the percipient in No. 10, Chapter 7, knew who was involved (his mother) and essentially what had happened to her, while in No. 13, another intuitive case, the percipient actually knew neither but acted compulsively, as if she had been informed. In short, differences in the amount of information yielded by individual experiences ranged from those in which a complete unit of information was transmitted, to others so incomplete as to constitute just a bare trace or "sign" of the message. And not only did individual cases vary in the actual amount of information they carried but the forms of experience also seemed to differ in general in their effectiveness as vehicles of communication.

These differences in the amount of information contributed in different experiences had been sufficiently impressive and intriguing throughout the collecting and classifying of the cases that I had routinely indicated on each case report whether it seemed to give a complete idea or not. A "complete" case, it will be recalled, was defined as one that yielded information as to the identity of the agent and the nature of the event in which he or she had been involved. If either of these items was lacking or if there were mistakes or misinterpretations of the actual facts, I had marked the case as incomplete.

Also, and as mentioned in Chapter 4, as the cases were classified, I had coded them as to their type, their form, and whether or not they had carried conviction. Some of these categories seemed more relevant than others to the present purpose.

The relative completeness of the message was, of course, of first interest because defects seemed comparable to the unsuccessful scoring of subjects in ESP tests. Here in the cases, however, it seemed that more hints as to underlying processes might be given than in the tests because the target material in cases was meaningful to the percipient while in tests using only numbers or symbols it was only marginally so.

The form of the experience also was important because it was the end product of the psychological process used in Stage II. The type, on the other hand, did not seem relevant in this study because types were distinguished only by the differing kinds of target material they involved (things, thoughts, future events) which it did not appear would directly affect the nature of the psi process. This impression was strengthened by the fact that each type included all of the forms.

The element of conviction, however, promised to be significant for in some instances the lack of it in itself suggested incompleteness. Also, as will be recalled from Chapter 6, no relationship was found between conviction and the amount of information the percipient received. It therefore was not the result of surmise or logic on the conscious level and very well might be related in some way to the unconscious psi process.

A total of 7110 case reports were available when the study was undertaken and a large number of them (72 per cent) had already been judged to have yielded a complete item of information. However, the percentages of completeness in the different forms varied greatly, the highest being in the realistic, the lowest in the hallucinatory. This, of course, showed that the forms were very different in the degree of efficiency with which they served as vehicles for carrying information to conscious attention, and suggested variations in the underlying psi processes as well.

The same thing was suggested even more strongly when the frequency of conviction cases in the different forms of complete cases was tabulated. In the complete intuitive cases it was the highest (87 per cent), in the realistic, it was much lower (24 per cent), and in the unrealistic, it was lowest (18 per cent).*

This difference between the percentage of conviction in the complete cases of the different forms showed that the form and the tendency toward conviction were independent. It indicated again that the feeling of conviction did not depend on consciously recognized information. The significance of this was that it therefore must originate below the level of consciousness and be affected by the specific processes that produced the individual forms.

No figures for conviction were cited for hallucinatory experiences because I had come to realize that it was impossible to judge it very reliably in this form. Usually the percipients were emphatic as to the reality of their experiences. They actually did see or hear the agent, but it was often unclear whether they believed the meaning of the experience in a way comparable to the conviction expressed in the other forms.

When the incomplete cases of the four forms were then examined for their frequency of conviction, a lack of obvious relationship to form was again shown. Surprisingly, the rate of conviction was even higher in the incomplete than in the complete intuitions. The reverse situation characterized the realistic form for it was *lower* in the incomplete than in the complete experiences. And this was true even though the amount of information in the incomplete realistic cases was greater than in the incomplete intuitive experiences. If some lawfulness or rationale could explain these peculiarities, it certainly was not at once apparent, but all of these irregularities, it seemed, were likely to be dependent on the processes involved. A study of each separately was called for and since the realistic cases were the most frequently reported of all, I turned to them first.

The Psi Process
in Realistic Experiences
(reference 26)

No. 1

It was night in an Indiana town. A young woman was having a frightening dream. Shivering and perspiring at the same time, she screamed and awakened herself and her husband, too.

"It was Jim. I saw him at the wheel of his car and then it spun out of control. I saw it turn over down an embankment."

Jim was her husband's young helper and also a close friend of hers. He had already gotten his driver's license and gone to his home in Louisiana for Christmas. Now he would be on the way back.

"He might be dead,"she continued excitedly. "He could be pinned under the wreckage out in the middle of nowhere and no one could find him for days!"

"But it was only a dream," her husband reminded her. He went back to sleep. She couldn't. It was too vivid. The least she could do was say a prayer for Jim's safety.

Jim called the next day. "I'm back again. But you should see my car. I guess I fell asleep at the wheel."

"Why Jim—do you realize that if you fell asleep the car might have gone out of control and down an embankment?"

"It did. That's just what happened."

"I knew it did," she told him.

"How could you possibly know it?"

"I dreamed it. I told Bob about it last night."

"Well, the car is all banged up all right. The front door won't open where it hit when it turned over, the window glass is broken where my head hit it. There was no one to help me. The road was deserted. But somehow I was not hurt too badly, just cut up a little."

"What time did it happen?"

"Wait a minute. What time do *you* think it happened?"

"It was about three a.m. when I saw it."

"That was just when it was."

How far can one analyze an experience like that? Certainly it appears that an actual event was apprehended in the dream. Somehow the wreck scene became "accessible." Somehow the percipient recognized or "selected" it as meaningful to her. Then, just as unconsciously, the construct or vehicle of realistic imagery was produced.

In Chapter 7, such dreams were characterized as similar to photographs. They seemed like copies of the actual event with the picture made up of visual imagery. But analogy or not, was it essentially a copy? If all realistic experiences were as correct as this, the answer might seem to be yes. But here the mistakes and incompleteness that sometimes were also shown, including the irregularities of the conviction element, must modify that interpretation.

A total of 3122 realistic experiences were available out of the entire list of 7119 cases. The large majority of these (91 per cent), like the one above, included also a wealth of correct detail. And yet, curiously, only 24 per cent of this number were conviction cases, like No. 1. The rest, while also including correct detail, did not carry conviction, as for instance:

No. 2

A woman in Texas, who was very fond of her father-in-law, one night had a disturbing dream about him. She thought she saw him laid out in his coffin. She thought she saw "his beautiful gray hair falling in waves on the pillow and the room in complete detail." But although she told her husband about the dream, she did not take it seriously. She thought it was "just a silly dream" because she knew her father-in-law was in good health. Besides, she knew he had a new brown suit and in the dream he had on his familiar dark blue suit.

Three days later, however, he was dead of a heart attack. When she and her husband went to the funeral parlor, all the details of the dream came rushing back. As she said, "It was like re-living the sight of the dream." His hair had been combed into beautiful waves over the pillow and his wife, thinking it a waste to bury him in a suit he had never worn, had decided on his dark blue suit.

The difference between the conviction elements in No. 1 and No. 2 seems clear, if not easily describable. Of course, dreams are familiar and usually even if disturbing, can be rationalized away as "just a silly dream." But in one that carries real conviction, a suggestion comes in that perhaps the origin is in some deeper level that rationalization fails to touch. But the content of those like No. 2 also presumably must originate in an equally deep level. The conviction element, however, is missing — or perhaps, not transferred? And if so, the tendency not to transfer this element seems relatively strong, for, after all, only 24 per cent of these complete realistic cases did carry conviction.

Among the incomplete realistic cases the actual kind of defect varied from case to case, and other questions besides those involving conviction were raised by the various omissions and mistakes, which in general, involved either the identity of the person or the nature of the event. An instance of imperfect identity was the following:

No. 3

A woman in Indiana had a very vivid dream one night of her neighbors, a young couple with an eight-year-old daughter. Although they had no baby son, in the dream she thought they had one and he was dead. She saw them bend over the bed, the man much taller than his wife. She and a group of neighbors watched helplessly and she thought, "There's just nothing we can do." The bed was in the corner of the room and although in real life she had thought the man rather brusque, she thought as she watched, that she had not expected him to be so nice and considerate to his wife.

When later her daughter came to visit, she told her about the dream. She said she was afraid something would happen to that family, but she didn't mention the baby boy for fear they might have plans for adoption. She didn't want to say anything that might cause worry.

About a month later, her own little fat and healthy (as they thought) grandson was found dead in bed—in the corner of the room. Her son is tall, his wife, short, just like the other couple. She thought, "I have lived through this once before in my dream."

Somehow in experiences like that one, the imagery, though seemingly modelled on reality, is such that it does not allow the real meaning of the message to be recognized in consciousness. Along with, shall we say, selection (or suppression) of the imagery which will carry the message, the element of conviction too tends to be omitted so that the full import of the item does not reach conscious recognition.

It would appear in cases like these that a sort of "screening" must go on as the imagery takes form. The result is not an exact copy, but one sufficiently altered or obscured to prevent the correct interpretation. It would be as if "this tragedy is coming up but let's not face it," a form of denial of reality and an evidence of the injection of an emotional influence into the imagery.

Another tendency sometimes shown is that of dreamers' substituting themselves for the persons actually involved, as in this instance:

No. 4

During World War I, especially in the latter years of the war in Europe and the American participation in it, the war was, as one might say, on everybody's mind so that war dreams would not have been exceptional. But one man in a city in New York State reported one that seemed to involve ESP.

It was the night of June 5-6, 1944. In the dream, he thought he was one of a band of paratroopers dropping into the darkness behind the German lines on the coast of France. He thought they landed, he extricated himself from his 'chute, the band advanced stealthily through the dark brush. Then they met the first sentry and silently overpowered him.

Then he heard the drone and steadily increasing roar of an approaching bomber-fighter squadron. Suddenly the night's silence was shattered by the shrill whine and explosions of tons of bombs falling from the skies and shells hurled from the naval armada off shore. The entire area was fitfully illuminated by the explosions and fires and he suddenly realized he was in a very precarious position. With the realization he awoke, badly shaken, but soon fell back to sleep. By morning he recalled it and dismissed it as "just another dream."

On the way to work the next morning, he received a jolt when, on the newsstand he saw in great black headlines the news of the Allied invasion of Normandy. It was D-Day, June 6, 1944.

Was it some unknown soldier's experience that person lived so vividly that night? Or only an imaginary paratrooper? Or an unrealistic fantasy based on the actual invasion and illustrative of an extraordinary imagination influencing the imagery formation process?

In all cases of mistaken identity, the conviction rate was low. Out of 70 cases, only ten showed conviction. Apparently, the unconscious "screening" process is quite effective here and, along with the identity of the person concerned, the belief that the episode is meaningful is also suppressed.

Conviction was somewhat more common when information about the nature of the event was imperfect but when the person involved was correctly identified. In 218 cases of this type, 23, or about 11 per cent, carried conviction. One instance which did is as follows:

No. 5

A woman and her husband were all packed and ready to start on a vacation trip from their home in Southern California to Oregon. But the night before she was disturbed by "horrible dreams—much crying, and in a vague way, our son," she wrote. When she arose next morning, her pillow was wet with tears and she looked so wretched her husband said she didn't look much like a person headed for a vacation. She replied, "I don't think I am, not today at least. Sonny is in trouble."

Sonny, although only 16, was a junior at USC in Los Angeles. Her husband, she said, "wanted to know all the answers and I couldn't give them." They did not leave, however, and that morning a phone call came from the university and the doctor at the hospital. The boy had collapsed in class and was rushed to the hospital for emergency appendicitis. Being a minor, his parents' consent had to be given before the operation. Had they left town as planned, his life might not have been saved.

Then in some instances the dream imagery might show a scene or circumstance which suggested but did not actually portray the reality of which it proved to be a part. This might be true regardless of whether the situation was contemporary or still in the future, as in this instance:

No. 6

After a family catastrophe, the children were separated and told that their mother was dead. One daughter, writing from Ohio, told of a dream she had had repeatedly over a period of years in her girlhood. It was always the same. It began with a long bus ride and when she arrived at the distant destination, no one met her. She walked over a railroad track, passed a feed mill and other buildings, a school, a church and a theatre. She then came to a house with a black covering all over it. No one was at home. She sat on the porch to wait. Eventually a woman came up the walk. In each dream she would awaken as soon as the woman got close.

When she was 20, she received a letter from her mother, who, it turned out, was alive and residing in a distant state. She invited her daughter to visit her and said she and her husband would drive to her home and get her. But the daughter decided not to wait but to surprise her mother and just drop in. She had never been to that place or state before, but when she arrived her dream came true in detail, even to the black covering. It was tar paper, as the house was being remodelled.

After that she never had the dream again.

In cases like that, a question arises, why, since the dream appeared to be truly related to the event, did it picture only an incidental scene, one which did not offer a clue as to its relevance? Is the answer to be found deep in the riddle of personality or in the mechanics of the psi process?

In a still more varied group of cases, the event was unclear for reasons that appeared more like the simple mistakes in observation that often happen in everyday sensory experience:

No. 7

A young man in Ontario had a married brother with a four-year-old son who lived some miles away. One night he had a most vivid dream about his little nephew. He saw him lying on the ground unconscious, his clothes and body all "black-looking." He thought the boy's father was looking down, grief-stricken, at the child.

"What's happened?" he asked his brother.

"It's Jimmie. He's been in a fire."

The dreamer awoke.

A week later, he was still worrying about the dream, but he did not meet any of the family until three weeks later and then he inquired, "Have any of you people been sick or had an accident lately?"

"Why?" his sister-in-law asked, surprised.

He told her about the dream.

"Ralphie fell out of an apple tree and broke his arm. He certainly was black in the face and his clothes very dirty."

Ordinary sense observation presumably could lead to a mistake on such a superficial level and apparently extrasensory "observation" too can be inexact. Or again, in a situation like this one:

No. 8

It was in 1932, just at the outset of the Depression with its bank failures and closings, when a woman in Washington, D.C., had an unusual dream. She thought she saw a man in jail shoot himself in the temple with a revolver.

She told her husband about it at breakfast, but as usual he just laughed at her for taking a dream seriously. Then, all at once she "knew" that it was the cage in the bank where the president sat and not a jail. The family was in very modest circumstances, with three small children, and their savings were in the bank. She told her husband they must take their money out of the bank at once.

He only kidded and teased her. She was so upset she cried and he finally consented to do it. He did go to the bank, drew out the money, but before he left the police were there. The president had gone down into the vault and shot himself with a revolver. He had squandered the people's money and suicide had seemed the only way out.

The mistake — a jail for a bank vault — again might suggest an inaccurate sensory impression. And the realization after waking that it was a bank, not a jail, was not part of the original realistic experience, but a waking experience, probably an ordinary intuition.

These various kinds of imperfections that may occur in realistic experiences show that this form is not necessarily nor entirely that of copying an original, as in photography. Even though the distinguishing characteristic is a photograph-like tendency simply to reproduce the reality, still, as shown in the incomplete cases, the dream-maker percipient can influence the process and shape it according to his or her own purposes.

The conviction aspect however appears to be different from and probably independent of that of the imagery formation. It would seem logically that it would arise in Stage I when the event becomes accessible. Certainly in accepting the accessible fact, the psyche would take it as true and thus conviction should appear along with the message when Stage II is inaugurated. However, the low frequency of conviction cases suggests that it tends to get lost in the process of imagery formation in Stage II.

A later aspect of the process of getting an ESP message into consciousness is the person's own final interpretation of the imagery. Oddly enough, although the person created it, by the time it comes into consciousness as a remembered dream, it no longer appears to be the person's own creation. It is a dream picture which, for all the person feels consciously, might have been constructed on Mars. This point is especially illustrated in an incomplete case like No. 3. The person herself created the imagery involving the death of her grandchild, but consciously she was no more able to interpret it correctly than if someone else had created it.

However, this need for a final interpretation of an ESP experience by the percipient himself does not apply only to realistic experiences, but to the other forms as well. It will come up again.

The Psi Process
in Unrealistic Experiences

No. 9

A girl in New York City had a curious dream one night about her mother back home and an event that seemed to happen there. Several years before while this girl was still in college (she had graduated now), her mother had been persuaded by the county nurse to care for an illegitimate baby girl, who otherwise would have had to be placed in an orphanage. As the girl reports, "Mother had a heart as big as herself—the little girl was later adopted by my sister."

The dream was that the baby's mother came to her parents' house with a small baby boy wrapped in a blanket and insisted that she give the little girl in return for the newborn baby boy. The dreamer was amused by the dream and thought it would amuse her mother too and so she wrote and told her about it. The day after she posted the letter, she received one from her mother, the two having crossed in the mail. Her mother's letter told her that two nights before (the night of the dream) a second illegitimate child, a boy, had been born to the mother of the little girl and in the same hospital.

The experience was the result seemingly of the (ESP) information in Stage I that the baby boy was born. But then Stage II did not produce photograph-like imagery, but rather a fantasy, a little drama based on the fact that her mother had taken the first baby.

Such fanciful unrealistic dreams vary considerably in the degree to which they reproduce the actual facts, so that the line between complete and incomplete information is not a sharp one. Still the dreamers do frequently get complete items of information, just as in the case above, even though at the time they cannot distinguish fact from fiction. Out of 1477 unrealistic cases, 1069, or 72 per cent, could be considered to be complete. But only a few of these carried conviction. To the majority of persons, as in the case above, the dream was "just a dream." Out of the 1069 complete unrealistic cases, only 197, or about 18 per cent, were dreams that carried conviction, as in the following:

No. 10

A woman had flown with her 10-month-old baby from her home in Florida to her parents' home in Indiana, mostly, she said, to get away from what she thought was a temporarily unhappy marital situation. Although pregnant, she went to work in a hotel where she had worked before her marriage.

Some weeks later she awoke one morning with a "terrible start" and recalled that she had dreamed that she and the baby had returned to Flordia without notifying her husband and had gone to the house he had rented. She thought she waited on the porch steps holding the baby until he arrived after work.

When he arrived he went around the car to open the other door and out stepped a lovely young girl and they walked up to the house together. When he saw his wife, he stopped short and asked what in the world she was doing there.

Then she awoke and the dream seemed so real that she telephoned her husband and asked if she could come back the next week. He gave a negative reply, but a little later, he phoned and said she had better come at once, "to see if we can make a go of our marriage, although I have many doubts as to whether we can."

When she arrived he told her that he was in love with another man's wife, who was more important to him than breathing. When he told the details of his romance, he said it began July 13, the night she had had her "horrible dream."

The list of unrealistic and incomplete experiences, just as the realistic kind, included some in which the identity of the person was omitted or mistaken and some in which the defect concerned the event instead. Again, conviction occurred very rarely in the former, somewhat more frequently in the latter, but even there in only 278 out of 1477, or only 19 per cent of the cases.

As already mentioned, the degree to which the fantasy departed from the reality varied endlessly so that some had to be considered symbolic because no element was factual. The next case illustrates this kind:

No. 11

A woman in Massachusetts who says that "somewhere along I learned that if I dreamed of water — if very deep and dark and muddy — something unpleasant would happen soon. But the tragic things come after I have dreamed of heavy black smoke."

The worst of such cases was after she dreamed of heavy black smoke, a column of it that seemed to be rising from a cranberry bog. She thought she was walking with her husband down the main road and called his attention to the smoke.

Next morning the dream was still in her mind and she felt frightened about it, so much so that she didn't tell her husband as he had come to have great faith in her "smoke" dreams. That night he was killed by a bus with a drunken driver.

A curious twist concerning conviction occurs with these symbolic experiences. Removed as the imagery may be from any hint of reality, still their rate of conviction is the highest of all the variations of incomplete unrealistic dreams. Of the 130 cases of symbolic dreams, 51, or about 40 per cent, were conviction cases.

This relatively high rate of conviction in symbolic dreams would seem inexplicable if it could be taken at face value. But as suggested in Chapter 7, the likelihood is too strong to dismiss that in many of them ESP is not involved. As with the person in

No. 11, above, and in most of the others, the dream recurred often, following which, sooner or later, a tragedy occurred, and then the person became deeply impressed. Whether or not these were actual instances of ESP then, or mere coincidence, one has no way of knowing. But the likelihood that ESP was not involved in many of them relieves the need to try to account for the high rate of conviction. But because in occasional instances the dream could reflect some deeply buried unconscious connection between an actual fact apprehended by ESP and a seemingly unrelated fantasy, the topic of symbolic experiences cannot be dismissed nor the possibility that, in some of the cases at least, the feeling of conviction has a genuine ESP basis.

In trying to trace the origin of unrealistic dreams one can safely assume that Stage I is the same as in the realistic form. The event becomes accessible and with it also comes the conviction that it is true. The difference comes in Stage II. Here, before the imagery is formed, an association of ideas seems to occur. It is as if the actual event leads to some associations which take the form of a drama or fantasy and this then becomes the basis of the imagery.

A tendency to so dramatize may well be a personality characteristic. But the fact that this kind of ESP experience occurs shows that an association of ideas, as well as the construction of a fantasy with subsequent imagery, can go on at a deeply unconscious level.

It seems then that the difference between realistic and unrealistic experiences is that in Stage II the imagery of the realistic form is based directly on reality, while in the unrealistic it is based on a fantasy suggested by the reality. But the fact that conviction occurs no more frequently than it does in either form (18 to 24 per cent) again would seem to mean that the feeling of conviction is not an objective item that can be expressed in imagery. Therefore, it tends to be omitted and lost. It seems reasonable that this tendency would be even greater when a fantasy intervenes before the imagery is formed than when a simple copy or reproduction of the reality takes place.

But the waking experiences also have a story to tell. This must be considered before any final discussion is undertaken.

The Psi Process
in Intuitive Experiences
(reference 25)

In the Chapter 7 classification of the forms of experience, it will be recalled that all those in which people reported that they suddenly just knew, felt or did something without a conscious reason but which later seemed to pertain to an event or situation unknown to them at the time, were put into the category called intuitive. They seemed the same as ordinary intuitions in that they broke into the ongoing stream of thought without preamble or conscious reason. The only difference seemed to be that in one, but not the other, the meaning must have been secured by ESP. Intuitions with or without ESP have no imagery and carry little or no detail, as in this case:

No. 12
A nine-year-old child was visiting a neighbor, Mrs. D., and was much absorbed in the activities going on there, when an ambulance could be heard on the highway about half a mile away. The little girl suddenly began to cry in fear. Mrs. D. was alarmed and questioned her. She said, "Oh, Mrs. D., that ambulance is going after Jim [her sister's husband]. He's been hurt bad."

The rest of the story was that Jim and her sister owned a small store several miles down the highway and, although they had never had any trouble there before, at that very time Jim had been shot in the back by a drug addict. He died a few days later.

Intuitive experiences like No. 12, in which an idea is received when the person is awake, are sometimes restricted to the bare meaning at most. One could even say that the information so received is often essentially just an abstract of the objective reality. And yet such cases do slightly more often bring a complete unit of information. With 1838 instances of intuitive experiences in the collection, 1021 (or about 55 per cent) are complete. This however, was a much smaller percentage than that of the complete realistic experiences.

The incomplete intuitive cases (818) varied considerably in

the relative amount of information they transmitted. As in the dreams, in many instances the identity of the person was not disclosed, but usually the impression was that "something was wrong," as in the case of an Ohio woman:

No. 13

She was at home preparing some ducks for supper which her husband had been given. He was at work in the shop of which he was a foreman. "All alone," she wrote, "Something told me something was wrong at the shop. I did not wait for coat or hat — it was cold — I ran all the way. When I got there I saw a crowd of workmen around someone lying on the ground. It was my husband. He looked up and said, 'Sue, I almost got killed.'

"I said, 'I know, that's why I'm here.' A workman had been trying to change a leaf in the spring of a truck. My husband had crawled under to help. The jack slipped and caught him through the back of the hips causing permanent injury."

Instances like the above suggest an emotional build-up below the conscious level. Presumably this reaction begins as soon as the information about the event becomes accessible. And again, in Stage I, when the item is secured it would seem that it must be taken to be true and the feeling of conviction is thus generated. In cases like No. 13, it would seem that both the emotion which the situation arouses and the feeling of conviction break through into consciousness because they are strong elements. In such occurrences, it is as if the two go together and make their way into consciousness even if the idea on which they are based does not, instead remaining blocked below the conscious level. Such experiences, then, and all those in which the person does not have an explanation for his sudden idea, emotion or compulsive action, make up the incomplete intuitive experiences.

These 818 incomplete cases vary in the degrees to which they are incomplete, from instances in which information is lacking about the person or the event to others, like No. 13, which include no specific fact at all but only an appropriate emotion or tendency to action. The likelihood of accompanying conviction also varies.

The kinds of incompleteness in these intuitions, just as in

the dreams, were those in which either the identity of the agent or knowledge of the kind of event was lacking. There were 259 cases of the former and of these 218, or 84 per cent, carried conviction. This was almost as high a rate of conviction as in the complete cases. This suggests that the level of incompleteness does not greatly affect the likelihood that the case will be taken seriously. Then, among a group of 138 cases, both the identity of the agent and the nature of the event were either unknown or only dimly perceived. Even so, there were 113 cases, or 83 per cent of them, which carried conviction, as in this instance:

No. 14

In a small restaurant in Utah, the cook, a young man with a wife and small children, working nights, once about 4 a.m. said to a helper, "Bea, do you ever have hunches?"

"Yes, sometimes."

"Well, I've got the awfulest feeling that something is wrong at home."

"Then get into your car and go home."

He did and found gas escaping, all his family unconscious. By quick work, he got them to a hospital in time, but it would have been too late had it not been for the hunch. He knew that something was wrong, and where, but not exactly who or what.

In two other groups of intuitive cases, the high rate of conviction in relation to the lack of information was quite striking. The first group consisted of only emotion, like this one:

No. 15

A woman in New Mexico was at work, expecting to work until 9 p.m. Her four children, ages 2 to 16, were at home. About 5:30 she became so agitated she could hardly sit still in her chair. Finally, she decided she couldn't work in that nervous condition, so she told her boss she had to go home. As soon as she was on the bus, she began to feel better. As she said, "It has always been my habit to pray at such times since my conscious mind does not know what is wrong, so I must be guided by something beyond me."

At her bus stop, it was necessary to go down an irrigation ditch bank to reach her back gate from the highway. In doing so, she would pass a telephone booth on the busy thoroughfare. This time she passed it and then thought she heard a baby cry. Going back to the booth, she found her two-year-old daughter had locked herself in the booth and couldn't reach the handle to pull the folding door open.

When she released the child and entered her house the older children were watching television and had not missed the little one. She thought her worst agitation had corresponded to the time when the little girl reached the dangerous highway and it prompted her prayer.

Then, when the child went into the phone booth and closed herself in, it seemed like the answer to prayer. That was the time, she thought, when she felt the release of tension.

To whatever extent that percipient's interpretation may have been correct, at least the emotional upset was the only sign that an ESP impression had been received. Yet, of 133 such cases, as many as 94, or 70 per cent, carried conviction.

In the last most incomplete group (194 cases) the experience consisted of a compulsive action only, as in the next example. But that action in itself, as well as the percipient's testimony about it afterward, was evidence of conviction. In 189, or 97 per cent of these cases, the situation could be assessed as indicating conviction.

No. 16

A family in California had just bought a beach house and the wife had taken the children and gone to spend the weekend working around the place. She was standing at the stove browning a roast for dinner when she had, as she said in reporting the ensuing incident, "the deepest feeling" to shut off the fire and walk to the beach.

She did shut off the fire, but before starting she did something else, which later seemed odd to have done. She went and found her binoculars.

The house was on a cliff 150 feet above the ocean. As she stood on the ramp that overlooks the sea, she decided to walk down the steep steps which lead down to the shore.

She stopped at the first level, about 75 feet down, and raised her binoculars and started to look out over the ocean. Then she caught sight of a little neighbor child down on the beach next to the high cliffs, frantically waving and screaming. She started running down the hill "as fast as my 210 pounds could go," she said. The child, when she reached her, pointed up the cliff, and there about 60 feet up, were two feet sticking out of the sand. The children, she learned later, had been digging on a ledge, when the cliff gave way, and tons of sand and boulders fell and the children were buried. From there on, she reported, "It was a nightmare. I dug and moved boulders until I was exhausted. I found a second and then a third child completely buried. They were unconscious with blue cyanotic swollen faces. I dragged them down the cliff, cleaned their throats of candy, gum and sand, and applied mouth to mouth resuscitation. It had not been a moment too soon."

She explained the seeming inhuman feat of saving them as possible because she was a nurse, knew she couldn't take time to run for help, and no one else was on the beach. She knew how important it was to get oxygen to the brain. Then, too, no small person could have moved the boulders, but by sheer weight she was able to push large boulders over the cliff. The binoculars had made it possible to see the frantic waving child which, without them, she could not have done.

But what made her leave her cooking, get the binoculars and start down the cliff? She says, "I definitely feel I was sent there to do a job." If so, an ESP impression taking the form of compulsive action could have been the mechanism for doing so.

As these examples indicate, the percipients had no factual information at all to go on, and yet the emotion they felt or the action they took was appropriate and could mean that an ESP impression had been received. Again, no relation appeared between conviction and the amount of information the percipient received. Apparently, the situation that allows or causes facts to be suppressed may still permit the feeling of conviction to become conscious along with emotional or compulsive tendencies. (The latter seem to occur when action would be fitting, emotion alone when, as because of distance perhaps, no action could be taken even if the facts were known.) Apparently, emotion or compulsive action, as well as conviction, can be separated from the facts and make their way into consciousness independently of them.

Both complete and incomplete intuitive cases thus give some idea of the psi process. In complete cases, entire items become known, but stripped of the nonessential details such as might be included in a realistic dream. Only the important idea with its appropriate emotion and conviction is recognized. But the information from unconsious levels must cross a barrier of sorts to get to consciousness and this ordinary psychological barrier could eliminate the nonessentials. In incomplete cases, the evidence even more strongly suggests that the difficulty is at the level of consciousness.

It seems in Stage II that even after the basic psi information has become accessible or has been selected as relevant and recognized as true (conviction) it may fail to reach consciousness intact. If this situation were to occur in an experiment, the result well might be a miss, but in these spontaneous cases it is still recognizable as ESP. If the situation persists in an experiment, a series of misses could occur that would become statistically significant and result in the effect known as *psi missing* (discussed in Chapter 16).

The incomplete cases by their variations show that their elements, namely the idea, its details, the emotion or compulsion it generates and the conviction about it, are separable. Each apparently makes its way into consciousness independently and sometimes one, sometimes another may be blocked below the level of consciousness.

In tests, subjects rarely know or have a feeling that a given call is correct. In that situation, it appears that the conviction element is blocked, and only the idea, which is of the target symbol, breaks through. On the other hand, in spontaneous intuitive cases, especially those involving highly emotional situations, the idea may be repressed, and only the emotion and conviction get into consciousness.

The situation in hallucinatory experiences, however, is quite different from that in intuitions.

The Psi Process
in Hallucinatory Experiences

Psi hallucinations are no different in form from hallucinatory experiences in general, except that, although no sensory target is present, one does exist somewhere and is accessible by *extra*sensory perception. Psi hallucinations appear mainly in the auditory, visual or somatic modalities and only these will be discussed here.

The total number of hallucinatory experiences at the time of this study (not including the call cases of Chapter 8) was 681. Of these, only 220, or 32 per cent could be considered complete and they were distributed unequally among the modalities. This percentage of complete cases was much the lowest of any of the four forms.

The auditory cases (excluding the call cases of Chapter 8) with a total of 348 items, included only 126, or about 36 per cent, which were complete.* The efficiency of the auditory form was low when it alone was involved, but was much increased when a visual element was added. In fact, in 44 cases of the auditory and visual modalities in combination, 37, or 84 per cent, were complete. This was the highest rate found in any of the hallucinatory modalities. One such instance is the following:

No. 17

After the Korean War, one young soldier had been returned to the Norfolk, Virginia, base. He had been able to visit his Long Island home for several weekends. The last time he had been there he told his mother that he expected to be sent to South America soon but did not know just when. He would know by the next Friday when he came home, however, and would let her know the date then.

---

*The call cases included only a few instances, for example Nos. 8 and 9 of Chapter 8, that were complete because the message included a sentence or two that carried the meaning. In the majority, however, the percipient only heard his or her own name called, as in the rest of the examples given there. Thus, in these cases, as in the rest of the auditory hallucinatory experiences, the percentage of complete cases was low.

That Friday his mother was dressing when she saw him standing between the beds. She turned and asked him what he was doing there. He answered, "Mom, I will not be home today and I cannot call you because we sailed this morning at seven a.m.," and then faded away. She stood, half stunned, and then decided she must have dreamed it while on her feet.

As the morning wore on, she became so upset she told a neighbor who happened to call. The neighbor suggested she call Naval operations in Norfolk and check on his ship. She did so and after identifying herself as the soldier's mother, was told that the ship had indeed sailed that morning at 7 a.m.

When a letter came from her son he said he had been very worried that morning because he knew she would be expecting him. He knew her health was not good and he feared the strain she would be under when he did not come home as she expected.

In contrast to the auditory, the visual modality alone, with 155 cases, included only 26, or 17 per cent, that were complete. This was the lowest percentage of all even though this modality—which, of course, includes apparitions—has been the most popularly recognized one. Of course, the low percentage of complete visual experiences might be expected since the mere "sight" of an individual does not in itself betray the nature of any crisis in which he might be involved. Occasionally, however, something incongruous about the appearance may enable the percipient to grasp the meaning of what has happened so that such a case may convey the essential information, as in this instance:

No. 18

The president, Mr. N., of a congregation in Galveston, Texas, was ill and had to go to St. Louis for an operation. The rabbi was requested to go to St. Louis to visit him and when he returned home, the report he brought was encouraging. He explained that Mr. N. was improving and would be able to come home soon.

The second night after the rabbi's return, his wife called to him: "Mr. N. just appeared in my room. He was dressed in white and said, 'I just came to pay a visit,' and then he disappeared. I feel that Mr. N. died."

In a few minutes, a phone call from St. Louis reported the death of Mr. N.

Here, although an auditory effect as well as a visual one was experienced, it contributed nothing to the meaning of the message. The appearance of the agent, Mr. N., in such an unusual place and "in white," conveyed the message, but the majority of visual cases were incomplete because they lacked supplementary detail. Thus, even though apparitional cases have deeply impressed those who experienced them, they actually represent one of the least effective forms of all as vehicles for transferring information to consciousness.

A third kind of hallucinatory experience to be considered here, besides the auditory and visual, is the somatic which consists of shared sensations. They are the opposite of visual experiences in the sense that the identity of the apparent agent is not disclosed. The situations, which usually involve a physical ailment or sensation that is felt by an agent, are experienced or sensed by the percipients as if their own. In 134 such cases, 31, or about 23 per cent, could be considered complete because some aspect of the symptom was specific for the given agent, as in this instance:

No. 19

A young woman in Minnesota was expecting her first baby. Her mother, who lived some 300 miles away, was planning to come and spend a month with her when the date the baby was expected, neared. However, the baby came 3½ weeks early and in the rush to get to the hospital, the young woman said later, she could not remember that either she or her husband even mentioned her mother.

However, that night her young brother who lived with her mother came home to find his mother pacing the floor, and she said, "Ann is having the baby."

"Did Charles call up?"

"No. But I know." She had suffered back pains. Incidentally, it was one of the cases in which the hallucinatory effect is shown to be the result of expectation or memory on the part of the percipient rather than a telepathic impression from the agent, for as the report continues, "my mother suffered with the pains all night while I did not have a single one. My son was born about 7 a.m.

"My husband called right away and was told about Mother's experience. If it was thought transference, how? I was not consciously thinking of her and if I had been I would have been glad she would not know about it until it was all over."

Of course, if this had been only telepathy, the mother's experience would not have included sensations which the agent did not have. (At the same time, a telepathic message would not depend on whether or not the agent thought of the percipient.) Instead, the awareness of the agent's crisis could be termed GESP and the pains, even though not part of the agent's experience, could have been hallucinated by the percipient as effects she *expected* the agent to have.

What then goes on in hallucinatory experiences? Obviously Stage I must be identical in this form to any other. The event becomes accessible to the percipient. In Stage II, however, the difference comes in. Because the person thinks he or she is awake, dream imagery is not evoked. Instead, it appears that (for those who can hallucinate) usually memory of past sense experience, visual or auditory, reproduces the customary view of the agent or sound of the agent's voice. It is as if they were being experienced sensorially.

In the somatic cases, however, the reaction in Stage II is somewhat different. Instead of a specific sensory modality's being used to convey information, the person seems to experience directly a sympathetic reaction which reproduces the symptoms being experienced by the agent or what the person expects the agent to have. These symptoms thus carry the information in these cases. As such, they of course give no hint as to the identity of the agent and consequently the percipients usually have to interpret the sensations they feel as being their own, except in instances like No. 19 when their peculiarity gives a clue.

In a very few instances, which may be more indicative than their numbers would suggest, the person may have an accompanying intuition, which tells what this pain means. Such an intuition accompanied by a somatic or other hallucinatory effect suggests that a relationship may exist between the two forms of experience, the intuitive and the hallucinatory. It could be that all hallucinations of whatever modality originate as an intuition at the start of Stage II and that in susceptible individuals the hallucinatory effect is then added to it. This could either block or at least overshadow the basic intuition to the extent that the person would become conscious only of the hallucination and not of the intuition.

However, experiences that combine both an intuition and an hallucinatory effect are rare, which could mean that only in a few individuals are both possible at the same time. Or, since the frequency of intuitions so greatly outnumbers that of hallucinatory experiences, it could mean that only a relatively small number of persons can experience hallucinatory effects.

After tracing the main steps that seem to be involved in the ESP process, a study of the process that appears to go on in spontaneous psychokinesis (PK) was called for. This follows in the next chapter.

Chapter 15

The Psi Process in PK

In March 1943 the *Journal of Parapsychology* carried an editorial by JBR which began, "In this issue we publish for the first time a report of an effect that belongs to a class called 'physical phenomena,' meaning of course physical effects of supposedly parapsychical origin. In the entire six years of the *Journal of Parapsychology*, no previous departure from complete attention to the research and issues of extra-sensory perception has occurred. Accordingly, this occasion marks a turning point, however great or small its significance may be" (reference 9).

The editorial continues with references to some of the early investigations of claimed physical mediumship, Home, Cook, Goligher, Eva, Stella, Marjorie, Kluski, and the Schneiders, and then goes on in these words, "The demonstration of detectable effects upon the physical environment claimed to have been made by many 'physical mediums' who came into public attention were dramatic and received wide publicity, but they fell far short of the goal of scientific acceptance even among those who were more or less giving themselves professionally to psychical research. This is not of course to say that we therefore regard this failure as equivalent to a classification as fraudulent or worthless. But in so far as the goal of scientific inquiry is the *establishment* of truth, the evidence in these instances was unsatisfactory."

The report referred to in the editorial as being published in that issue of the *Journal of Parapsychology* was the first of a series on the topic of physical effects (reference 33). This one was the report of experiments on the direct effect of mind on matter.

The results of the series indicated that the human mind had produced a statistically significant physical effect, mainly on the fall of dice.

With the psychokinetic effect established, this series of experiments tended to throw a favorable light on the exploits of the physical mediums of the past. Even though they did not guarantee the genuineness of all of them, they did make it seem more likely that some of them may have been genuine.

Besides that, they made it possible to assume for PK, just as the laboratory results on ESP had done for that ability, that if the effect occurs in the laboratory, then surely it also occurs spontaneously in life situations. It would not necessarily be in such spectacular ways as reputed to a Home or a Kluski, but more likely, as with ESP, in the less conspicuous personal experiences reported by individuals of the general public. It was because of this possibility that I had accepted for the case collection all reports of experiences that *could have been* instances of spontaneous PK. They were cases in which an unexplained physical effect occurred that seemed to be relevant to a human situation. On that basis, these case reports had been collected but over the years from 1948 on the number of them had been small in proportion to those suggesting ESP.

However, the fact that relatively few possible PK experiences had been reported to the Parapsychology Laboratory may not very truly represent the actual rate of spontaneous PK occurrence. If it is difficult to recognize ESP with certainty, it is much more difficult to identify PK. In the first place, the possibility of PK is even more incredible to almost everyone. Even if this is so only because very few persons have seen any evidence of it in daily life, those that have experienced something that suggested telepathy or other ESP effects are by comparison much more numerous. As one result, since frequency affects familiarity which in turn could affect the readiness with which a strange and inexplicable effect might be reported, ESP-like occurrences have been used in literature, especially in fiction, much more frequently than those suggesting PK.

Another reason the occurrence of PK has remained relatively more incredible than ESP is because it is always difficult to be certain that no ordinary physical cause operated to produce it, one that simply had not been detected. For all these reasons, the number of PK-like effects that were reported and accepted for this or any other collection may well be inordinately low in relation to their actual rate of occurrence. This is not to say that the occurrences may not also be relatively infrequent. At any rate, these cases accumulated so slowly that by 1963, when reports of over 10,000 experiences that could have involved ESP were in the files, still only about 100 presumptive instances of spontaneous PK were on hand. It seemed that even though the number of them was smaller than desirable, their study should not be put off any longer and that even though they were few they should not be ignored. As I wrote in the report I made of the subsequent study, "In the jigsaw puzzle which the field of para-psychology still is, every little piece may be important" (reference 28).

To augment the number of items for the study, I gathered all the accounts of possible PK effects I could find in the literature of psychical research and some kindly loaned by the American Society for Psychical Research, so that all together a total of 178 cases were assembled, a number large enough at least to offer suggestions. The question to be explored, of course, was if these were PK experiences, what was the psi process involved and how was it related to those that produced ESP effects?

Upon first inspection, the accounts seemed to vary so greatly that it hardly seemed possible that any common threads of meaning would be found in them. They had been assembled, however, because of one common characteristic. It was that an unexplained physical effect had occurred that seemed to be connected with someone in a crisis. Observation showed it usually was a person emotionally connected with the one who observed the effect.

In general, the effects involved household objects. Clocks starting or stopping and objects falling from walls or shelves seemed to be most common, but in some instances an object broke or exploded; in some, doors opened or shut "by themselves"; in others, a chair or other object rocked or shook. In all of them, however, the situation was different in at least one respect from that in laboratory experiments of PK, even though presumably the same process would be operating in each. The difference was that the subject in an experiment consciously willed the PK effect to occur. But in the cases no one willed such an effect or apparently was even aware that it was occurring.

However, it could be that the "trying," the conscious willing, was not actually necessary. Tests in which subjects tried to cause the effects to occur, when compared to others in which they merely wished them, had not consistently shown differences great enough to be conclusive.

The process, if it was actually going on, was obviously entirely unconscious. In the tests an experimenter as well as a subject was usually present, but the presumption was that the subject caused the effect, even though the experimenter too knew the target and was interested in the outcome.

In the cases also two persons were usually involved, one who observed the effect, and another usually at a distance and undergoing a crisis, as in this example in which the mother observed the effects and her dying sister was the one in crisis.

No. 1

A woman in New Hampshire reported that when she was a girl of about 12 she came home from school one day and her mother told her about a queer occurrence.

Her mother said she was sitting knitting in the kitchen about 2 o'clock that afternoon when the clock stopped for no apparent reason. It was not run down for soon it started running again and kept going until evening, the time it usually was wound.

Three days later a cable came from overseas saying that her mother's sister had died. It was the day and hour the clock stopped.

The question was, if PK was involved in a situation like that, which of the two persons "did it"? Who was analogous to the subject in a test, the one who observed the effect or the one undergoing the crisis?

With that question in mind, definite terms to distinguish the two seemed necessary. In a way, the two might seem analogous to the percipient and agent, as those names are applied in ESP experiences. But, as discussed earlier (Chapter 11), those terms are probably misnomers and at any rate, they do not fit the PK situation as viewed in the context of a PK test.

The question here was that of trying to decide which of the two was the psi-person. So instead I chose to call the one who had the experience, like the mother in the case above, the experiencing person (E person); the other, the aunt who was dying in that instance, the target person (T person).

In the past, just as with apparitional experiences, occurrences seeming to be marked by PK effects had usually been interpreted as signs or signals from the T person to the E person. But now the question was, is such an interpretation necessarily correct?

The first step was to separate the cases according to the condition of the T person to see if any indications were given under any of them to show whether or not he was the one to exert the PK. This separation yielded 95 cases in which the T persons were dying, 46 in which they were deceased, 32 in which they were living and five in which no T person was included.

In instances like No. 1, in which presumably the T person was dying at the time of the effect observed by the E person, I could find no indication to show whether or not the T person could have exerted the effect, but since she was in the crisis, and since the two were close relatives, she very well might have been motivated to communicate the fact. But, on the other hand, the E person was equally involved emotionally and I could find no reason to exclude the possibility that this person, instead, was responsible. The issue thus could not be decided on this basis.

Turning then to the 46 cases with deceased T persons, in 31 of them the situation appeared to be such that the T persons had a definite and specific reason to initiate the effect, as for instance to inform the E persons of their survival of death.

No. 2

A woman who was very close to her father, in a discussion with him on the subject of life after death one night, asked him if he believed in it. He replied that he did. She asked if he would try to come back and give her a signal when he died.

On the day of his funeral, as she was going out of the door, a large mirror fell to the floor but did not break.

The rest of these 46 cases, although the situations did not directly involve the survival of the T persons, were such that it seemed that motives that more or less plausibly could explain the occurrences, were ascribable to them.

No. 3

A young girl in California—like many others elsewhere—had a habit of reading in poor light. Her father often would say, "Evie, you'll go blind," and then he would turn on the light.

One evening after his death the girl was reading in the dwindling daylight and, although straining to see, she did not take the trouble to get up and turn on the light. The memory then came to her of her father saying, "Evie, you'll go blind." Just as she thought it, the light snapped on.

In all of the 46 deceased T person cases, the E person was in a situation that was relevant to the deceased T person, who in effect appeared to be bringing the E person needed information or advice. The emotional involvements were the same for each of the two, for the relationship was reciprocal, so that on that score either of the two could have been motivated to cause the PK effect. But here the *T persons were deceased.* Now PK has been shown to be an ability of living persons. But that the deceased also have it—if indeed they do survive, also a question still unsettled—cannot be assumed. Instead, it is the question to be answered. In this group therefore one can only say that the E persons could have been responsible. Whether or not the T persons were responsible must remain an open question. The issue cannot be decided on this evidence.

Turning then to the 32 cases with living T persons, it seemed that these should be particularly enlightening because in these as in none of the others, the T persons could report for themselves. Since in each instance they were undergoing a crisis at the time of the E person's experience, it would seem that they might report an acute awareness of the E persons at the time, and thus confirm the idea that they "did it," just as the E persons had generally assumed in the cases when the T persons were dying. Presumably, if the T persons were the ones responsible, they would at least have been strongly oriented toward the particular E persons and one could therefore expect that something of the kind would be indicated.

However, this did not turn out to be true. Invariably, the E persons were the ones who reported the cases and little or nothing was said about the state of mind of the T persons. The following case is typical:

No. 4

One night in the bedroom of a girl away from home, the light went on when no one was near the switch. She reported that she just knew then that something was wrong at home.

The next morning her sister called her that their father, a miner, was in the hospital. At the time her light came on the night before a motor down in the mine had fallen on her father and crushed his pelvis.

In none of the other cases was there any information given as to whether the T person had this particular E person in mind or even whether this one would have been the person to whom the T person's thoughts would likely have turned in a crisis. Neither was it clear in most of the cases whether or not the T person was conscious sufficiently to have thought strongly of anyone. At the same time, the E persons, just as in that case, were not thinking especially of the particular T person. The relationships, as in the other groups, were close and reciprocal so that a crisis for one would create an emotional reaction in the other. In fact, the situations were no different than those in which the T person was dying except that here the kinds of crises varied.

Finally, in the remaining five cases, *no T person* was involved; the effect simply occurred in the presence of the E person, who, however, was usually in an emotional state, as for example:

No. 5

A woman was reading an article on Jimmy West, a crippled orphan who did so much for children's welfare when he grew up. As a child he had a tubercular hip and he was accused of malingering. The hospital discharged and refused to readmit him, and as she read, she was deeply stirred.

As she put the article down a loud sound came from the living room, though no one was in it, not even a dog or cat. But, a book had fallen from the bookcase. It was a book on surgery for children.

The fact that no T person was involved in these five cases and that therefore the E person must have been responsible for the effect was the most revealing fact that examination of these cases uncovered. Unfortunately, however, the number was too small to be other than suggestive. But in each instance the effect occurred when the E person was in a definite emotional state, which presumably could at least have accounted for the timing of the effect.

With the question still undecided, I next tried a different angle of observation. I noted the nature of the effects under the three different states of the T person. As the cases already given show, the kind of effect varied from case to case. In No. 1 a clock stopped. In No. 2 an object fell. In Nos. 3 and 4 a light came on. But when the effects were listed under each T person condition, each kind of effect was represented in each condition: when the target persons were living, when they were dying, or when they were dead. Also, although in a number of cases the object affected, clock, picture, or whatever, was one particularly reminiscent to the E person of the T person, no information was added by this fact, again because these situations too were reciprocal. If it was an object especially reminiscent of the given T person, often for instance because it had been a gift from that person, it was similarly familiar to both T and E persons. These observations then did not give any basis for distinguishing between the two.

I next tabulated the locations of the two persons relative to the object affected, to see if any suggestions would be raised thereby. I found that in the majority of cases the T person was at a distance from the E person and the PK effect, sometimes a great one, happened while the E person was quite close to the object affected. In only four instances was this reversed. All that these observations or relative distances showed, then, was that distance apparently was not important, especially the distance of the T person from the scene. (Laboratory experiments have shown no limitations as far as the distances that have been tested indicate.) If the E person were the one involved, however, then in the majority of the cases presumably the short distance might be advantageous. But on the other hand, if the phenomenon was a signal from the T person, he or she naturally would want it to occur in the vicinity of the E person. Again, nothing definitive was added by these observations of relative distance nor was any basis for differentiating between the two persons even suggested.

After these various examinations of the PK cases, the answer to the question of which person exerted the PK effect was still undecided for neither the cases with dying T persons nor the kind of effect had permitted a distinction. Those with deceased agents could not be assessed because the PK effect has only been shown in the laboratory to exist in living persons. It was only in connection with cases with living T persons that a suggestion could be found: none of the T persons seemed to have reported being strongly oriented toward the E person at the moment of crisis and in a few instances no T person was involved. The suggestion then was that the E person had been the active party rather than the T person. With this I had to leave the question.

If the E persons should be decisively shown to exert the PK effect then presumably they would be analogous to the subjects in a PK test. But if so, their role could easily be misinterpreted, just as with apparitions of the dying and the dead. In these PK cases too the naive interpretation, that the T person "did it," could well be the reverse of the true one.

One other kind of experience needs to be mentioned here for completeness, if nothing else. That is the auditory effect in which a sound that could have physical or mechanical cause is heard at a significant time. The auditory experiences of Chapter 8 were vocal sounds, but these were mechanical, like the striking of clocks, the ringing of bells, and raps, knocks and the like that did not seem to have an ordinary cause, as for instance:

No. 6

A woman in Illinois was awakened one night about midnight by hearing two knocks on a bookcase. She was frightened and told her husband she thought something had happened to their son who had not come home.

About 2 a.m. he came in "white as a sheet" and told her he and his friends had been doing some backward somersaults on a floor without any mats for tumbling. So he had thought that if he stood nearby he could protect the boy doing the tumbling from falling on the hard floor. But instead of saving him, the boy came tumbling backward and the heel of his shoe caught her son square on top of the head and knocked him out for two hours. He said before passing out he thought of his mother. They thought the two knocks on the bookcase could have been his signal.

When I made the study of the PK cases I did not include these auditory experiences involving mechanical sounds, although it seemed possible that they might be instances of PK too. However, since the call cases of Chapter 8 had been classified in general as instances of auditory hallucinations it seemed best to make a separate study of those with mechanical sounds and to try to find a method of separating the origin of the two.

In 1963 I had 621 cases that involved auditory effects of both kinds and, of these, 510 were call cases and 111 were characterized by nonvocal sounds. In order to try to distinguish between the possibly different origins of the two, it seemed that hallucinatory sounds would seldom be heard by anyone but the experiencing person since this form of psi tends to be private. On the other hand, if sounds were produced by PK, it should be expected that everyone within auditory range would hear them.

Accordingly, I made a study along this line (reference 27). The vocal and call cases I listed as Group A, and the mechanical ones as Group B, and divided each into those in which other individuals besides the E person were present. This division immediately hinted at a difference in the two kinds, for Group A, with its 510 call cases, included only 68 instances in which more than one person was present at the time. This was only about 13 per cent of the total. The 111 Group B cases, however, included 63 instances in which more than one person was present, or about 57 per cent of all. This suggested a tendency for Group A cases to occur most frequently when the person was in solitude, and solitude presumably might favor the hallucinatory form.

The next question was, if a second person was present,

whether this person too heard the sound. In Group A they did so in only 28 per cent of the 68 cases but in 92 per cent of the 63 Group B cases the sound was heard by everyone within range. These differences too of course favored the idea that the two groups were different and that Group A cases were largely hallucinatory while Group B cases were the result of an actual physical effect on the clock, bell or other mechanism involved.

The idea that PK might so affect mechanisms did not seem too farfetched in view of the manifold kinds of PK effects that have already been substantiated. But the mechanism involved in instances like No. 5, when the sound is a knock or rap, was and still is difficult to explain. Whatever may be the physical action represented, it is more subtle than those involving a known and recognizable mechanism. The manner by which such sounds could be produced on doors, walls, tables has not yet been investigated in depth and so this problem is one of those still awaiting futher exploration.

Returning now to the question of the person responsible for PK effects of whatever specific kind, and the likelihood that the E person is the one, it would mean, of course, that physical effects as well as those involving ESP are modes or forms by which information is relayed into consciousness, a method in addition to the four ways by which ESP information may be brought to conscious attention, the fifth form already mentioned in Chapter 7.

What would this addition of a PK effect to those involving ESP mean about the process by which all of them are produced and how would it be related to the ESP process? The process of course would be unchanged in Stage I. The information would become accessible and be selected by the E persons as of interest to them. This would basically be *an idea*— and just the same regardless of whether PK or ESP results.

But in Stage II, the difference would come in. In this stage, the possible range of vehicles by which the information would get to conscious attention would be increased to include PK effects as well as the psychological constructs of ESP. Of course, since PK appears to be less frequently used than the others, it very well may be a possibility for only a few persons and besides, as suggested earlier, it very likely may also tend to be overlooked in real life, explained away and never reported.

However, in a few instances, a suggestion is given that is similar to the one mentioned in Chapter 14 in connection with hallucinatory experiences. It is that the PK effect too may be a concomitant of a blocked intuition. It is suggested in cases like No. 5 above, when the woman hearing knocks on the bookcase seemed to take them (intuitively?) as referring to her son. Sometimes the sign of a blocked intuition, in the form of an emotional crisis only, is even more marked, as in No. 7.

No. 7

A woman reported that she was sitting in her office adjoining her shop one Friday at 3 p.m. when suddenly she started to cry. Her employer kept asking her what was the matter, but she could not tell him and neither could she stop crying.

At 3:20, a huge decorative vase fell off the shelf when no one was near it. The next morning she received a call telling her that her father had died on Friday. He was alone and was only found on Saturday (reference 28, page 112).

Again, with this PK process as with the hallucinatory, it could be that the intuitive form is initiated at the beginning of Stage II but that then it is in a sense diverted, this time into the release of PK. This then would tend to block the passage of the intuition into consciousness. Possibly too the PK avenue of expression may only be activated when, for whatever reason, the information is blocked at the level of consciousness. In such instances it would be, as it were, an alternate route by which an indication of the psi information is given. At any rate, it would mean that PK effects are in a way side effects, fragments, signs of repressed information. But even so, they must be counted as representing one form of psi since they become a form recognized in consciousness.

As a form, however, PK effects are obviously very ineffective. The information they transmit is always incomplete and only a sign that information is blocked. The message is not disclosed specifically.

In spontaneous PK, just as in the four forms of ESP, the

unconscious operation of the processes must be emphasized. It is clear that nature does not do it consciously. But since tests cannot well be conducted unconsciously, it probably is only lucky that any results at all have been achieved by laboratory methods.

Of course, in contrast to the reports of outstanding physical mediums as those mentioned in JBR's editorial, it would appear that such minor effects as stopped clocks and fallen pictures are only very small tips of a very large iceberg. But even so, as the editorial stated, those reports were not sufficient to establish the occurrence of PK. It was necessary to have controlled experimental conditions to do that.

Today, however, after the establishment of the reality of PK nearly half a century ago, a new phenomenon has appeared on the horizon, one which, if it were fully authenticated, would suggest a larger role for PK than its actual occurrence in the laboratory and in personal spontaneous cases would have suggested. It is the so-called "Geller effect" in which, by mind alone, the strongest metal, it appears, can be bent or distorted (reference 5). Just as JBR said in his editorial that the announcement of the establishment of PK in the laboratory "marks a turning point," so would the establishment beyond question of the Geller effect mark a turning point in the development of knowlege of PK. But even without it, should that not prove reliable, the fact of PK as an adjunct of human personality poses a great challenge to the scientific mind. The personal experiences seem to say that whatever the total function of PK ability may be, it is one that those experiences hint at and offer their suggestive bit. But it remains for proper experimentation to determine not only the perimeters of PK in the physical world, but also its meaning and function in the living personality.

* * * * * *

In this chapter and in Chapter 14, I traced the steps in the psi process as they appeared in numerous spontaneous cases. By considering what the process must be in view of its known end product, whether experimental or spontaneous, some logical inferences could be drawn and, I believe, an inclusive perspective of the way psi operates, glimpsed.

But one more characteristic of the psi process, or at least of the process as it has been observed in the laboratory, remains to be considered, the one called psi-missing. It is one whose absence in spontaneous cases is logical enough once the possible process that goes on in intuitive experiences is recognized. It is presented next in Chapter 16.

Chapter 16

Psi in Reverse

A peculiar characteristic of scientific discoveries often observed is that by answering one question, they raise a host of others. Parapsychology runs true to form on this. When, as outlined in Chapter 2, the reality of psi ability could be considered as established, it answered in the affirmative the old original question, then phrased as whether telepathy — the transfer of a thought from one person to another without sensory mediation — can occur, and answered it so broadly that the question itself, so far as the old idea of telepathy was concerned, had to be phased out. But the inquiry could not stop there. It had to go on to the establishment of psi ability. Then the questions had to be asked: How does the ability operate? What controls it? What affects it? What are its dimensions? These and many others that had not come up before now all called for answers. But the attempt to answer them in the laboratory was slow and difficult and particularly so because of an effect that came to be known as "psi missing." In this, it frequently happened in an ESP test that a subject attempting to identify symbols on concealed decks of cards, would miss instead of hit so many of them that his score was so much below the level to be expected by chance that it was statistically significant. What did psi missing mean? It seemed like a road block on the way to discovering the nature of the psi process. It took considerable time and research before its true meaning could be recognized and also the fact that it was an important characteristic, the understanding of which would throw new light on the psi process itself.

When early in the experimental work psi missing occurred

it often involved a situation in which one part of an experiment might be significantly positive, another just as significantly negative and the two sections thus seemed to cancel. It meant that results were difficult to confirm. Of course, anyone who knows anything about the experimental work knows that one experiment alone, even if it produces results well above the level expected by chance, cannot be taken as proof of the point in question. It needs to be confirmed either by the same or different experimenters in the same laboratory and eventually by those in other places too. However, in these parapsychological experiments, all too often the results the second time around were different from or even the reverse of those the first experiment yielded. While a number of the reasons why such experiments did not succeed were eventually found, the psi missing effect when it occurred was one of the most baffling and pernicious.

This failure of psi experiments to be easily confirmed understandably gave much ammunition to the ever-present critics of parapsychology. In a way their attitude was, "Before you can impress us you must have a repeatable experiment." By this, as I remarked in an article on the topic (reference 31, page 260), "they meant a formula, a simple one. Something like in chemistry when an acid and an alkali yield the same salt on Monday that they yielded on Friday. They did not mean a formula that says subject A on Monday, just back from a weekend at home is a different person than he was on Friday, and consequently his results on delicate psychological tests like those of ESP cannot be expected to be the same as they were on Friday. Such a formula ... is too complex for quick and easy assimilation." But just because the formula for a psi experiment that will yield "positive results" is not a simple one, does not mean that none exists. It means instead that the formula is complicated and affected by innumerable conditions, some obvious, some obscure, some controlled, some uncontrollable. And, in the bargain, when psi experimentation began, all of them were unknown. Nothing but sheer patience and willingness to go the extra mile and sometimes many extra miles kept the field alive for decades in the face of test results which, although they showed *something*, often did not tell what that something was because another test made to confirm the first might even be contradictory. If neither had shown anything, but had yielded scores at chance, then all rational investigators would surely have quit the field soon after their first disappointment. But the reversals seemed to have a meaning. The puzzle was what that meaning could be.

In some of the reversals, both results might be statistically significant but one deviated above the chance line, the other below it. The laws of statistics are based on the average amount of deviation from that line that occurs when chance alone is operating. When the test results are greater than those to be expected by chance and greater by a commonly accepted amount, they are considered to be significant, which of course means that something more than pure chance is involved. That rule applies just the same if the amount is consistently below as if it is consistently above the mean chance expectancy.

Originally, when ESP tests first began, the idea had been to find persons, if such existed, who "had" ESP, much as in a different situation, it might have been to find those with blue eyes, or those who were right- or left-handed. The idea of ESP (or telepathy, as it then would have been called) was that it was like a characteristic which the person did or did not possess. But instances continued to occur when subjects yielded test scores that were significantly below the chance level instead of above it. The psi missing effect, then, had to be recognized as a real one and not due to some ordinary fault in procedure. Eventually, it became clear that ESP was not an ability that was or was not present in an individual, but instead it was a process which, as it were, could run either forward or backward. It meant that subjects could hit the target by ESP, or miss it the same way. Experiments had been carried out to show that when subjects were told to miss instead of hit the target, they could do so and produce scores that were significantly below chance expectation. But in the psi missing effect, the reversal occurred when subjects missed when they were trying to *hit* a target. And, as I said above, it could show up even in a single experiment if in it two conditions were to be contrasted. The result was that one tended to be positive, the other negative, and so results would cancel; so far as the total scores were concerned, experimenters could not easily say whether one of the two conditions was better than the other.

Later, the possibility of such a reversal from a positive result to a negative one came to be recognized in advance. Then the strategy was developed of planning the experiment in such a way that it would be statistically admissable to consider the deviations in either direction as valid if the difference between them was in itself great enough to be significant.

For instance, an experiment was carried out by Rao (reference 6) in which he contrasted two kinds of card decks to see on which the subjects would do better. One was the usual ESP deck with five standard geometrical symbols. The other was a deck made up for the purpose by each subject who selected as his own list of five symbols, certain ones that had personal meanings for him.

When the subjects were tested in that experiment they were told which deck was being used. The result was that the total scores with the cards of the person's own chosen symbols averaged well above chance and those with the ESP symbols averaged about equally much below. The difference between the two was great enough to be statistically significant. It was the result he expected to get, but it needed to be repeated and confirmed.

He then repeated the experiment and the results were at once baffling and, as it eventually proved, enlightening. In this second experiment one change was made in the procedure. This time the subjects were not told when the ESP deck or when the "choice" deck was being used. The result was a reversal. The experiment using the ESP deck yielded a positive deviation, the "choice" cards, a negative one. The experiment was a success. But what did it mean?

The enlightening element was that the two experiments together showed that changes in conditions, even seemingly slight ones, might cause reversals. But the basic question still was what could be the reason for reversals? The problem was a serious one and caused a baffling road block on the way to learning how to control psi. It, of course, had long been realized, however, that psi is an unconscious function and the person in a test does not know either how he hits the target or how he misses it. It was also realized that whether he hits or misses the target could be caused by differences in the conditions, whether external or internal and whether great or very small. It came to be recognized that the effect occurred especially when subjects were asked to make comparisons, as in Rao's tests. Generally, the results would differentiate between the two but the reason why they did so was seldom clear, just as in Rao's experiments.

The time came about 1965 when I thought I could see a possible bearing on this question from my study of the psi process in ESP (Chapter 14). Since the function of the case studies was especially to produce tips for experimenters, I undertook to see what could be found in the cases to bear on the reasons for, or explanation of, psi missing.

Of course, any bearing the case studies might have on the topic could not be direct because psi missing would not produce a recognizable psi experience. It would be one that *did not* happen. Evidence of psi missing therefore would have to be indirect. But "guessing" in experiments in which the missing occurred involved the intuitive form of response and that form had been one of the major ones analyzed in my study of the ESP process (Chapter 14). It, therefore, seemed to be the form in which to look for hints as to the way the missing might occur.

The study of intuitive experiences had brought out the fact that in contrast to the other major form, the realistic, the intuitive experiences reproduced no detail. Besides that, a large number of them, 45 per cent, contributed less than a complete item of information. Out of 1839 intuitive experiences, only 1021, or 55 per cent, were complete, while, in contrast, out of 3122 realistic experiences, 2834, or 91 per cent, were complete (reference 30, page 93). Therefore, as mentioned in Chapter 7, the intuitive form showed a tendency to produce information considerably narrowed down in comparison to the realistic—a narrowing at times almost to extinction. This narrowing first as to the details and even as to meaning suggested a kind of process that involved difficulty, presumably in the transfer of material from unconscious levels directly into the waking level of full consciousness.

More than that, the kind of incompleteness was different in realistic and intuitive experiences. In the realistic, for instance, Nos. 1 and 2, are typical.

No. 1

While in the army a man on maneuvers at Fort Dix in New Jersey dreamed about his sister's friend, Barbara. He thought she was getting married and was dressed in a beautiful white gown and veil. A large number of people were in attendance but he didn't see his sister among them. He dreamed that he did see his sister later and said to her, "Barbara was married and why weren't you at the wedding?" His sister answered, "I didn't know anything about it until it was all over. I felt so terrible about it."

Later when at home he asked his sister for the news and she said that her friend Barbara had passed away suddenly. He asked her if there had been many at the funeral, and she replied, "I don't know. I didn't know anything about it until it was all over. I felt so terrible about it."

No. 2

A woman in Washington dreamed very vividly that her husband's uncle had drowned. She could plainly see his body floating on the water, face up against some weeds.

That same morning, to her horror, they received word that this uncle, the evening before, had committed suicide by shooting himself. His body was found face up in the sage brush and weeds.

Characteristic of incomplete realistic experiences, a mistake was made in each dream. In No. 1 a funeral was changed to a wedding. In No. 2, a shooting and a drowning were interchanged. The rest of the scenes, however, were pictured sufficiently correctly to identify the episode. But the following intuitive cases show that their incompleteness is of a different kind from that of realistic dreams.

No. 3

The 70-year-old mother of an anesthetist who worked in a hospital in Gary, Indiana, lived with her daughter and son-in-law, and while they were at work she stayed at home about 22 miles from Gary. One morning about 10 a.m. the anesthetist had just finished one case and was about to start on another when she got a terrible worried feeling and a heaviness in her chest as if she were badly frightened. She, at once, went to the phone and placed a long distance call home.

Her mother answered gasping with a severe chest pain and said to get a doctor. She hung up and called her mother's doctor who went to the house immediately and found the mother suffering from a heart attack. By the time the daughter could arrive her mother was on her way to the hospital.

No. 4

A woman from Fairbanks, Alaska, was visiting in California. She had been in San Francisco and had gone to Santa Rosa when suddenly she knew she must call her married daughter who lived in Anchorage. As she reported it, "It simply came to me that I must call her although I had not been thinking of her particularly. And so when I got to Santa Rosa, I put in a long distance call to her. She asked me how on earth I had known she needed me. Her husband had been seriously injured and since I had been traveling she did not know how to reach me. I had just known, that's all. Her great need and troubled thoughts had come straight to me and since I was receptive, I got the message."

In both of these intuitive cases the experiencing persons did not know what the circumstance was which disturbed them. In No. 3, the effect was mainly emotional. The daughter did not know why she should call home. In No. 4, it was a compulsion. The mother did not know why she should make the phone call. In other cases, the actual imperfections were largely differences in degree of incompleteness. It seemed that even the kind of incompleteness in the intuitive cases suggested difficulty in getting information into consciousness and, as suggested in Chapter 14, it appeared that the message itself or part of it could be suppressed, or blocked, below the conscious level and the only sign that an ESP message had been received was the emotion, or the compulsion to action. It appeared, therefore, from the study of intuitive cases in general, that a tendency to blockage was a characteristic of the intuitive form.

Blockage, of course, is not a peculiarity of ESP alone. Memory, or recall, too offers frequent instances of it. Sometimes it is only temporary, and the item can be retrieved by effort, or it may appear spontaneously later, as when one is unable to remember a name, perhaps when trying to introduce a well-known acquaintance. But what if blocking occurs in an ESP test? If for some reason the identity of the correct target is suppressed, the person will not be aware of the blockage, as he is in conscious situations like introductions, but he will simply call one of the other symbols, and the call will be certain to be a miss. If the reason for the blockage persists, he will make a series of misses. And he will be unaware that he is doing so. If this kind of situation continues sufficiently long it will, of course, produce a significantly negative deviation and that will be psi missing.

It seemed thus that this result of the analysis of the process that produces the intuitive form of experience could very well suggest the way in which psi missing can occur. It does not, of course, tell why the blockage of the correct target should take place, but only how it does so.

In the cases, a large percentage of those in the intuitive form have emotional overtones. Even though persons react differently to emotional stress, the blockage of incomplete intuitive experiences practically always occurs in connection with highly emotional situations. This fact, however, would not explain blockage resulting in psi missing in tests because under laboratory conditions emotional factors even at the best certainly are minimal. In them, the circumstances are more comparable to noncritical and nonemotional situations. A survey of the apparent reasons for blockage in the tests has indicated that almost any kind of unpleasantness in the test situation, even when it is so slight that the subject himself may scarcely be conscious of it, can cause psi missing.

Approaching the question from the angle of psi hitting rather than psi missing, however, has shown that hitting occurs when all conditions are favorable so that the subject can fall into a "set" or state of mind free from even slight disturbance. But when something changes even slightly—boredom, a less preferred method, a distraction of any kind—no evidence of psi may result and the test scores will be at the level of chance expectation. But if the disturbing factor is greater, blockage and psi missing rather than simply chance level scores may result.

An experiment that would illustrate this was an early one

of Schmeidler's (reference 35) in which she found a tendency for subjects who believed in ESP (sheep) to score positively, those who did not (goats) to score below chance. In this situation, presumably the sheep react naturally without inhibition, but the goats tend to be under a degree of conflict and hence they "forget" the correct target and call a different one, so that their scores fall below the chance line.

If the reversals seemed at first to mean simply that ESP is an inconsistent and unpredictable ability, it seems now that the mistake was simply that of expecting an unconscious mental process to operate according to the rules of conscious processes. As already observed, the unconscious processes have their own rules and when once understood one can see that they have their own logic. But in the formula for producing a "repeatable" ESP experiment, account of those rules must be taken. Unfortunately the formula for doing so can never be as simple as that for combining an alkali and an acid, a process which does not go into reverse upon the slightest provocation. But nevertheless, the formula is not unworkable and these hints from the way psi seems to operate spontaneously seem to be quite applicable. It might be added that an understanding of psi missing, while it did not answer all the questions about psi, did help to clear the way toward those answers, too.

These observations on psi missing and those of previous chapters on the psi process, I think, add to the concept of psi, even though they do not touch on the larger problem, the one that is central in Stage I. These observations may tend to "humanize" psi experiences and make them seem less unaccountable but they are basically psychological observations and do not deal with the parapsychological question raised by Stage I.

However, before confronting the question of Stage I, it might be well to ask what spontaneous psi experiences *do for* the percipients, what function they serve. That question is pursued in Chapter 17 by the study of the subject matter of the cases in an attempt to see what this subject matter tells about human beings and about the function of the psi process.

The Subject Matter of
Psi Experiences: Its Significance

Accounts of psi experiences have been sprinkled liberally over these pages. Anyone who has read them knows that they cover a broad range of subject matter. But they were not selected on the basis of their content. Instead, they were chosen only to illustrate the way psi seems to operate. However, their content, the information they bring should also tell something about psi. It should suggest its reason and function in human life; that is, it should if one could know all the topics of psi experiences. But this, of course, is not within the realm of possibility, for as discussed in earlier chapters, probably not all psi impressions reach consciousness and certainly only a few of those that do ever get reported. On that account single cases or even the thousands of them in the Duke Collection would still seem to be very incomplete material on which to base an inquiry about the scope of subject matter of psi. However, on that point, the value of these in the collection, it seemed to me, might in a way be comparable to that of a poll taken before an election, or in an attempt to assess the popularity of a television program. I thought it could be that any marked trend that a complete list might show would at least be suggested in a portion of experiences, unselected as to topic, like those in the collection. It would seem that even the relative frequency of one general kind of topic over another should give suggestions about the motives and interests that psi serves. And since the origin of psi is deeply unconscious, any insights such comparisons might permit should reflect a quite elemental level of human nature.

By reasoning such as this, I decided to make a survey of the subject matter of a representative portion of the cases in the collection. It seemed possible at least to test some of the commonly held general impressions about it, in an effort to see how well they would be supported. One of these is that psi experiences tend to be on critical, highly emotion-stirring topics. Another is that they usually involve people who are closely linked emotionally.

Both of these impressions, of course, mean that psi, as it is expressed in daily life, is largely a purveyor of critical information. They do, in fact, often lead to the question, "Why does ESP always bring bad news?"

I knew, of course, that many cases in the collection did just that. They brought news about deaths, accidents and tragedies of many kinds, often concerning the percipients' close family members. But I also knew that not all of the cases were on critical topics. How frequent, relatively, were the critical versus not critical topics? And so, I undertook a survey to see to what extent the result would show that these general impressions were correct, and, more broadly, what would be suggested as to the function that psi serves in the lives of the percipients.

The Subject Matter
of Realistic Experiences

For the study (reference 29), I decided to use only the realistic cases in the collection rather than the entire number which had become large and unwieldy. Also the subdivisions of the total collection varied considerably in the degree of reliability that one could feel as to whether psi rather than only chance coincidence was involved in individual experiences (discussed in Chapter 7). Besides, realistic experiences were the most frequently reported of the forms and nearly three thousand cases (2878) of that one form were available.

Of course, judgments about the relative emotional impact of the information of each case would have to be made and also about its relative importance. Both judgments, too, would have to be made from the viewpoint of the percipients themselves. Four levels or groups of emotional intensity and four of level of importance of the event seemed to cover the range satisfactorily. Those of emotional intensity were:

Group I: The highest emotional level. This included all experiences which brought information that applied only to, or mainly to, the E person. An example is:

No. 1

A girl in Illinois dreamed that she saw an elderly woman holding a tiny, crying baby. Beside her was a man and a woman. Suddenly a shower of rice fell on the couple. The girl woke up with a start.

She remembered the dream but did not give it much thought until over a year later she was "compelled" to get married. Her mother held her four-weeks-old baby boy. He was crying while the Justice of the Peace performed the marriage ceremony.

Group II: The next highest emotional level. This included experiences involving mainly members of the E person's immediate family. The agents thus would include the spouse, children, parents and occasionally a very special friend of the percipient. Many foregoing examples fall into this category, as does the following case:

No. 2

A woman in Minnesota was working in an old people's home and dreamed that her daughter, who was in California, came up behind her and threw her arms around her, and that she (the mother) said aloud, "My God, it's Mary Jane," and then she saw the girl's face was gray and drawn and realized too that she was very cold.

The dream worried her. She told her employer about it. Three days later it came true exactly, and Mary Jane was cold, gray and tired out. She had driven from Los Angeles to Minnesota in three days. She had come through a snow storm and two near accidents.

Groups III: This included all the E persons' less emotional relationships, their more distant relatives, friends, and acquaintances, neighbors, business associates and pets. An experience in this group follows:

No. 3

Two small businesses in California occupied the same building. Mr. A. and his wife, on the right, had a sewing machine sales shop; Mr. B. and his wife, on the left, had a similar set-up for typewriters. A young man named Bob Mitchel would bring his typewriter into the B's shop for repairs and Mrs. A. occasionally saw him. She had met him incidentally perhaps a dozen times when he came in one morning when both Mr. and Mrs. B. were out and so he sat down in Mr. A's side to wait. In a few minutes Mrs. B. returned and the two were engaged in conversation when Mrs. A. turned toward them with, as she said, "what must have been a look of terror on my face," for Bob Mitchel asked if she had seen a ghost.

Incautiously, she answered, "No, but I just remembered that I had a dream about you last night and it wasn't good." Of course, after that she had to tell them what it was. In the dream she had seen the young man and his wife driving down a local highway and as they went through an underpass, he ran into a truck and although the wife was only hurt, he was decapitated. They all said it was a terrible dream, and then the subject was changed.

A few weeks later it happened, just as dreamed. Mrs. A. was most upset. Why did she have such a dream? She only knew the young man slightly.

Group IV: The T persons here were strangers to the E persons, in some instances persons of whom they knew, as in the next example, and in others not.

No. 4

A private nurse in England was sent by a doctor to an urgent case. The patient, a man who was employed as a country school inspector, had suffered an epileptic seizure, his first, and had fallen in such a way that his face had struck the bars by an open fire resulting in severe burns and lacerations.

The man's physical state was bad, his mental state was

even worse, because the doctor could not guarantee he would never have another seizure and he feared he would lose his position.

As he convalesced and discussed his situation with the nurse, he hoped he would soon be able to call upon the Superintendent of Inspectors and try to find out what his prospects were for continuance. The nurse suggested that they might ask the superintendent to call the patient instead. However, the patient objected that the man was much too busy. She offered to write the superintendent, but he would not permit that either.

One night the nurse dreamed that the superintendent did come, that she opened the door to him, that she recognized him, that she said, "Oh, you are Mr. W.... Come in, Mr. R. is in here." Then in the dream, she escorted the visitor into the dining room and left the two men together.

Next morning when telling the patient her dream he laughed and said, "That's not likely to happen." She described the superintendent as about 40 years old, wearing a brown suit and tie and carrying a valise with initials in gold, W.W.W. The patient said, "I don't know what he looks like. I've never seen him. And anyway, why would you be going to the door? The maid does that."

One Sunday later on, other family members were away and it was the maid's day off. The patient and nurse had finished a leisurely evening meal and were chatting over final cups of tea in the dining room, when the door bell rang. Of course, the nurse went to the door. She saw the man of her dream. Automatically, she said, "Oh, it's you, Mr. W. Please come in," and showed him into the dining room.

When they were alone the superintendent asked the patient how the nurse had known his name, and was told of the dream and how exactly the details fit. It turned out that the superintendent had not intended to make the call but had been in the **neighborhood unexpectedly and decided on impulse to drop in**. And, of course, on any other day the maid, not the nurse, would have admitted him.

These four groups covered the range of emotional involvement of the percipient with the agents, but the other dimension to be taken into account was the relatively critical nature of the events in which the agent was concerned.

Those events, too, could logically be considered as falling into four levels of seriousness. The cases accordingly could be divided into the following sections. *Section A* concerned death; *Section B* included other serious personal crises including all nonfatal illnesses, operations, accidents, births and marriages; *Section C* covered all other generally important events; and *Section D* concerned trivial topics.

The four examples above which illustrated the groups of varying emotional relationships also illustrate the four levels of seriousness, although not in the same order. Thus, No. 1, the marriage of the percipient, listed under *Group I*, was here placed in *Section B*. Case 2, the arrival of the percipient's daughter, in *Group II*, was here placed in *Section C*, while No. 3, the death of a casual acquaintance, *Group III*, here in *Section A*, and No. 4, the arrival of the superintendent, a stranger to the percipient, *Group IV*, here belonged in *Section D*.

Besides these divisions, it seemed as if it might be worthwhile to see if subject matter was affected by timing—in other words, whether differences in the subject matter of precognitive versus contemporaneous experiences, or at least in their frequencies, would appear. That information, I thought, might raise the question why percipients look ahead in precognition rather than staying within the habitual limitation of sense experience which of course is to the present. Would the subject matter of precognitive experiences perhaps show underlying tensions, anxieties or other hidden motives to account for its selection, motives that did not surface in experiences that referred only to the present situation? Or would such a survey make any suggestion as to the general reason for the selection of any specific topic regardless of the timing?

The cases, of course, were already filed by type so that the precognitive ones were already isolated and a contemporaneous group could be made by simply combining the clairvoyant, telepathic and GESP groups. In order to catalogue the numbers of experiences falling into the various relationships, I constructed a 16-cell matrix using the emotional groups, *I, II, III,* and *IV* as abscissa and the seriousness of the event section *A, B, C,* and *D*

TABLE I
Frequencies of Subject Matter of Realistic Experiences (2878 dreams)

EMOTIONAL RELATIONSHIPS Groups		RELATIVELY CRITICAL NATURE OF EVENT								Total No. of Cases per Group	% of Total per Group	% Precognition Cases per Group
		Section A Death		Section B Illness, etc.		Section C Important Topics		Section D Trivial Topics				
		No. Cases	% Pcg	No. Cases	% Pcg	No. Cases	% Pcg	No. Cases	% Pcg			
I.	Self	27	100	197	100	484	69	253	92	961	33	82
II.	Family	365	71	416	41	277	65	65	75	1123	40	58
III.	Remote Relationships	175	56	108	54	107	56	19	90	409	14	57
IV.	Strangers	85	48	91	56	125	69	84	94	385	13	67
V.	Total Cases	652		812		993		421		2878		
VI.	% of Total Number	23		28		34		15				

as the ordinates. In each cell, I made two entries, one for the total number of cases that fell into it and one for the percentage of each that was precognitive. These entries, of course, constituted the data for which the study was made. They are presented in full in Table I but it can be skipped if desired for I will discuss below all of the points that seem of interest.

The results did and did not bear out expectations. True, the two groups in which the emotional linkage was the highest, *I* and *II*, did contain nearly three-fourths (73 per cent) of all the cases and of these, *Group II*, involving the percipient's close relatives and friends, was the largest of all (40 per cent). This gave some support to the idea that emotional linkages are very important. But two considerations rather diminished that importance.

One was that over a quarter of all the cases were in the nonemotional groups and nearly half of them involved strangers. These figures seemed to show that emotional linkages were not always as important as reputed to be. The other consideration involved the total number of cases (33 per cent) in *Group I*, which was nearly as large as *Group II*, which with 40 per cent of the total had only a few more.

Curiously, although *Group I* cases were in the high emotion category, until I made this study I had not noticed how frequent they were, nor had I even seen any observation to that effect in the literature. On the contrary, it seemed that traditionally, psychic experiences were considered as mainly bringing information about tragedies occurring to the percipient's closest circle of relatives and friends, cases that in this classification would fall into *Group II*. The fact, of course, was that *Group I* cases must have been frequently reported all the time but why had I — and apparently everyone else who noticed tendencies in psychic experiences — missed it? The reason was one of which I finally became aware as I studied the percentages in the groups showing the relative seriousness of the events, *A, B, C* and *D,* as I will point out in discussions of those studies below.

The overall numbers of cases that fell into categories *A* and *B,* the most critical, again only partially fulfilled expectations for, instead of including nearly all of the entries in the group, they made up just over half (51 per cent), and of these, death (*Group A*), which so often has seemed to be one of the main topics of psychic experiences, turned out to number less than a quarter (23 per cent) of all of the 2878 experiences. The largest single category was the next one, *C*, which included other than critical but still important events. These events were distributed fairly widely over the spectrum of human interest, as will be illustrated below, and it included "happy" occurrences as well as "unhappy" ones. It appears, however, that in contrast to critical topics, the "happy" topics simply do not make as strong an impression as their frequency of occurrence deserves. This, of course, is a commentary on human nature rather than on para-psychological tendencies.

As it turned out, the variations in overall numbers of precognitive versus contemporaneous cases also either "made sense" or raised interesting questions. For instance, the groups that included the highest proportion of precognitive cases of all, were those involving the person himself, *Group I*. Why should this be so? It is a point for later discussion, for only part of the story is told by these general percentages. The rest of it is shown by the interaction of all three classifications, the emotional, the nature of the event and the timing. Taking each of the groups, *I, II, III, IV,* in turn, these variations are:

Group I, The Person Him or Herself. In this group of cases, the topics of death and other critical events, *sections A* and *B*, made up scarcely a quarter of all (3 and 21 per cent respectively), while *Section C,* important but not critical topics, were half of the total, and the final group, *D*, trivial topics, had a relatively large number of entries (26 per cent). The variations in percentages of precognition in each of these subdivisions were also of interest. First, the low numbers of critical cases affecting the percipients themselves was, to some extent, the result of the fact that they were all precognitive, and had to be, because the persons could not have contemporary experiences involving their own death or serious illness. This, of course, somewhat artificially increases the frequency of precognitive experiences in this group (82 per cent).

However, even without a contemporaneous component in

the two sections, *A* and *B*, the numbers of cases they do include, even though precognitive, seem inordinately low since every person has crises of these kinds in his or her future. The numbers are low enough in fact to suggest that a repressing influence is operating. People apparently tend not to look ahead and contemplate these crises of their own. Instead, it seems that they are much more likely to get information about their own affairs of general but not critical importance and even of quite unimportant and trivial topics.

Of course, one can surmise reasons why critical topics might tend to be avoided. A healthy refusal of the percipients to dwell on painful subjects in their own future or on the unavoidable reality of death could do it.

(But, if such repression does occur, at what point in the psi process does it take place? Would it be in Stage I and mean that such unwelcome topics are simply not apprehended and turned over to Stage II? Or would they be apprehended, turned over to Stage II, but be repressed there and not processed as an item in consciousness? However, as discussed in Chapter 14, the basis on which psi items are selected in Stage I is entirely uncertain and unknown so that conjectures here are not likely to be very profitable. One had better ask about the situation in Stage II where conjecture seems a bit more feasible. As shown in Chapter 14, evidence exists to show that an item of information arriving in Stage II is by no means certain of being apprehended intact in consciousness. Any part of it may be distorted or suppressed by personal and emotional influences like anxiety, need, expectation, preference, so that entire topics, if selected in Stage I, presumably could be suppressed in Stage II. It seems possible then that suppression could occur in this stage and that topics like death or serious illness might therefore seldom get into conscious attention.)

The topics under *C,* however, being of general interest and less acute emotional value, would be much less likely to be suppressed and therefore their total percentage might well be greater.

The topics under *C* varied widely and can only, imperfectly, be illustrated by generalizations like the following (with numbers of each):

1.	The locating of missing articles	95 cases
2.	Fires of major concern to E person	20
3.	Outcome of bets, races, contests	52
4.	Job or professional incidents	79
5.	The elements, floods, earthquakes, etc.	19
6.	Ceremonies, speeches of E person	11
7.	Scenes from later life	76
8.	Miscellaneous	132
		484 cases

About two-thirds of these cases were precognitive. Most of the topics are self-explanatory, but for several reasons the "scenes from later life" call for special discussion. Of course, they are all precognitive, in contrast to the locating of missing articles, the "finding cases," which are nearly all contemporaneous. The scenes from later life, however, as will be shown later, have a rather special characteristic which is that they depict a specific scene which the person will later come upon and recognize as the original of this experience. But more than that, at the time of the experience, he has no explanation of the setting of the scene or of its relevance. The experiences are dreams and the situations to which they prove to be relevant may or may not be of importance to him.

The scenes from later life made up a fairly large number of items in both *sections C* and *D*. The basis of their distribution into either *Section C* or *D* was that of the relative importance of the subject matter to the E person.

For example, one that was of some importance is the following:

No. 5

A woman writing from California described a dream she had had when about 12 years old in which she thought she was in a room in which a grand piano stood covered with green silk with long gold fringes in the center of which was an ivory plaque engraved in silver. From a door behind her a stately woman entered dressed in white with a brown sash, her dark auburn hair parted in the middle. The girl somehow had the impression that this woman would start her on a musical career.

Three years later the girl had an audition with the accompanist of a well-known Philharmonic choir who was "the woman of my dream." The explanation came with the accompanist's apology for her appearance saying that she had just shampooed her hair and had not had time to set it. Therefore, she was still in her bath robe (white, with a brown sash) and her hair was still parted in the center.

I called this particular kind of case, because of its detailed reproduction of the scene, often an outdoor one, a "landscape case." Those in which the relevance seemed of sufficient importance to the percipients to be placed in *Section C* included items like places that would later become significant to them. Sometimes these were homes they would later live in, as in the next case.

No. 6

A woman in Indiana, the wife of a lay pastor, dreamed the family was living in a different house and in a strange town. She saw her familiar furniture in various rooms, even her dishes in a strange dish cupboard in the dining room. Then she saw the family in the yard outside and noticed that the house was very plain. The dream was sufficiently impressive that she told her husband about it.

About six months later, the superintendent of the church sent her and her husband to a new church. They were shown the parsonage. It was "the very same house I had seen in my dream and we were living in it within two weeks."

The importance of the situations of which the scenes were a part tapered off, as mentioned, and many had to be considered to be of trivial nature and were placed in *Section D*.

As already remarked, *Section D* in *Group I* was unexpectedly large, just as *A* and *B* seemed unexpectedly small. This number in *D*, about a third of all of the E person's own experiences, was large, not only in relation to the rest of his or her own experiences but also in relation to the numbers of cases in *Section D* of the other groups, *II, III* and *IV*. Whatever the reason for so many experiences with unimportant subject matter, their largely precognitive content (92 per cent) was also unexpected, for only the remaining 8 per cent of the trivial topics were contemporary. Often the scene portrayed was so casual and lacking in any general importance to the percipients that they themselves commented on it, as in this case:

No. 7

A school teacher in New Hampshire dreamed one night that she was standing on the steps of the school house, two children on the step above her, one on the one below on the opposite side, and that the sun was shining brightly through the maple leaves making a lovely pattern. Then seven-year-old Billy, who usually arrived on the school bus, came walking into the school yard.

Six months later, Billy had a sore throat one morning and was left in the care of a neighbor. But later he felt better and since it was a nice day, he was allowed to walk to school.

As the teacher said in reporting her dream, "It happened exactly — but such a silly topic — nothing dramatic."

The "landscape" kind of case, particularly those that fell into *Group I, Section D*, needs some emphasis because it has gone so long generally unrecognized in parapsychology and it seems to provide a good explanation for a kind of experience that has puzzled many persons, lay and professional alike. It is the feeling of having "lived this moment," this situation before, the *déjà vu* experience.

Of course, until the occurrence of precognition had been established, precognitive dreaming had only been suspected to occur but was not widely accepted as a reality. However, early studies like one made by Saltmarsh (reference 34) had done their bit to show that such a phenomenon as precognition very well may be an actual facet of human experience. But without the recognition of precognitive dreaming, the experience of seemingly having already lived through a present situation is inexplicable, as shown by all of the psychological attempts to explain the *déjà vu* experience, which at best must be considered less than successful.

One point about the majority of reported *déjà vu* experiences is their banality. Usually the feeling concerns some undistinguished scrap of daily living, just like the many trivial dreams in *Section D*. But in the cases of *Section D* in the collection, the percipients usually did recall that they had dreamed the scene, as in this case:

No. 8

A young girl in New York State had a recurring dream that she was driving by a stretch of railroad on the right with several particular houses on the left. Later, attending college, and in a car pool, the occupants were delayed by a train one day and decided to take a short cut. It was by a railroad track on the right and the particular houses on the left. The same as in the dream, she said, "Every house and curve in the road as familiar to me as if I'd known it all my life, though I'd never been down it before then."

However, sometimes the percipients were uncertain whether or not they had had a previous dream, as in this instance:

No. 9

A young man in North Carolina was much puzzled over a episode which he said he may have dreamed, but "The only thing I can remember is that I had done it before it took place. The trouble was that the person I was talking with was a person I had never met until that very day.

"I was in my car behind the wheel. The car was parked. The young man was about 18. He was married. He was leaning through the window on the other side of the car and I was saying things that I know I had said before. Everything fit down to the last detail of me leaning my right arm in the middle of the seat. His face was the same face I had seen before. I knew that I could not stop what I was saying and doing but I knew I had done the exact same thing before."

In other instances the person might report that after such an experience, he or she did recall the dream which had preceded it. Then again, in still others, no memory of a corresponding dream remained, but only the feeling of familiarity. In view of the frequency of precognitive dreams that were remembered and especially of the large numbers of them on unimportant topics, they form the perfect backdrop for the feeling of having "lived this situation before" in those instances in which no memory of the dream remains. Many dreams, of course, are poorly remembered. No doubt many too are not recalled at all, especially if their subject matter is very commonplace.

In general, then, the experiences of *Group I* seemed to show several unexpected aspects. In the first place, they covered such a diversity of topics that they raised the question, why and on what basis were they selected? Certainly, to account for their selection no single reason like anxiety or emotional need was suggested. However, they were all topics of interest to the percipients, though it varied from the least to the greatest. Even the great frequency of precognitive experiences, which might have indicated a degree of anxiety for the future, did not actually do even that because the subject matter so often was not on an anxiety-producing level. However, the contrast between the situation in the *Group I* topics and those of *Group II* was striking. It suggested a reason why experiences involving oneself have tended not to make the general impression of those involving one's relatives.

Group II. The Person's Immediate Family. Here almost every observation was in contrast to the comparable one in *Group I.* I had expected the great majority of all the cases to fall into this group and although more of them did so than into any other (40 per cent), the number was lower than I had expected and especially so since so many possible individuals might be included, the percipient's spouse, parents, and children, while *Group I* cases only could refer to the percipients themselves.

However, although these *Group II* cases begin with high percentages in *sections A* and *B* (27 and 33 per cent respectively) they taper off rapidly to low numbers in *D* (5 per cent). In *Section A*, the death cases, at 365, are about 34 times as frequent as were death cases in *Group I*. This, instead of suggesting suppression as it did there, seemed instead almost as if the person was courting trouble by registering a comparatively large number of deaths, and nearly three-fourths of them (71 per cent) precognitively. While this could suggest an anxiety element in choice of topic, that idea does not hold up well in regard to the topic of serious illness of *Section B* where, among the total large number of cases, precognitive ones (41 per cent) are in the minority. (Of course, as remarked earlier, with all numbers in this survey it is difficult to judge what the size of a difference must be in order that it be considered as having overall significance.)

In *Group II, Section C,* which, of course, includes important but non-critical topics, the number of entries is smaller than those of the deaths and serious crises of *A* and *B,* instead of being the largest of any section as it was in *Group I,* in which only the percipient was concerned. About half of the cases here were precognitive. The topics are considerably different from those in *Section C, Group I,* given above.

1.	Scenes at location of agent	70 cases
2.	Miscellaneous troubles of agent	44
3.	Arrival and return to the percipient of the agent	64
4.	Fires of major concern to agent	9
5.	Ceremonies involving the agent	8
6.	Miscellaneous	82
		277 cases

Notably, although these topics concern the agents, they often actively involve the percipients too and speak for their interest in and concern for the other.

The distribution of agents among the members of the percipient's immediate family shows sons first, husbands second, with father, brother, daughter, mother, sister and wife in decreasing numbers. Male agent-persons were twice as numerous as females. Presumably this could be because a greater number of females than of males report their experiences. But also, male relatives, no doubt, are absent more than females and more often, as in war, in danger. Possibly numbers here could be an indirect indication of anxiety.

However all this may be, it seems apparent too judging by the numbers that the percipients' interest in the noncritical affairs of their families is much less than in their own affairs of comparable seriousness. This suggestion is strengthened by the small number of trivial entries in *Section D.*

Even in this group the cases are predominantly precognitive, although less frequently so than in *Group I*. This fact, along with the general high proportion of precognitive cases in almost all cells of the table, seems to say that the experiencing of events still in the future does not necessarily mean that they were selected because of anxiety. It seems that a different motive must be assigned to them. But the reduced number of experiences in *sections C* and *D*, in comparison to the similar ones in *Group I*, suggest that the percipients are mainly concerned only with the important, even tragic events may befall their close relatives. One could say that they betray considerable concern for those they love but are content not to follow their lesser affairs very closely.

And so, it seems to me, experiences involving the persons themselves are, on the whole, less spectacular than those that concern their relatives. It is their deaths and tragedies, not one's own, that one reflects. The percipients' own major involvements are in their less than critical affairs and these run the gamut of greater to lesser importance and taper off into a large number of episodes of slight or even negligible significance. All of these, of course, add to the total number of cases in which the percipients themselves are the principal participants, but they are not the kind that, in reports, would add up and be remembered. That very well may be the reason they have so long escaped emphasis and almost even, recognition.

Group III. Remote Relationships. This group involving, in general, only slight or no emotional relationship to the percipient, still did include some individuals, grandparents, aunts, uncles, and others, that do represent a certain degree of emotional linkage. This may account for the fact that distributions here resemble those of *Group II* even though the numbers are smaller. Even precognitive cases still predominate although not so strongly.

Taken as relationships regardless of the number of individuals in each who could be involved, the number of cases in this group, in order, concerned grandparents, grandchildren, aunts, nephews, nieces, cousins, in-laws, fiancés and boyfriends, acquaintances and business associates, neighbors, servants and employees, and finally animals. The animals were mainly pets, but farm animals and even a few wild ones appeared. The most frequent event in which an animal was concerned was death or accident.

The percentage of crisis cases here, *sections A* and *B,* is about the same as in *Group II.* The range of topics in *Section C* is similar too, though slightly reduced:

1.	Scenes at the location of the agent	33 cases
2.	Miscellaneous troubles of the agent	14
3.	Arrival of the agent	13
4.	Fires of concern to the agent	7
5.	Miscellaneous	40
		107 cases

The number of trivial cases is small, and the percentage of precognitive experiences in *Group III, Section C* is only slightly lower than that in *Group II.*

The idea that anxiety might be a factor in the selection of precognitive cases in *Group III* seems hardly indicated, although the death or serious illness of persons of all the relationships represented here would have a degree of shock effect. This, rather than anxiety, possibly could explain the fact that over half of all the cases in the group are in *sections A* and *B* and could mean that little but crises among these persons would claim much attention.

Group IV. Strangers. I had classified experiences as involving strangers if the person was perceived and described as a distinct individual, not just as a shadowy "unknown" in *Section I.* Perhaps it might have been expected that the topics and distributions here would be quite different from those in the others. However, the total number of cases (13 per cent of all) was about the same as in *Group III* (14 per cent) and the distribution among the sections was not significantly different except in *Section D,* of which more later. The proportion of precognitive cases (67 per cent) was slightly higher than in *Group III,* but probably not significantly so.

Entries both precognitive and contemporary occurred in both of the critical sections, *A* and *B.* One from *Section A,* and involving a stranger, comes from a woman in Tennessee:

No. 10

In a dream one night, she saw two little boys fishing. Then she saw one kill the other with a rifle. She saw the dead boy being carried to a nearby store and being placed in a large box.

The next day her brother-in-law went to the store of her dream, and when he came back he told her that a little boy had been in a fight and was killed. She added, before she was told, that the dead boy was carried into the store and put in a large wooden box. He said, "Yes, but how on earth did you know that?" And then she told him of the dream.

The cases involving other important events in *Section C* covered a somewhat reduced range compared to those in *Group III*. But they included scenes from the location of the strange agent who often was an individual reported in the news as missing. In a number of instances, an agent played a role of some slight significance to the percipient, as for example:

No. 11

An elderly woman in Nebraska had to have a delicate surgical operation for which she had to go to Rochester. After leaving the hospital, she roomed for a time in a private home on the north side of town.

One night she dreamed that she had decided to walk to the hospital instead of taking the bus. It was a long way and she began to get tired. Her steps were lagging when she came to the business area.

Suddenly a door on her left opened and out came an intoxicated elderly man. He was disheveled and bare-headed, with graying, sandy hair standing in all directions. He focussed his bleary eyes on her and with a broad grin he came lunging across the walk to her. She was so frightened that she awoke.

Occasionally she had had bad dreams before and so she did not take this one too seriously. Not long afterwards, on a lovely April morning, she was tempted to walk to the hospital. She was enjoying the walk but by the time she entered the business district, she realized she had better slow down as she was getting a little breathless and so she walked leisurely along, window shopping as she went.

Suddenly a door on her left burst open and out came the drunken old man of her dream: sandy gray disheveled hair, bleary eyes, the same broad grin, outstretched arms, and coming as fast as his unsteady legs would carry him. She was very frightened, but, as she said, "This time I could not awaken. It was real.

"I swung out around him and ran as fast as I could until I felt sure I had left him behind. What a queer circumstance to have come true. It still seems uncanny to me."

As in this circumstance, the majority of the cases in *Section C* were precognitive (69 per cent), a somewhat higher percentage than in Group III (56 per cent), but the significant fact perhaps is that precognition continues to occur even when involving strangers and even when the situations are less critical than those under *sections A* or *B*.

This same observation applies even more cogently in the cases of *Section D* in which the precognitive type (94 per cent) is the highest of any of the *D sections*. These are essentially "landscape" cases and in a way could have been placed under *D* in *Group I*. However, I separated them because the strangers were identified to a degree that seemed to call for emphasis, even though in most of them the episode in which they were involved, in itself, had general interest only for the percipient.

Another situation came to light in examining these cases involving strangers, one that could have a bearing on the reach of psi as suggested in spontaneous experiences and also on the question of why given topics are selected in Stage I. This was that, in certain instances, no *present reason* seemed to exist for the given item to be selected.

On this distinction, these cases could be divided in such a way as to leave one body of them in which a link or connection even though tenuous did exist between the percipient and the stranger. In some instances the percipient knew of the agent, or at least that individual was from a place familiar to the percipient. But in about two-thirds of the "stranger" cases (261), no such link existed at the time the percipient had the experience.

In some of these instances, when no connection between the two existed, they later did meet and the relationship that ensued became significant, as in this case:

No. 12

A girl on Long Island dreamed she was walking down a street with a person she later could describe perfectly down to his brown slacks and suede jacket, except for his face, which was not visible. They were in a town which she did not recognize either, although details of the street, the name of which she somehow knew was Tennessee Street, and a grocery store, hedges, etc., were also clear. The dream seemed strange but she passed it off as just a dream.

A year later she went with her parents on a vacation to Florida. While there, she met a Navy man home on leave visiting his parents. A romance developed and five months later the two were married in California.

One evening a month later she and her husband went to a little grocery store. She began to feel she knew what her husband would pick next and the exact amount that the groceries would come to. When they left the store, they went on Tennessee Street. They passed an odd hedge that grew to the sidewalk, skipped it, and then went on to the street. Just then it all came back, the grocery, Tennessee Street, the odd hedge, her husband whose face she now could see, and it was all the same down to his brown slacks and suede jacket.

In such cases, in some of which the degree of significance was much less than in this instance, still one could say that the only reason for the selection of that topic *was in the future*. Or at least, the scene as dreamed was related to a situation that, in time, made it significant.

In the rest of the cases, however, the reason for the selection not only did not exist at the time of the experience, but no reason, except at the most casual level, ever did exist. In some instances, the agents were or became public figures and the percipients eventually heard of them in a news broadcast. Or they eventually saw the agents of whom they dreamed. The following is one of 133 cases in which this was true.

No. 13

A man left England and after some travels, arrived in Western Australia from which he reported that three years before leaving England he dreamed he was walking down a side street into a sort of public square in a large city in India.

The scene was very clear. There were dark, thin people dressed in dirty white and among them he noticed especially two people walking diagonally across the square. They were paler than most, one woman in a shabby pale green sari. The other he did not notice further. Across his path then sauntered a young native with tattered white sarong, European shirt hanging out, and a loose untidy head cloth, almost a turban. In the dream, he noticed the man's hooked nose, slow swinging gait, sinewy calves and the gray dust on his ankles. He also noticed white buildings at the side of the square.

The dream impressed him and he told it to his family. It was about three years later when he left England. But he did not go to India. However, in Colombo, Ceylon, the dream came true, although long out of mind. There, among a crowd in a square, he suddenly recognized it all, though the young man must have looked younger at the time of the dream than now when he was the exact counterpart of the dream, as were all the other details.

And so, even experiences several years in the future, it would seem, can be picked out and individuals in them of no significance to the percipient visualized sometimes as clearly as if of present importance. In fact, cases like these are apparently only an extension of the trivial experiences of *Group I, Section D,* and the point they make is that no obvious connection be-- tween the two individuals needs to exist. Psi can bridge the gap.

Apparently psi can also bridge the gap between the affairs of those persons (agents) who are emotionally close and those who are utter strangers. It can bridge it whether the strangers are personalities in their own right or simply in a future scene with no particular significance to the percipient. This apparently means that the content of psi experiences can range in seriousness over the entire spectrum of personal interests no matter whether the percipients are themselves the major figures or if, instead, those figures are strangers with whom the percipients have no link, present *or* future.

TABLE II
Frequencies of Subject Matter of Intuitive Experiences (1,441 Cases)

E-PERSON'S EMOTIONAL RELATIONSHIPS Groups	RELATIVELY CRITICAL NATURE OF EVENT								Total No. of Cases per Group	% of Total per Group	% Precognition Cases per Group
	Section A Death		Section B Serious Crisis		Section C Other Important Events		Section D Trivial Events				
	No. Cases	% Pcg	No. Cases	% Pcg	No. Cases	% Pcg	No. Cases	% Pcg			
I. Self	5	100	82	73	277	36	17	-	381	27	42
II. Family	172	45	318	14	148	13	1	-	639	44	22
III. Remote Relationships	163	45	72	22	84	21	15	-	334	23	32
IV. Strangers	26	58	19	71	29	18	13	-	87	6	38
TOTALS	336		491		538		46		1441		134

The Subject Matter
of Intuitive Experiences

After finishing the classification of the realistic cases which, as explained above, had been selected on the assumption that the subject matter of psi experiences would not be affected by their form, I decided to test that assumption by treating another form in a similar way (reference 30). I used the intuitive form this time both because the number of cases available was the next largest of all (1441) and because it contrasts strongly with the realistic, since in it the person is awake and no imagery is involved.

I used the same divisions into emotional *groups I, II, III,* and *IV,* and the same division of seriousness of the event into *sections A, B, C,* and *D* with a similar matrix including both contemporaneous and precognitive entries. The results are given in Table II, which again can be skipped at will, for the main points will be discussed below.

Comparing the numbers in the various categories of Table I and Table II, both similarities and differences are noticeable. The similarities are that in both, the numbers in the *A sections* of *Group I* are low, in *Group II* they are high and they taper off in *groups III* and *IV.* It is less clear in Table II than in Table I that the actual number of *Group I* cases per individual is larger than that of *Group II.* But in both, *Section C* is the largest of all in the group.

In *Section D,* however, a great difference between the numbers in the two forms comes in. The number of dreams of trivial subject matter of Table I (253) was over half as large as that of *Section C* (484) while in Table II, the number of trivial topics in *Section D* was so small as to be practically negligible. Another difference was that of the relative percentages of precognitive cases. In Table I (last column) the average percentage of precognitive dreams was 66. In Table II, for the intuitions, it was only about 34 per cent.

This difference, however, certainly may not mean just what it seems to say, that precognitive intuitions are much fewer than intuitions about contemporary events. After all, the validity of an intuitive experience, even when it concerns a contemporary event (and so can be confirmed quickly), is more difficult to establish if the experience cannot be confirmed until a future time. Even the person having it may come to doubt the accuracy of the hunch and almost certainly his or her friends will do so, in this case.

No. 14

A woman in Oklahoma in February was obsessed with the feeling that a family tragedy was ahead. The family consisted of her husband, four sons and two daughters, all grown. As she wrote, "No one seemed to sympathize or be interested in my fears. But in March our oldest son, 38, was killed by an intruder at his place of business."

No doubt many such hunches (often even less specific) are discounted. Even if a person believed the feeling to be meaningful, a case collector like myself might very well not. In fact, for such a precognitive intuition to be recognized, remembered and reported, it would almost have to include objective evidence of some kind like a mention of it beforehand to another person, as for instance, in the experience of a woman in Maryland:

No. 15

A cooking school in one of the department stores had been going on one afternoon a week for ten weeks. A Mrs. A. and her friend had attended, and even though every night a bag of groceries was given to a "winner" neither one had ever won any of them. Now the next afternoon would be the last and an electric refrigerator was to be the prize, as they had all known it would be.

On the evening before that meeting, Mrs. A. said to her husband, "When I win this refrigerator do you want me to phone you at the office or wait until you come home from work?" In reporting, she wrote, "I *knew* I was going to win. It was not wishful thinking, although we did not have such a refrigerator. Without a smile, my husband said, 'Phone me.' "

The next day before the drawing, Mrs. A. took out her compact, powdered her nose and thought over what she would say over the radio. Her neighbor beside her asked, "What are you doing?"

"I have to go up on stage and thank them for the refrigerator." Her neighbor just laughed.

Then someone on the stage said, "The lucky winner is Mrs. A." She recounted, "I went up, gave my little speech of thanks, went back to my seat and then shook so hard I rattled my chair."

It thus seems likely that the differences between the frequency of precognitive intuitions and precognitive dreams, as shown here, cannot be presumed to be very reliable insofar as they give an indication of the actual rates of occurrence of the two forms. One other reason besides this difference in ease of recognition of the two might be an innate difference in the tendency of the human mind to drift across the barrier of the present, as one might say, and invade the future. Possibly that could occur more frequently, more easily, in the relaxation of sleep than when the person is awake. But if so, no other data yet exist to support the idea. The recognition of precognition as a reality is still too recent and too limited for the questions even to have been asked, much less answered.

The situation shown in the intuitive cases thus did not very clearly support the initial idea that the subject matter of psi experiences would be independent of the form. It failed to do so, particularly in *Section D,* and in connection with the landscape dreams in which a real scene is reproduced in terms of visual imagery. No counterpart of this occurs in intuitive experiences. Besides that, a large number of landscape cases involved quite trivial subject matter. But, intuitions on trivial topics were very rare. And after all, considering the apparent genesis of intuitive experience, it should be expected that this would be so. As discussed in Chapter 14, the evidence suggests that in intuitions, material rising from unconscious levels directly into consciousness must somehow be possessed of considerable urgency (or meaning?) in order to cross into consciousness. Such urgency from all signs is closely associated with the emotional significance to the percipient of the content of the message. Unimportant items thus would surely seldom break through.

And so, in this respect, the content of intuitive experiences would tend to be more serious, more emotional and meaningful to the person than that of the realistic. To that extent, the form and subject matter would not be independent. At the same time, because of their form, the relative numbers of precognitive experiences would tend to be greater in the realistic than in intuitive cases. Also, because of their form, the percentage of precognitive dreams would be greater than that of precognitive intuitions, just as the observed percentages indicate.

* * * * *

These studies of the frequencies of kinds of topics in psi experiences have, of course, been made on only the segment of all recognized, reported — not to say experienced — cases that appeared in the collection. But even in this sample, the fact stands out that almost any kind of topic that a normal human being would recognize as of even passing interest might turn up as the subject matter of his or her psi experience. The main point these studies show is the uneven distribution of topics. While highly emotional topics are frequent, they are well balanced by others much less important, and while the subject matter concerns first of all the percipients themselves, it also, to an unexpected degree, may involve persons who are not even close to them emotionally.

And so it is that the frequencies of topics observed in over 4000 cases suggest some commonly accepted ideas and some too that are quite novel. For instance, as mentioned at the outset, one of the commonly assumed ideas is that emotion plays a considerable role; another, the fact that crises are often involved. Less expected however, at least by me, was the fact that the percipient's own affairs would make up the subject matter of so large a proportion of all. In fact, as mentioned earlier, when I first realized that a category for the person's own affairs was necessary, I did not expect many entries in it. Instead, I thought the largest number of cases would concern the person's family members.

As I mentioned earlier, the relative frequency of *Group I* cases, to my knowledge, has not been noted before. It suggests an elemental self-centeredness in the percipient, which the amenities of civilization tend to conceal. After all, although each of us finds oneself the most interesting person, we seldom acknowledge it even to ourselves. But psi, being unconscious, turns out not to be so restrained.

This impression of self-centeredness is reinforced by the relative frequencies of the various kinds of topics in the percipient's own experiences, and especially by the fact that nearly a third of them were not even important. They are (embarrassingly?) trivial and their main claim to the percipient's interest is the fact that they are his or her own.

It was no surprise to me, however, to find at the other extreme few *Group I* cases involving the person's own death or serious injury, for as the reports came in and were filed originally, those involving these topics were noticeably rare. Necessarily, also, those concerning the percipient's own death were likely to seem of low reliability because they were nearly always secondhand. They depended largely on the testimony of a second person to whom the percipient had told of the dream or premonition before the crisis occurred.

Although, as already mentioned, this paucity of experiences portending the person's most serious crises seem to indicate repression. Whether this is healthy or unhealthy is not clear. If healthy, it would indicate a refusal to dwell on the less happy side of life; if unhealthy, a hesitation to face it.

But at the other extreme one's involvement may cover individuals with whom one's emotional ties are weak and in these another motive seems to substitute for personal involvement, one that tapers down to — sympathy — curiosity — and finally it would seem, to no specifiable motive at all, for strangers appear who not only lack a present connection, but seem not even to have a future one. All this means, it seems, that although no topic is too great nor too intimate, so, too, is none too impersonal, too insignificant to be the subject matter of a psi experience.

As I said at the beginning of this chapter, I undertook the survey to see how relatively frequent would be the topics of various kinds and whether the general impressions about the role of emotion and the critical nature of the information would be borne out. I also hoped to see what would be suggested as to the function of psi in the lives of the percipients.

In a way, I think, these ends were achieved and to a higher degree than I ever anticipated. As a matter of fact, this survey, almost more than any other in my long years of study, seemed to me to show not only that psychic experiences do occur, but that they have inner regularities and significance in human life, of which our grudging and limited attention to them have as yet permitted only the barest glimpse.

Chapter 18

The Total Picture

The studies reported in this book show, I hope to the reader as they have to me, that psi experiences in their simplest, most basic forms are more than just coincidences between a thought and the objective world. Together the studies show, instead, that spontaneous psi is a definite part of the personality. Single cases could not do it but numbers of them in perspective could.

They turned out to be like dabs of color on a canvas that take on form and meaning as they accumulate. They could do this because the majority of them, whether every single one or not, are fragments of a larger whole. That whole on this canvas is the result of the mental process by which psi functions in the personality. For it the canvas had to be large enough to show the process in entirety because the pieces came from all parts of it. They were not selected for a single segment, but were a jumble of all the basic ways in which psi appears spontaneously.

Like any jigsaw puzzle, the pieces scattered did not show the picture of which each was a fragment. They had to be assembled, sorted, arranged so that they all made sense even though the place where some of them fitted was not obvious at first and remained, for years, a question. But now, it seems to me at least, that in the background a rational and intelligent concept of spontaneous psi must be entertained by any fair and open-minded inquirer. And since these "pieces" are real and actual indications in consciousness of the ability to which they bear testimony, they even give added strength to the experimental results on which they relied for support initially. But besides that, they amplify those results and show that the ability is an active functioning aspect of personality and not just a hidden trace of a nearly extinguished one carried down from our primitive ancestry.

Whether or not the picture to be glimpsed herein is correct and true in all details, it is a panoramic one, a total overview of territory much of which is still unexplored in the laboratory and which, accordingly, still awaits experimental validation. But, at least at this stage, as far as the two lines of investigation, the experimental and the anecdotal, overlap and cover the same territory, they agree.

I have presented this account of the terrain of spontaneous psi as it appears from the vantage point of the experiences themselves with the implicit understanding that this is the way it looks. At the same time, I remember that the earlier researchers and especially those trying to interpret such unrevealing and inherently misinterpretable topics as apparitions, based their conclusions too on the way the material *looked*. As later methods and new approaches have modified and changed the interpretations they made, so too, these made now may have to be changed or modified in the future. But, if so it be, so be it. For today, the glimpse given here of the psi process in its entirety, I venture to suggest, is the broadest and most comprehensive one presently available.

Parapsychology has a peculiar need for a comprehensive glimpse of the processes by which its phenomena are created. Most of the other and older sciences, based on commonly observable phenomena, have well defined and generally accepted conceptual backgrounds, but parapsychology began with no framework into which its research findings could fit. The distinguishing feature of the early research was that the results did not belong in any then recognized area. Psi is elusive, sporadic and hidden, so that the rules governing its expression in consciousness are only slowly being discovered. Only relatively few persons are aware of experiencing it so that those who have not done so usually can only be convinced of its reality, if at all, by argument, illustration and experimental data.

Because of the obscure and unobjective nature of psi, its experimental demonstration had to begin with only a very dim and imperfect concept of its phenomena to guide it. The research

had to be diffficult, its results piecemeal and more or less un-
coordinated, because in order that anything could be learned
reliably, the phenomena had to be forced to occur in circumstances that nature did not intend. As in any science, the conditions
under which it would occur had to be controlled, so that the
causes of the results achieved could be determined. In nature psi
occurs spontaneously. In the laboratory, on demand. In life, psi
is intimately linked with personal influences. In the laboratory,
however, such influences can be duplicated only to a slight
degree. With the limitations of both the anecdotal and the experimental methods so obvious, investigators have been fortunate that something of nature's secret in the psychic area has,
even at this late date, been disclosed.

I feel, as a consequence of all this, that the value the
studies outlined here may have lies first of all in the emphasis
they place on the discovery and meaning of psi ability and, after
that, on the perspectives they permit, perspectives broader and
more general than those that the slow careful experimental approach can offer now or probably for years to come. But even
so, as already emphasized, the experimental approach was
necessary to validate the anecdotal material sufficiently that it
could be given even the weight of suggestion offered here and
which will be just as necessary too in years ahead to validate or
negate impressions like these offered here. The experimental
method, however, has established the basic fact that at least some
human beings show a psi potential and that therefore psi ability
is probably a natural part of the human personality. Even
though its evidence in tests is relatively slight, it is definite. That
evidence shows that the objective world is not totally hidden to
the human psyche by space and time because psi ability trans-
cends the limited sensory faculties. Psi messages may bring information about inanimate objects and events, even the thoughts of
other persons — and this regardless of their time or place.

No person is actually aware of all of this, however. As
with all one's other human abilities, with psi too one does not live
up to his or her full capacity. We are not all Olympic winners. No
one knows how many of those who never try could be. By quite a
different token, very few of us consider ourselves to be clair-
voyants, prophets or mediums. And that is just as well for in this

kind of contest the rules are not yet set up and so we have few guidelines by which to judge a winner. Those guidelines and those to govern the practical application of psi in the affairs of life still await a more complete understanding of the phenomenon than has yet been achieved. The degree to which application can ever be reliable will depend no doubt on the extent to which the ability can be brought under conscious control. However, the time when such control can be achieved seems remote, considering the unconscious nature of the function. But until such time no attempt at application, regardless of good intent, can be certified to be reliable.

The case study project described here began, as outlined in Chapter 4, with a considerable heritage from the past. The most important part of that was, of course, the body of fact that had been established by experiment. The reality of extrasensory perception, and of its types, had also been carefully distinguished. Psychokinesis, too, had been demonstrated so that no longer did the ancient concept of mind-over-matter depend on what had been highly suspect testimony that, in "dark-room" seances, furniture sometimes moved around "by itself." Now, whether or not any truth resided in those claims, at least it had been shown that dice tumbling down prepared chutes obeyed the human will to a statistically significant degree.

And so it was that when my case studies began, the accumulated experimental results constituted a wall, a background firm enough to give a measure of support to case observations. It permitted the logic: if psi is a laboratory phenomenon it is likely one that occurs in nature too. It was because of this that I could regard individual instances that conformed to the definition of psi as *possibly* involving it. I could at least give them the benefit of the doubt and undertake a study of them even in the experimentally oriented Duke Parapsychology Laboratory of 1948. And more than that, for my project of trying to observe the mental processes involved in their production, I could use—in fact, I had to use, as outlined in Chapter 4—a different method of handling the cases than the time honored one of extensive validation of individual reports. It was that of validation by numbers instead.

In the background, accounts of earlier case studies were scattered over the preceding fifty or more years. Each in its separate way had kept alive, if only for the small circle of psychical researchers, the idea that psychic occurrences represented an unexplained human phenomenon.

In a few of these studies, I had found, especially those by Saltmarsh and Tyrrell, that a degree of insight had been shown into the processes that might be involved. These researchers had **gone beyond the implications the experiences might have for the** survival question, which had limited the perspective of most of the others. Tyrrells' ideas especially had advanced the concepts of possible explanations for psychic occurrences. My own research, like that of anyone coming later, had the advantage of earlier suggestions as well as those arising from the years of laboratory research that had preceded.

With these and other initial advantages for my own project, just what has it accomplished? In the presentations chapter by chapter of this book, my intention was to trace out each general contribution and give samples of the evidence on which it was based. But it well may be that in those more detailed accounts the "trees" have, to an extent, obscured the "forest," and that in order to reverse that effect, a summing up is necessary. It must begin with Chapter 5 in which the "reach and types" of psi in cases were compared with those established in the laboratory. Ten years earlier, before precognition had been shown by experiment to be a reality, all the precognitive cases would have been extras, or they would have had no "ready made" place of classification. But now I found no extras. The study had shown that the two lines, experimental and anecdotal, coincided as far as the types were concerned. Each method, in its own way, not only testified to the diverse types of psi but, in so doing, the difference between psi abilities which operate without time and space limitations and the sensory ones which are confined by them was emphasized again.

In Chapter 6, the study of conviction introduced a real **unknown, an enigma. What did its irregular but occasional oc-** **currence mean? The study of the topic turned out to be a con-** tinued story that had to be left dangling. It took many more years of other studies before it fell into place and I came to realize that because it is not objective it would not be transferred by imagery and also that it must be an item that can cross into consciousness independently of the facts on which it is based. This first round of observations served only to set the stage. They showed that the feeling of conviction occurs so erratically as to seem to lack a reason. But in time when the reason became clear, then I found it to occur with a regularity that helped to explain other puzzles, like the fact that precognitive cases tend to be experienced as if in the present.

The next and perhaps the most basic of all the studies, as reported in Chapter 7, involved a fact that had long been noticed, of course, which was that psychic experiences take various forms—hunches, dreams, apparitions, emotional states and compulsive acts—but no study had ever been reported to sort them out on the basis of the mental processes that seemed to be involved. Now with a collection of all the forms that are reported as my material, I could and did make such a study.

On the basis of the differing mental processes that must have been involved, the distinctions were reflected in the imagery that was or was not present and, when present, was of different kinds. Each kind, then, obviously was the result of the individual process which created it. Since only four such differences were found and since PK, too, represented a specific psi effect, the catalogue of psi forms was complete and now each one of them could be observed separately. Before this no attempt to explain the psi process in daily life could have been successful since it is not one but five related but separate processes.

This is one reason why a catalogue of all the forms was necessary in the attempt to understand psi experiences. Another was that until this delineation had been made it was not easy to distinguish which were basic forms and which were only superficial variations of them. And until that distinction could be made, the mixture of variations certain to occur in any comprehensive collection of cases caused psi experiences to seem more mysterious and complex than they really are.

Then in Chapter 8, by actual observation of cases of the same kind ("call cases") something of the mechanics of psi was shown—that it is not in any sense a stimulus-response action but a percipient response operation instead. This finding was basic and of greater and more far reaching importance than I could recognize at the time. It was one that had not been decided in the laboratory, but had been suspected occasionally from historical to present times, even while in survival research the assumed need for an active "sender" had been a biasing influence against it.

The roles of percipient as necessarily active and of sender as functionally passive are the opposite of those in sense perception that superficially seem analogous, as, for instance, when one person calls to another. In that exchange the agent, of course, is active and the percipient, passive.

This difference in the mechanics of sensory and extrasensory perception was only one of the examples I found of the fact that ESP processes not only are hidden but may well run in contradiction to those of sense perception. It was natural enough and almost inevitable, one can see now, that the supposition should have been that the two, the psychical and the psychological, operate according to the same general laws. The fact has only slowly been grasped that instead, since one process operates unconsciously, the other for the most part consciously, they obey different rules and must be interpreted differently accordingly.

In Chapter 9, I struggled with the question whether precognitive experiences differ from contemporaneous ones in any way except that of timing. I found no difference other than the seemingly inexplicable excess of precognitive realistic dreams. It was in the course of this study that the point came out that the timing element in them was seldom indicated. It was the recognition of this fact that led in turn to the realization of the reason, which is that time is not an objective item and hence does not appear in imagery.

But none of this, of course, explains why this particular form, the realistic precognitive dream, should occur in great excess over other forms. The question raises the suggestion that an innate tendency of the human mind may be showing here, a tendency, when in sleep and freed from customary mundane restraints, to look ahead to experiences yet to come rather than be limited to situations of the past or present. Could it be, then, that our ordinary attitude toward the present compared to that toward the future is one imposed by the sensory limitations of the personality rather than one of nature itself?

The phenomenon of precognitive ability carries with it the age-old question of free will versus fatalism, but my study of cases of attempted intervention of precognized events, in Chapter 10, did not support the old idea of an immutable future. The cases seemed rather to suggest merely the imperfect functioning of psi ability. Detailed study of the general telepathy cases supported the idea, from the call case survey of Chapter 8, that in a telepathic case the percipient is the active party, with or without active "sending" by an agent. The same conclusion covered a more detailed survey of apparitional cases as well. These, like the telepathy cases, are instances in which superficial appearance is misleading. Although it seemed obvious that the agent, or target person, "did it," and although that was the preferred interpretation, it did not stand up that way under analysis.

In chapters 14 and 15, I attempted to put together the insights gained by the preceding studies and to trace out in some detail the processes that go on in each of the forms of psi. For the purpose of analysis, I used Tyrrell's classification of the process into a Stage I in which a psi message is secured and a Stage II in which it is processed into consciousness.

In Stage I, however, the question of how the information could be secured offered no easy answer. This is the distinctive process of parapsychology. In sensory experience, information comes via the well-known channels of sense, but not so in ESP. Even the best of philosophers and psychologists have been baffled to explain the method here.

The facts, however, show that somehow the psyche does interact with the external world and acquires information regardless of time or distance. And this carries with it another question. How is the specific pertinent information selected? Evidence shows that it is purposively oriented and directed by the percipient. But, as discussed in Chapter 17, no theory for this selection that does not raise a more difficult problem than it answers has been proposed. Suffice it here merely to state the obvious, which is that selection somehow does occur and the information becomes available for processing in Stage II.

How will it be processed, and why? Does the psyche somehow give it impetus toward consciousness? Is the psyche at this unconscious level at one with the person's need to know? If all the messages were important ones, the easy answer might be yes, but what about the unimportant topics? Do they just move themselves into consciousness?

However all this may be, psi information, insofar as it ever comes to conscious attention, at this point becomes channeled into one of the four ESP forms or that of PK. Taking each of the forms in turn, then, it was possible to trace back and see the kind of process that must have produced the result. In general if the person was sleeping, dream imagery carried the message, whether it was a kind of copying of the reality in the realistic form or whether it involved fantasy, as in the unrealistic. But if imagery was employed when, instead of sleeping, the person thought he or she was awake, it was modeled on that of sense perception and so produced an hallucinatory effect. If, on the other hand, no imagery was formed, the psi message apparently arrived directly at the threshold of consciousness, where it might or might not cross intact into consciousness. If not intact, the elements of emotion, or compulsion to action, and conviction, apparently acting independently of the factual psi message itself, were sometimes able to become elements in consciousness even though the fact itself was not. Then, in the PK cases, when none of these ESP effects occurred, it appeared that the psychokinetic response instead was released at the start of Stage II.

After this analysis it was easy to see why conviction was low in dreams in comparison with intuitive experiences. The feeling of conviction, like that of the time element in precognitive experiences, is not an objective item and hence does not get transferred by imagery.

The tracing of the origin of ESP experiences through the four ESP forms (PK adding nothing essentially different) thus suggested the mechanisms that are involved. The psi process thereby becomes less obscure than is recognized by those who say that parapsychologists "have no theory." There is no theory to explain the extrasensory acquisition of knowledge, it is true. This lack of a theory, of a tentative explanation for an unknown, of course, is not a defect of the parapsychological concept only. Many still unsolved and theory-lacking concepts afflict other fields as well as parapsychology. Even such an everyday occurrence as the transformation of sense impressions into mental constructs is still a baffling problem for psychologists. In fact, the forefront of advancing science in any field is likely to abound in questions that precede the theories that will have to be formed as the field advances.

In parapsychology, the processes that occur in Stage II, however, do have a theory. They are not unknown. They are not new or specific for parapsychology, as the analyses here have shown. Instead, they are relatively simple, almost common sense deductions, once the situation in each can be observed separately. In these deductions the incomplete cases in each form added suggestions as to what apparently caused them and showed perhaps even more than the complete cases the psychological and personal influences that affect, divert or modify the psi message as it works its way into consciousness.

In Chapter 16, I attempted an analysis of the psi-missing effect based on the earlier study of incomplete intuitive experiences. The incompletenesses in that form, already shown to be caused mainly by a blockage occurring at the level of consciousness, seemed to be at the basis of psi missing. While complete blockage in cases would of course leave no trace, in experiments it would tend to be recognized if it persisted long enough to be statistically significant. Various experiments in which it occurred showed that it might result even when the strong emotions of life experiences were absent, if the experimental situation was less than entirely satisfactory to the subject. It might even be slight as when, in comparisons, one condition was preferable to another or if a bit of boredom was involved. It was another illustration of the fact that unconscious mental processes do not necessarily operate like conscious ones.

In Chapter 17, a key question about psi came up even though it did not have to do with the psi process *per se*. The question was, what is the significance of the content of psi experiences? Put another way, what is their general value to the percipient? The survey of the subject matter of thousands of cases then showed psi information as covering practically all areas of human affairs. And even in a sample—so large, so small—as the cases used in these studies, a recognizable picture emerged. Their content covers a broad and believable human spectrum. It is one that shows the experiencing persons interested most of all in themselves. Not even their closest ties equal the level of their self-involvement. This is natural, normal, unadorned and, although it could be common knowledge that it is so, it is a fact not too often recognized as underlying the veneer of altruism with which civilization attempts to cover its more primitive tendencies.

Once granting this strong underlying self-interest, the rest of the psi experiences show the individuals as deeply involved emotionally with their family ties, but only where they matter most. Living their own lives to the full, they do not attempt the unnecessary and actually impossible spread of attention to all aspects of the lives of those close to them. They do not follow the affairs of others in detail like they do their own but only the high spots. Possibly one could say that a person attends to others' crisis situations, those that in the last analysis are crises of their own, so that even in these self-involvement shows through.

Another unexpected fact the survey of Chapter 17 revealed had to do with the inclusion of strangers in psi experiences. The surprise was not that strangers should appear, particularly in precognitive experiences, for considering all future scenes and events, the inclusion of persons too might well have been expected. Instead, the *reasons*—or lack of reasons—why they occasionally were included were unexpected, for sometimes they apparently were selected only for a *future* reason. Then those cases in which no link, or no identifiable one at any rate, could be found between the two seemed to say that on this level it is not only time itself that is not necessarily involved, but even our ordinary cause-effect logic. That logic leads to the expectation that the percipient must have an identifiable reason for the choice of subject matter. The experiences involving strangers thus considerably widen the list of possible reasons for that choice. They widen it to include future as well as present reasons. Then, most disconcertingly, they add some cases that appear to have no perceptible reason at all.

But upon consideration what should be so strange in that, for psi? Reasons, in a way, are timed. They precede effects. First the reason, then the effect. But psi escapes the time sequence as both experiment and anecdote have shown.

And so, here again, perhaps we all have been led astray *by appearances*. Perhaps, after all, reasons for all of the psi effects are illusory. Perhaps they just *look* necessary because of our timed thinking habits. Perhaps here again, just as in the matter of excess of precognitive dreams, we mistake our psychologically oriented concepts for the real world when actually that world knows nothing of the time limitation.

The surprise here then seems to be the strong realization of the degree to which our present concepts are superficial and too tightly bound to the time-space perspective, to easily permit the complete realization of the meaning of psi in the extended universe, but also in the personality and its relation to the universe.

Concepts such as these, of course, are not easily imaginable, much less entertainable. Like the idea of potential omniscience for the human mind mentioned earlier, they are unassimilable in the present materialistically and physicalistically oriented world outlook. But they arise here from the very "stuff" itself of human experience, and experience which in its very content has a built-in measure of verity to show that the picture on this canvas is not one painted by an imposter. This picture could derive only from a living situation for which no imposter could have the necessary insights, since even the wisest have so generally missed it.

The study of spontaneous psychic experiences shows psi to be, in general, a healthy aspect of the human being. Although it has long been one of humankind's best kept secrets about itself, it shows us realistically as not too overwhelmed by life's inevitable tragedies but absorbed instead in the commonplace affairs of life. Both our faults and our virtues are suggested and our panoramic interest in the world around us.

In its own way, psi in human life thus seems to reflect that life as it is—high, low, strong, weak, important, unimportant. Even though the picture so suggested is fragmentary, not really visible, it is revealing all the same. It shows the psi process fitting so smoothly into the personality that it has gone almost unrecognized. And even at this late date in the history of our study of human nature, our present knowledge of this hidden aspect of it must surely be only a fragment of a larger whole.

That larger whole, it seems to me, glimpsed through these natural spontaneous experiences, takes on a "feel" of reality that experimental results alone can scarcely give. In this way each approach, the anecdotal and the experimental, supports the other and together they add up to more for humankind than this mundane life alone suggests. This life, the sensory life alone, turns out to show but half a human. The other half is shown, by both approaches, to represent a different level, one as yet too much unknown. That is partly, of course, because it has been so long held to be beyond investigation—to be an area for religion, not for science.

But in this modern age, scientific method is necessary for authority. It is that method which in parapsychology is slowly discovering this hidden side of personality and the cosmos into which it fits. And toward that end even the modest reconstruction reported here I hope can have some value.

References

1. Gauld, A. ESP and attempts to explain it. In Shivesh C. Thakur (ed.), *Philosophy and Psychical Research*. London: Allen & Unwin, 1976. Pp. 17-45.

2. Gurney, E., Myers, F.W.H., and Podmore, F. *Phantasms of the Living, Vol. I*. New Hyde Park, N.Y.: University Books, 1962. (Originally published, London: Trubner, 1886.)

3. McDougall, W. *Body and Mind*. Westport, Conn.: Greenwood Press, 1974. (Originally published, London: Methuen, 1938.)

4. Myers, F.W.H. Report on the census of hallucinations. *Proceedings of the Society for Psychical Research*, 1894, *10*, 25-422.

5. Panati, C. (ed.). *The Geller Papers*. Boston: Houghton Mifflin, 1976.

6. Rao, K.R. The preferential effect in ESP. *Journal of Parapsychology*, 1962, *26*, 252-259.

7. Rao, K.R. *Experimental Parapsychology: A Review and Interpretation*. Springfield, Ill.: C.C. Thomas, 1966.

8. Rhine, J.B. Experiments bearing on the precognition hypothesis. *Journal of Parapsychology*, 1938, *2*, 38-54.

9. Rhine, J.B. "Physical phenomena" in parapsychology. *Journal of Parapsychology,* 1943, *7*, 1-4.

10. Rhine, J.B. The value of reports of spontaneous psi experiences. *Journal of Parapsychology*, 1948, *12*, 231-235.

11. Rhine, J.B. *New World of the Mind*. New York: William Sloane Associates, 1953.

12. Rhine, J.B. *Extra-Sensory Perception*. Boston: Branden Press, 1964. (Originally published, Boston: Bruce Humphries, 1935.)

13. Rhine, J.B., and Pratt, J.G. *Parapsychology: Frontier Science of the Mind*. Springfield, Ill.: C.C. Thomas, 1957.

References

14. Rhine, L.E. Case books of the last quarter century. *Journal of Parapsychology*, 1949, *13*, 292-296.

15. Rhine, L.E. Conviction and associated conditions in spontaneous cases. *Journal of Parapsychology,* 1951, *15*, 164-191.

16. Rhine, L.E. The relation of experience to asssociated event in spontaneous ESP. *Journal of Parapsychology,* 1953, *17*, 187-209.

17. Rhine, L.E. Subjective forms of spontaneous psi experiences. *Journal of Parapsychology,* 1953, *17*, 77-114.

18. Rhine, L.E. Frequency of types of experience in spontaneous precognition. *Journal of Parapsychology,* 1954, *18*, 93-123.

19. Rhine, L.E. Precognition and intervention. *Journal of Parapsychology,* 1955,*19*, 1-34.

20. Rhine, L.E. Hallucinatory psi experiences. I. An introductory survey. *Journal of Parapsychology,* 1956, *20*, 233-256.

21. Rhine, L.E. The relationship of agent and percipient in spontaneous telepathy. *Journal of Parapsychology,* 1956, *20*, 1-32.

22. Rhine, L.E. Hallucinatory psi experiences. II. The initiative of the percipient in hallucinations of the living, the dying, and the dead. *Journal of Parapsychology*, 1957, *21*, 13-46.

23. Rhine, L.E. Hallucinatory psi experiences. III. The intention of the agent and the dramatizing tendency of the percipient. *Journal of Parapsychology*, 1957, *21*, 186-226.

24. Rhine, L.E. The evaluation of non-recurrent psi experiences bearing on post-mortem survival. *Journal of Parapsychology*, 1960, *24*, 8-25.

25. Rhine, L.E. Psychological processes in ESP experiences. Part I. Waking experiences. *Journal of Parapsychology*, 1962, *26*, 88-111.

26. Rhine, L.E. Psychological processes in ESP experiences. Part II. Dreams. *Journal of Parapsychology*, 1962, *26*, 172-199.

27. Rhine, L.E. Auditory psi experiences: Hallucinatory or physical? *Journal of Parapsychology,* 1963, *27*, 182-198.

28. Rhine, L.E. Spontaneous physical effects and the psi process. *Journal of Parapsychology,* 1963, *27*, 84-122.

29. Rhine, L.E. Factors influencing the range of information in ESP experiences. *Journal of Parapsychology*, 1964, *28*, 176-213.

30. Rhine, L.E. Comparison of subject matter of intuitive and realistic ESP experiences. *Journal of Parapsychology,* 1965, *29*, 96-108.

31. Rhine, L.E. Toward understanding psi missing. *Journal of Parapsychology,* 1965, *29,* 259-274.

32. Rhine, L.E. *Mind Over Matter.* New York: Macmillan, 1970.

33. Rhine, L.E., and Rhine, J.B. The psychokinetic effect: The first experiment. *Journal of Parapsychology*, 1943, *7,* 20-43.

34. Saltmarsh, H.F. Report on cases of apparent precognition. *Proceedings of the Society for Psychical Research*, 1934, *42*, 49-103.

35. Schmeidler, G.R. Separating the sheep from the goats. *Journal of the American Society for Psychical Research,* 1945, *39,* 47-49.

36. Sidgwick, Mrs. H. On the evidence for premonitions. *Proceedings of the Society for Psychical Research*, 1888-1889, *5,* 288-354.

37. Tyrrell, G.N.M. The "modus operandi" of paranormal cognition. *Proceedings of the Society for Psychical Research*, 1946-1949, *48*, 65-120.

38. Tyrrell, G.N.M. *Science and Psychical Phenomena and Apparitions.* New Hyde Park, N.Y.: University Books, 1961. (*Science and Psychical Phenomena* originally published, New York: Harper & Bros., 1938.)

39. Ullman, M., and Krippner, S., with Vaughan, A. *Dream Telepathy.* New York: Macmillan, 1973.

40. West, D.J. The investigation of spontaneous cases. *Proceedings of the Society for Psychical Research*, 1946-1949, *48*, 264-300.

Index